DATE DUE			
⸺			

IN AND OUT OF THE IVORY TOWER

In and Out of the Ivory Tower

THE AUTOBIOGRAPHY OF
WILLIAM L. LANGER

NEALE WATSON

ACADEMIC PUBLICATIONS, INC.

NEW YORK

First published in the United States by
Neale Watson Academic Publications, Inc.
156 Fifth Avenue, New York, N.Y. 10010
© William L. Langer 1977
Printed and manufactured in the U.S.A.

Designer Ernst Reichl

Note: *In and Out of the Ivory Tower*, despite minor changes and a more comprehensive title, is essentially the same unpublished autobiography copyright in 1975 by William L. Langer under the title *Up From the Ranks*.

The Publishers wish to express their gratitude to Professor Ronald Coons of the University of Connecticut whose devotion and expertise greatly facilitated the preparation of this volume.

Mr. Langer's portrait courtesy Fabian Bachrach

Library of Congress Cataloging in Publication Data
Langer, William Leonard, 1896-
    In and out of the ivory tower.

    1. Langer, William Leonard, 1896-   2. College teachers—Massachusetts—Biography. 3. Harvard University—Faculty. I. Title.
LD2137.L33   378.1'2'0924 [B]   77–20035
ISBN 0–88202–177–X

TO MY DEVOTED MOTHER

In Memoriam

Contents

Preface

THE NOTION of setting down the chief events and impressions of a long and chequered life came to me initially from the younger members of the family. At first, it had no appeal to me, for it seemed that any number of more prominent men could tell more interesting and important stories.

My reasoning changed, however, after the stupendous tide of unrest among the students and other youths of the 1960s, which I am convinced will loom large in the historical studies of the future. The inability of so many of our young people to "find their identity" and, even more, the widespread and to me quite uncritical rejection of the "Establishment" shocked me as it did many others. My generation still believed that our country had for centuries been the land of liberty and opportunity, peopled largely by immigrants who had little to offer but their labor. Most of them were able not only to find a decent living, but also to make a substantial contribution to American society in many fields. I have yet to meet an immigrant or even an immigrant's child who does not think this the greatest of all countries. Of all patriots they have seemed the most patriotic.

I have thought this to be worth recalling in a concrete case, and so I literally took pen in hand and wrote out my recollections and impressions, only rarely referring to a document and relying almost entirely on my head and my heart. I do not offer these memoirs to suggest that my career was that of the average American of my generation, but, nonetheless, as a record representative of countless others who have helped to preserve the fundamentals of our democracy and to make this great country what it still is: the most free and most rewarding land in history.

William L. Langer

IN AND OUT OF THE IVORY TOWER

CHAPTER I

Tragic Beginnings of a Happy Childhood

MY PARENTS were among the hundreds of thousands of Germans who, in the closing decades of the last century, deserted their native land in the hope of finding a better and richer life in the New World. For them, as for countless other young people, the great event was their transatlantic romance.

My mother, then about twenty, was a native of Zweibrücken, a delightful eighteenth-century town in the Bavarian Palatinate, within a stone's throw of the French frontier. French writers like to call it Deux Ponts, revealing perhaps a secret Freudian desire. In the eighteenth century it had been the residence of Stanislas Leszczynski, the father of the French queen, and it retained much of the French flavor and elegance. Unfortunately, as a key fortress in Hitler's Siegfried line, it was later all but destroyed in the heavy bombardments of the Second World War.

My maternal grandfather was a well-sinker by profession, itinerant over a large area. He succumbed to the smallpox epidemic which followed the Franco-Prussian War in 1871, leaving a wife, a son, and two daughters. My grandmother supported the family by keeping a few cows and selling milk and by engaging in small-scale market gardening. My mother would often tell us of a serious flood in the 1880s that carried off the cattle and washed away the crops. The government, it was said, provided relief for the poor, while property owners, like my grandmother, were put off with a mere pittance. It seems that even the Imperial German government, world renowned for its efficiency and honesty, failed to satisfy all sufferers from disaster.

My mother's family was not well-to-do, but it managed reasonably well. Her brother was apprenticed to a cabinetmaker and emigrated to the United States chiefly to escape compulsory military service. Settled in Chicago he eventually prospered as a foreman in the instrument-building division of the telephone company. My mother, the older of the two daughters, had only a primary school education, yet always impressed her children with her knowledge of literature and nature. She became a dressmaker and at an early age was induced to cross the Atlantic to New York, where an aunt, a most kindly and charming lady, had a prosperous dressmaking establishment, somewhere around Union Square, if I am not mistaken. Unfortunately, my mother soon contracted a serious case of erysipelas. The doctor insisted on a change of scene, and it was decided that she should briefly return to Germany, if only for the benefit of the ocean voyage.

I have always found it impossible to decide on the appearance of persons I love. I think my mother was probably a very attractive girl, well built, agile, and alert, with comely features. Her eyes, as I remember them through life, were unusually deep sunken, giving her the appearance of a perhaps too sober and serious person.

On the voyage home, my mother made the acquaintance of a young man slightly older than herself. He came from the further end of Germany, from Silesia, now a part of the German Democratic (Communist) Republic. The family, which belonged to the devout Moravian Brethren, was evidently typically petit bourgeois. A late eighteenth-century ancestor was a cabinetmaker and church organist in the town of Gnadenfrei, six miles from Reichenbach in Lower Silesia. Within walking distance of his home was the establishment of an Englishman named Rushaway, who built only the finest furniture and may well have been the master and later the employer of my ancestor. Being entirely literate, the latter, quickly promoted to noncommissioned rank in the Prussian army, was grievously wounded in the battle of Leipzig (1813), but recovered to live at least for another twenty-five years. His sons thought him so remarkable that they finally induced him, in his old age, to dictate his autobiography, a manuscript of some forty beautifully written pages which is still in the family's possession.

My father, Karl Rudolf, was born, I believe, in 1866, one of a family of three sons and a daughter. When and how the father died I do not know, but my aunt Martha, who long survived him, agreed that he was a prosperous maker of the highest quality furniture and a devoted musician. He would, she said, come home for lunch and then take a nap upstairs while she was expected to practice the piano. Any malingering or careless playing on her part would invariably lead to sharp raps from father's cane.

My father was the second of the three sons. His older brother (Ernst) was a passionate naturalist who, at an early age, was killed in a fall from a cliff. My father shared his love of plants and animals, but was evidently something of a bookworm. He was destined for the Moravian ministry, but was so frail of health that the doctor urged that he be sent to sea.

For two years he shipped on a square rigger and journeyed around South America to Japan. His letters to the home newspaper are still extant and reveal a remarkable power of narrative and description for so young a man. How he ultimately came to the United States I do not know, but he decided to settle in Philadelphia and was evidently on his way home to make arrangements when he met my mother. They seem to have fallen in love quickly and made a solemn compact to return to America together on the same ship. By the return voyage they had decided on marriage which, I believe, took place in Boston, in 1888.

I have no reason to suppose that my parents were not happily married, though I gather from occasional remarks of my mother in later years that she was somewhat troubled by her husband's flights of imagination, his exuberant disposition, and his exaggerated generosity. Though I have no personal memory of my father, I gather from photographs and from the comments of those who knew him that he was an exceptionally handsome man, with a wiry pompadour hairdress and an impressive moustache. He opened a small florist shop on Broadway, South Boston, somewher near F Street, where he soon attracted attention by unusual floral displays and tropical settings with miniature swamps, baby alligators and turtles, drooping lianas, and other features. He must have had many friends, for his business prospered, and for years after his early death people would still address me as "Charlie Langer's boy" and sing the praises of his short career.

I am impelled, at this point, to say something of my natal site, and if possible to correct erroneous impressions that have become deeply rooted. South Boston is a flat area of some five or six city blocks, separated from Old Boston by the Old Fort Channel. This part of the town was, even in my childhood, rather run down and poor; but it was dominated by Dorchester Heights, which overlooked both Boston Harbor and the Old Harbor of Dorchester Bay. Dorchester Heights is a fairly steep hill, occupied on one side by the Carney Hospital and on the other by residential streets so precipitous that only lighter wagons could negotiate them. At the summit was a circular road enclosing an elevated park and a marble monument commemorating the evacuation of Boston by the British in 1776.

Broadway, to the east of Dorchester Avenue, must once have been a delightful residential area, for in my childhood it was still lined with large, beautiful homes, each with its stable and carriage house. In fact, I have never been able to understand why the Heights, close to Boston, with salubrious air, and splendid views over the Old Harbor toward Quincy and the broken coastline, has not been redeveloped and covered with high-grade apartments. Its poor reputation must have been derived entirely from the unattractive in-town area, for in my boyhood Dorchester Heights was definitely a solid, lower-middle class community, inhabited chiefly by second-generation Irish, intermingled with pockets of German immigrants. The Irish were, naturally, devout Catholics, while the Germans were both Catholic (from Westphalia) and Protestant and, to my childhood surprise, also atheist (socialists from the Ruhr and other industrial areas). I cannot recall any racial troubles. The Irish were the majority and pitied those who did not attend Mass or have a brother in the priesthood. It was taken for granted that "the Irish can beat the Dutch," so there was no need to repeat the demonstration. Almost without exception our playmates were Irish, who were particularly well disposed on Saturday afternoons when the fragrance of my mother's newly baked cake began to permeate the neighborhood.

I believe it was during the 1890s that arrangements were made to bring my father's sister and mother to this country. My aunt Martha, even in old age an extremely good-looking woman, soon married an equally impressive Swiss German named Walter Strickler, who was a master confectioner. They had no children and compensated by being very kind to us. I can never forget the impression made when they appeared together riding a tandem bicycle and garbed in the latest styles. I cannot recall ever having seen a more beautiful and jovial couple. Their arrival was always something of an occasion, though they lived with my grandmother no farther away than Roxbury. Grandmother died when I was eleven, but I have the most vivid recollections of a sweet little old lady, somewhat lame, with the usual violet-covered little hat. She was convinced that all the Irish streetcar conductors at least understood German, for when she asked them in that language to let her off at a certain street, they invariably did so.

There were four children in our family. The oldest, a girl named Elsa, died of diphtheria at the age of two, an event all too common in those days and certainly an ordeal for the unhappy parents. The remaining children were all boys: Rudolph Ernest born in 1894, myself born in 1896, and Walter Charles, a posthumous child, born in 1899. I naturally have no memories of events before the turn of the century. I have a vague recollection of hearing about the assassination of President McKinley in 1901, and of the prolonged artillery salute on March 17, 1901 celebrating the 125th anniversary of the evacuation

of Boston by the British. But of the great tragedy in our family
—my father's death—I could not, when two years old, have
any recollection.

I had been born on Seventh Street, South Boston, between
D and E Streets, just a stone's throw from my father's shop.
But by 1898 his business had so prospered that he could buy
the house at 81 Old Harbor Street where I was to spend seventeen years of my boyhood. The house was a sturdy frame structure with three tenements of five rooms each. There was no
central heat and, naturally, no electric light or telephone. Indeed, there were no bathrooms—only two toilets, neither of
which had outdoor ventilation. Standing on the side of a steep
hill, the house had three stories in front and five in the rear,
counting the cellar and the basement kitchen. There was a
small plot of very indifferent land behind the house, so steep
that my mother kept trying to shore it up and fill it in.

According to my mother's sad tale, the family had only just
moved into its new home when my father began to complain
of severe headaches. Presently, he was obliged to take to his
bed which he never left. He suffered intensely from what the
doctors finally concluded was cancer of the liver, and in a few
months died at the age of thirty-three.

It takes little imagination to fill in the details of the tragedy
which occurred in the gloomy days of mid-November, while
my older brother was seriously ill with measles and my mother
was expecting another child in a few months. Financially, the
situation was also grim, for the family had scant savings and
extremely modest insurance. To complete the disaster, my
mother, at her husband's advice, entrusted money matters to a
friend or acquaintance who enjoyed the enviable nickname of
"Honest John." His reputation was soon belied for he promptly
defrauded my mother and a dozen other victims of whatever
money he controlled. Indicted on fifteen charges, he was tried,
convicted, and sentenced to five years at hard labor. He died
before his term had expired, but my mother, and I think his
other victims, never recovered any of the funds entrusted to
his care.

This meant that my mother, at age thirty, was left with

three small boys and no money. I am sure that my father's relatives were a great support to her in these times, as was the old German doctor who arranged to have her exempted from paying the property taxes while she was supporting minor children. As I recall, the Boston property tax rate was then about $20 a thousand, and the house was valued at only a few thousand dollars. In our present affluent days, these sums seem piddling, but at the time they loomed formidably, at least to lower-middle class people.

Some time after the recovery of my brother Rudolph from measles and the birth of my younger brother Walter, two of us children contracted whooping cough, a most unwelcome addition to the grief and confusion. At this juncture my mother's kind New York aunt urged her to bring us all there, if only for a change of air, which was reputed to be most beneficial. Since she offered to pay all the fares both ways, my mother quickly accepted the invitation, and we traveled by railway coach to the great metropolis. I must have been four years old at the time, for I have at least hazy recollections of our New York visit, and especially of my mother's cousin William, after whom I had been named. I recall his showing us the horse-cars on Fourth Avenue and rushing down stairs with me on his shoulder to see the fire engines go by. Among other good things, we enjoyed an excursion to Coney Island, where I distinctly remember being horrified to see a restaurant cook take a pigeon from a cage and turn its neck to fill an order for roast squab. More agreeable, was a long trip we made to some relative who had a home or small farm on the outskirts of New York, I think around 125th Street!

I have no doubt that we all benefited from our New York visit, and I suppose it was then that my mother settled down to the redoubtable task of earning a living for her brood. To accept relief was, I am sure, too abhorrent to her to be even considered. She might, of course, have remarried, and I am sure that she had several favorable opportunities. But she never entertained the idea seriously. Her three boys were everything to her, and she could not contemplate interference in the close family relationship by any stepfather, however kind and understanding he might be. If our conduct called for a spanking, she was sure to inflict it. Punishment at any other hand, even a relative's, was utterly out of the question.

For some years my mother found employment as a home dressmaker. She had several well-to-do clients who were evidently well satisfied with her work. But it involved rather long streetcar rides to the Back Bay for fittings. As we grew older, mother became more and more uneasy about leaving us alone. No matter where she concealed the matches, she was sure we would find them and burn down the house along with ourselves. She therefore gave up dressmaking and decided to take in roomers and boarders.

Our tenement or flat (one hesitates to call it an apartment) was the lowest of the three in the house. It consisted of a fairly generous and attractive parlor with a bay window on the street side, which, however, was too remote and unheated to be of much use. Behind it was the largest bedroom, in which my brother Rudolph and I, and, when necessary, our youngest brother or even our mother, would sleep. The third room on the upper level was a small hall bedroom, frequently rented to some single man who was mostly absent at work or lodge. Downstairs, there was a front dining room below street level, rather dim and clammy, and rarely, if ever, used as a dining room. On occasion it served as a bedroom with a folding bed when the other rooms were rented.

In retrospect I am rather impressed that of the five rooms, two were next to useless, chiefly because of the problem of heating in winter. Each room had a cast iron stove which functioned well but consumed much fuel and required considerable attention. So much more important was the rear kitchen, easily accessible through a back entrance. It was a generous room, with a large coal range and a three-burner gas stove. There was usually an old sofa or davenport along one wall, occupied by any member of the family who could get onto it. The kitchen was the scene of my mother's activities and hence the center of our lives. A rather large, plain table seating as many as eight, stood in the middle. The stove was always fired, making the room cozy in all weather and redolent of good cooking.

My mother always maintained that before her marriage she knew very little even about simple cooking. But my grandmother took her in hand and made her, by common consent, a chef de cuisine *sans pareil*. When I was a student in Vienna later in life, I was interested to note the cultural affinity between Silesia and Austria, even after almost two centuries. In the first place, the name *Langer* is not at all common in Germany proper, while in Vienna or even in Prague one would find it in almost any street. My mother thus learned a cuisine from her teacher that was more in the Viennese style than in the somewhat heavier German. In any event, she never lacked for boarders. For board and room she charged five dollars a week, but one could have lunch or dinner for fifty cents, and it was worth three times the price.

Our table, then, was usually full, and as children we were trained to be seen and not heard. This did not prevent my brother Rudolph, a big, strapping lad, from heaping his plate and devouring his helping in record time. I myself was smaller and lighter and could never manage more than half my brother's helping. This troubled my mother, although I never lacked good health and abundant energy. The doctor explained that I simply had a somewhat small stomach. I could not eat much at a time and should therefore be fed more frequently. He recommended that my mother buy a bottle of Rhine wine ($1.00) and give me a glass a day. Furthermore, he suggested beef, iron, and wine, to say nothing of sulphur and molasses. These recommendations were followed faithfully, despite my protests. Looking back, I think the doctor was right. As a student in high school, I could never eat enough breakfast to carry me through to lunch. I was a good student and well liked by the teachers, but they were infuriated by seeing me surreptitiously lift the cover of my desk to take a big bite of my lunch-time sandwich. Most of the penalties meted out to me were for this horrendous offense, due entirely to the teachers' ignorance of my constitutional idiosyncrasy, which has continued throughout my life.

The circumstances of our existence turned our kitchen into a veritable beehive. While my mother was cleaning, making beds, mending clothes, and preparing meals, we were setting the table, drying endless dishes, filling the coal hod, running up and down the hill on errands, splitting wood for kindling, and doing other chores. I dreaded nothing so much as having to go to the cellar in the evening to split wood. My brother and I went down into the cave of mystery with a small oil lamp which cast many weird shadows. Neither of us dared look behind, for fear of the monsters who were surely lurking there.

I was certainly not more than nine when my brother and I landed a weekend job with a neighborhood grocer. On Friday afternoons we were to distribute large stacks of handbills advertising the bargains of the morrow. We did very well at first, but it was a tedious job, and we soon found effective methods of lightening our task. We tried putting batches of bills down the sewers, but their capacity was limited. More effective was to use the bills as a coaster on which we could slide down a large mound of fill. But this left heaps of scrap paper in the vicinity. Our most rewarding discovery was that any vacant house would serve as a receptacle for the major part of our stock. This solved our problem, but only until people began to complain to the storekeeper about the lack of advertisements. When the truth came out, we were read the riot act in no uncertain terms; but evidently our other services were valuable enough to spare us loss of the job.

Saturday seemed at least as long as any other two days. We were on the go from 7:30 a.m. until 9:00 or even 10:00 at night. Our main task was to help customers carry home their purchases, but lest we become lazy, the proprietor had other useful tasks for us. There was the weighing out of potatoes (15¾ lbs. to the peck, if my memory serves me well after seventy years), and the filling of bags with coke, which invariably cut the fingers and was therefore avoided in any way possible. By evening we were both ready to drop in our tracks, but stores stayed open late, and customers would come in at any hour. Besides, for the joint effort of two boys for a day and a half, the proprietor paid $1.25, not an unfair wage considering our ages and the general wage scale. The big thing, however, was the satisfaction we derived from contributing, in hard, cold cash, to the family income, which was never much more than adequate.

Although we were kept on the jump from an early age, it would be misleading to suggest that our life was one of misery and tribulation. Quite the contrary, the very plight of the family and the example of hard work set by our mother, led to a feeling of mutual sympathy and solidarity. Furthermore, our neighborhood offered countless opportunities for juvenile activity, far beyond what modern suburbia can offer its children. In the days before automobile traffic, residential streets were the children's playground, where on summer evenings we would play hide-and-seek, duck-off-the-rock, puss-in-the-corner, and other games until darkness set in. At the foot of our hill, there was a large public playground, much used by young men for late-afternoon baseball, but rather too distant and not needed by us. Dorchester Bay, or the Old Harbor, was a huge mud flat at low tide, fragrant to those who have spent many years along the seashore. Occasionally, we would dig there for clams, but mostly for seaworms needed for fishing. Along the bay a good sand beach ran far beyond the low water mark to the various Boston boat clubs and the famous L Street baths. This fine public facility consisted of three divisions: one for women and girls, one for men, and one for boys. Each was set off from the other by a high fence running far out into the water. Both men and boys bathed in the nude without, to my knowledge, this having ever provoked sex incidents. The baths were well kept and policed and were a joy on hot summer days, whether in the clear salt water or on the rich, yellow sand. It was something like a mile's walk to the baths, but for boys of our age this was unimportant.

Beyond the baths the beach ran out to City Point, the tip of the peninsula, where there was a Head House for refreshments, another bathing beach, and a long pier in the English style for promenading. This pier formed one arm enclosing Pleasure Bay, the other being a long wooden pile bridge or causeway connecting the mainland with Castle Island, on which stood the huge harbor fort which was no longer in use but served as a great tourist attraction. "The Castle" commanded every approach to Boston by sea and had served as British headquarters during the occupation of Boston. First fortified in the early years of the colony, it was rebuilt on several occasions, with the present fort dating, I believe, from the 1840s.

The Castle Island causeway had a small drawbridge, no longer operative, under which was a platform designed for fishermen. Although I later lost interest in fishing, as a boy I was passionately devoted to the sport. The water was shallow, and fishing, to tell the truth, was poor. If, along with an assortment of bull-heads and skates, one could take home two or three flounders, the day was well spent. There was, moreover, the added pleasure of watching the shipping in Boston harbor. Sailing vessels of three to six masts, usually loaded with lumber, were a common sight, while the proud transatlantic steamers were a special treat and a great stimulus to the imagination. Recently I began to wonder whether there ever were six-masted sailing ships, except in my imagination. So, even more recently, I was overjoyed to see in the Peabody Museum in Salem a splendid model of such a ship, built at Bath, Maine, as late as 1909.

Despite the rigors of a New England winter, South Boston provided all that youngsters could desire, except perhaps skiing, which was then virtually unknown. The playground at the foot of the hill was flooded at the first sign of frost, and throughout the season was kept free of new snow. Parts, indeed, were kept shaved in preparation for hockey games. We all loved skating, although our skates were a constant affliction. They were the old type that clamped onto the soles and heels of the shoes and usually ended by either coming off or by tearing off the sole or heel. I have warm recollections of the kindness of older boys and young men who were constantly trying to remedy our predicament, either by tightening the clamps or by using straps. The older boys for the most part had the new long, narrow "racing" skates that were screwed into the heels and firmly secured with cross straps at the forward end. A few men even appeared in the amazing new shoe skates, which were riveted onto special, heavy boots and provided security and stability theretofore unknown.

In the days before automobiles the streets were not plowed. On the contrary, sleighs of all sizes and types, including the heavy trucks or camions which we called "pungs" soon had the snow hard-packed. So it remained throughout the winter, providing a firm if somewhat slippery pavement that was ideal for coasting or sledding. Our own street was far too steep, and in any case too dangerous since a streetcar line crossed it at the lower end. Telegraph Street, which ran from the top of the hill down to Dorchester Avenue, was perfect for coasting, the more so as the lower end was reasonably flat and regularly sanded so as to stop all sleds. When the coasting was good, the three or four cross-streets were closed off, so that sleds had a clear run of several city blocks down a steep incline. We made full use of our opportunities, lying prone on the low sleds that could be steered only with the tips of the shoes, an effective but not very desirable method. On moonlight nights we were sometimes allowed to go coasting after supper and above all to watch the young men and women go down the hill at breakneck speed on their double-runners. These were two ordinary sleds connected by a plank and usually by running boards, the front sled being designed for steering. Six or even eight passengers would risk their lives on these contraptions, which provided plenty of thrills, without, to my knowledge, ever having occasioned serious disaster. Thinking back on my boyhood days of swimming, fishing, skating, and coasting, to say nothing of hastily contrived street games, including marbles, I sometimes pity present-day children, who have so little opportunity to work off energy.

In these early years my record in school was, to say the least, undistinguished. In kindergarten I was convinced that the teacher favored a little boy dressed in a velvet suit, thus destroying my prospects of successful competition for her attention. Of the first years of primary school, I have almost no recollection, while in the third grade I was constantly under a cloud because on return from lunch I could never resist playing a few games of marbles and consequently arrived in school with dirty fingers. The teacher, a strict lady with a French name, had me stand in the corner with my back to the class. It was an unpleasant penalty, but not nearly as effective as having one's marbles confiscated. This, I think, proved a permanent remedy.

The fourth of the nine grades of school involved transfer to the grammar school, an attractive, new building not far from home. Unfortunately, my debut there was again inauspicious. The teacher began each morning by reading from the Bible and on an early occasion observed me busy with other concerns. On completion of her reading, she summoned me to her desk and, without a word of explanation, gave me a sharp rap on the open hand with the rattan rod which she always had nearby. It hurt so much that I have often recalled it when reading Dickens, whose characters were treated more frequently than I to this simple mode of punishment. In my own case, my feelings were even more hurt than my physique, for I felt innocent of any intentional misdemeanor and much humiliated before the class.

I think I should say that after this initial episode I got along very well with the teacher, who was highly competent and certainly aroused in me much interest in my studies, especially in geography, history, and spelling. Corporal punishment in the schools has, of course, long since been abolished, but I have never been able to make up my mind on the wisdom of this move. When used with discretion and moderation, I think it was useful, but it was easily abused. As I remember my school years, I would say that most of the teachers exercised effective discipline, and that there were but few instances of physical correction. On the whole, the boys were a decent lot, and there was relatively little fighting even outside the school. But there was, as one would expect, a hard core of really tough boys who were so troublesome that they had to be disciplined by the headmaster. In one case the boy's family brought suit for damages against the headmaster, claiming that the boy's hearing had been impaired.

As I review the first decade of my life, I am keenly aware of the difficulty of marking the tempo of life, especially as reflected in everyday existence. Our family and our neighbors were not concerned with the great affairs of the world of even of the country. To be sure, Teddy Roosevelt, under the tutelage of Admiral Alfred Mahan, sensed the growing importance of the country in world affairs and would on occasion dabble in international issues. But there was certainly very little concern in this country with the vagaries and problems of other countries. One of my early memories is of the Russian-Japanese War of 1904–1905. The newspapers would occasionally print maps with tiny flags showing the position of the armies in Manchuria, but I never heard anyone get excited about the Japanese victories or discuss the revolutionary events in Russia, or even show more than a fleeting pride in Roosevelt's arrangement of the peace conference at Portsmouth, New Hampshire.

While the President was busily "busting" the trusts (always represented as incredibly obese gentlemen smoking huge cigars and with "devil may care" expressions), the country was enjoying prosperity and stability. It was indeed the "horse and buggy age." I saw my first automobile in 1906 or 1907, a vehicle modeled on the genteel carriages of former days. People walked more than can now be imagined. For longer trips they used bicycles (it was the golden age of the bicycle), or the streetcar (standard fare five cents, with ample provision for transfers), or the fast interurban streetacars or trains.

The conditions of life were so fixed as to seem unalterable. The electric refrigerator had not yet supplanted the old icebox, and automatic dishwashers were undreamed of. The only air-conditioning known to man was the electric fan. A loaf of bread cost five cents and so did a quart of milk. Children paid one cent for their candy, or for a sizable pickle, which was much in favor. Clothing, of course, varied in price according to quality, but people of modest means could get a decent suit for $20 or $25. The average workman earned $14 or $15 a week and, if married, had a comfortable flat for $15 per month. Although most houses had toilets and city water, only a few were centrally heated or equipped with electricity. Gas was much used for cooking, but was very unsatisfactory for lighting, as the "mantles," which alone provided an acceptable light, were constantly breaking. Most people used kerosene lamps of varying size and beauty according to the uses for which they were intended. A fine, big, porcelain lamp with circular wick gave out a rich, warm, yellow light, easy on the eyes and soothing to the spirit.

There are probably more than a few old timers who even now would prefer the favorite oil lamp of their youth to the harsh light of modern electric fixtures.

Bathing was a real problem given the lack of proper bathrooms. In our family my hard-working mother would, on a suitable afternoon or evening, heat kettles of water on the coal range, bring out the large, wooden wash bucket and give each of us in succession a good, thorough scrubbing. As we grew older and this procedure became embarrassing, she managed to buy at second hand, a metal bathtub, which could be used by one or another of us in the warm kitchen at times reserved for this purpose. Although we were far from having the daily morning dip so favored by English writers, I can say without reservation that for my mother cleanliness was next to godliness. None of us ever went to school unwashed or improperly clothed. Only a woman of genius could have accomplished so much and done it so well.

One way of making both ends meet was to be on the alert for every favorable opportunity. In the days before the present fantastic and infuriating food packaging, eggs came into the stores in large crates, and some were inevitably cracked or broken. We bought the damaged ones at one-third the regular price, and they served mother's purposes as well as any perfect specimens. The bakeries also made it a practice to get rid of remaining stock on the very next day. We were able to buy pies (normally ten cents) at three for ten, and doughnuts at five cents a dozen. Since three growing boys could consume an impressive quantity of such goodies in an amazingly short time, our "stale" pies and doughnuts were almost indistinguishable from the freshest product.

We liked to read and even more to be read to, which happened occasionally when my mother could find a few spare moments. Fortunately the Boston Public Library maintained a really good branch in South Boston, and we spent many a rainy afternoon there. Among the magazines were *Harper's Bazaar* as well as high-brow journals such as the *Atlantic*. Like all children we looked at pictures whenever we could, but we also checked out numerous Henty and Alger stories, along with Mark Twain and poets such as Whittier and Longfellow, who still wrote intelligible English. In the early years of the century, the great African explorations were quite recent. We read Stanley and many others and got the needed horror thrills from the pictures of savages dancing the war dance at night before stewing their captives in the huge cauldron which the white man had providentially provided.

Among the great days of the year was the seventeenth of March, which celebrated the evacuation of Boston and completely overshadowed my birthday on March 16. Not that my good grandmother, in her little violet cap and with her very lame leg, did not arrive on my birthday with a huge cake in the shape of the appropriate numeral and some highly desired present such as a sweater, but March 17 meant a grand parade, led by our last Indian fighters such as General Miles, surrounded with prancing horsemen, followed by bands and marching soldiers. The day was usually raw and cold, but we shivered rather than miss the splendor. The Irish had appropriated the day as St. Patrick's Day, so the mayor and city notables rode in elegant carriages followed by the Knights of Columbus, the Hibernian Order, and other organizations which, in guady costumes, supplied the pomp and circumstance.

The identification of Evacuation Day with St. Patrick's Day undoubtedly explains, at least in part, the cavalier treatment with which so many history books deal with Washington's first great military success, an event which marked the beginning of systematic war between the colonies and the mother country. True, the skirmishes at Lexington and Concord in April 1775 had demonstrated the determination of the colonists to resist, and the battle of Bunker Hill in June 1775 had marked the first attempt at offensive action. But the evacuation of Boston, the focal point of the revolutionary movement, was the first carefully planned and executed operation and the essential first step toward victory in the War of Independence.

Because I grew up on the slope of Dorchester Heights, I will ask the indulgence of the reader if I embark on a short excursus to establish a proper balance of events. The British had begun the military occupation of Boston in 1765 and in the ensuing

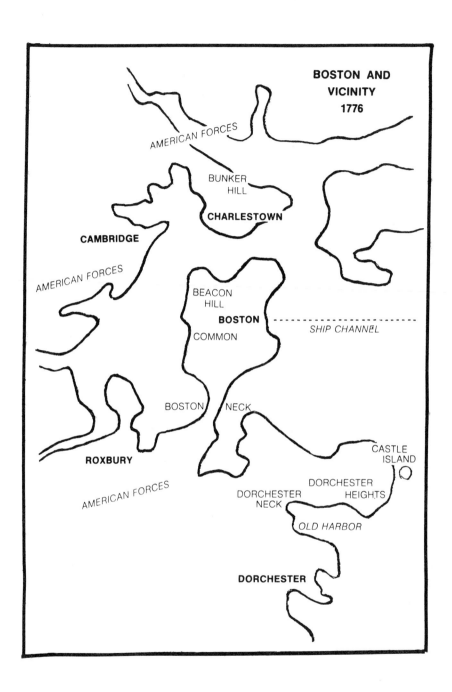

BOSTON AND
VICINITY
1776

AMERICAN FORCES

BUNKER
HILL

CHARLESTOWN

CAMBRIDGE

AMERICAN FORCES

BEACON
HILL

BOSTON

SHIP CHANNEL

COMMON

BOSTON   NECK

ROXBURY

CASTLE
ISLAND

AMERICAN FORCES

DORCHESTER
HEIGHTS

DORCHESTER
NECK

OLD HARBOR

DORCHESTER

years had completely blockaded the town, which at that time was still practically an island with a population of 20,000, connected with neighboring Roxbury by only a narrow strip of land, hardly more than a road, known as Boston Neck. No bridges connected the town with the surrounding communities such as Charlestown, Cambridge, Roxbury, or Dorchester. With a substantial fleet and an excellent base at Castle Island, the British could interdict all communication with the city and eventually starve it into surrender.

Boston was full of British troops and there were many strong posts, notably the forts on Beacon Hill. How to force them to evacuate was a crucial problem. Washington, who had taken command of the Army of the United Colonies in July 1775 and had established his headquarters in Cambridge, spent the winter of 1775–1776 not only in reorganizing, training, and equipping his army of 12,000, but also in planning an assault on the city. Lacking cannon, he had sent General Henry Knox and an appropriate force, to bring cannon from Ticonderoga on Lake George, which the Americans had captured in May 1775. In what was certainly an amazing feat, Knox and his men between December 1775 and February 1776 hauled over the snow on sleds over fifty cannon and mortars, which were indispensable for an offensive. Washington had hoped at first to cross the Charles on the midwinter ice and attack the forts on Beacon Hill, but the ice in the tidal basin was never deep or hard enough to support an invading army. He then altered his plan completely and decided to seize Dorchester Heights, on what was then Dorchester Neck. This area, on the south side of the city, had been neglected by the British, who were diverted by the various engagements fought in the north and west.

Making full use of his newly acquired artillery, Washington had his forces open a formidable bombardment of the British positions on the three successive nights of March 1–3. Then, during the principal bombardment in the night of March 4–5, General Thomas with a force of some 2,000 men, advanced with cannon and defensive equipment up the steep hill (probably along Old Harbor Street on which we lived), occupied the crest and hastily threw up provisional fortifications.

General Howe, the British commander, taken wholly by surprise, at once saw all the implications of the American operation. He promptly organized a counterattack, only to be foiled by a great gale and torrential rains which broke over the area on March 5 and made all action impossible. Seeing that the Americans, firmly entrenched on the Heights, were now in a position to bombard the British positions and fleet anywhere in the area in and around Boston, he made his decision. Rather than see the city destroyed, he decided to evacuate. On March 17 all troops, plus about 1,000 Loyalists, were embarked on British ships and on March 26 sailed for Halifax.

The forced evacuation of the key city in the colonies was a great American achievement, which marked Washington for the eminent general he proved to be and brought the decisive turn which had only been foreshadowed by Lexington, Concord, and Bunker Hill. It was actually an event transcending in importance these earlier engagements, an event well worthy of commemoration.

I do not claim that as a boy I knew this entire story. And in fact, it was not particularly stressed even in our public school. Nonetheless, we knew that South Boston had played a significant role in the Revolution. Dorchester Heights had remained essentially unchanged, though much of it was laid out in transverse streets. Even in my day there were only two important vertical streets: Telegraph Street running from the west directly up to Thomas Park and the beautiful evacuation monument, and Old Harbor Street, running up steeply from Dorchester Avenue on the north, past Thomas Park and down to Eighth Street and the Old Harbor on the south side. For a future historian this was an appropriate setting for the beginning of his career.

The Fourth of July, although the great national holiday, lacked the local appeal of St. Patrick. As a boy, it filled me with feelings of both fear and delight. The firecrackers and blank pistols became larger and louder with every year, so one never knew when one might be scared to death. After dark there was illumination and fireworks displays. These were always impressive, though in children's hands anything more than a roman candle might be dangerous. I remember setting off a skyrocket and forgetting to let go, so that a good part of the skin of my hand went aloft, and I suffered for days while oil and other medicaments were applied to what was, in fact, a rather serious wound. In later years, when cannon crackers were thrown at automobiles, causing panic and accidents, the sale of such devices was forbidden, and only public fireworks, increasingly innocent and unimpressive, remained.

Christmas was, among other holidays, the happiest and most meaningful. In our family it was always celebrated in the German fashion, either at our home or at my aunt's home in Roxbury. The fir tree was decorated with real candles in deep secrecy, and we were warned that anyone peeping through a keyhole might have sand blown into his eye. On Christmas Eve, as soon as night had fallen, we trooped in to see the tree ablaze with lights and dazzling with ornaments. A grown-up would read the Christmas story, and we would sometimes look out to see whether by chance choirs of angels might again be bringing tidings of comfort and joy. We then sang the German Christmas carols until the arrival of Santa Claus. It seemed to us a great misfortune that our Uncle Walter could never be present, as his work as confectioner in the Charlesgate Hotel allegedly required his presence at odd hours. We never guessed that this impressive and rather frightening Santa Claus, who in his deep voice began to inquire as to our past conduct, was none other than our Uncle Walter. Eventually, after the inter-rogation, his huge sack was opened and all kinds of good things emerged. One particular Christmas I shall always remember: He had produced from his sack a wonderful pair of hip-length rubber boots for my older brother and, to my great relief, he ultimately found a similar pair for me. But he seemed unable to find a third pair for our little brother Walter. The tears were soon welling in the round little face, and we all began to lose joy in our wonderful presents. Then, after all the grief, Santa did discover, at the very bottom of the sack, a third pair. Joy was then unconfined, the more so when we were given permis-sion to go out in the dark, to test our wonderful boots in the largest and deepest puddles we could find.

Uncle Walter's little joke, however well intentioned, was a poor idea, particularly when dealing with a young child. It struck my young brother in a sensitive spot, for he could not help feeling like an unwanted child. Born less than three months after my father's death, he was a child of sorrow. One can readily imagine that to my bereaved mother he seemed like an unwelcome addition to an already desperate situation. Moreover, my brother Rudolph, who would never undertake anything without my support, was quite autocratic in excluding Walter from all our undertakings. At an early age the difference of three years in itself presents problems. I often regretted seeing Walter unceremoniously rejected. While quite young I probably sensed that he was, in a way, a fifth wheel. To make amends I decided one day to take him on a tour of the surrounding world. He was perhaps four years old and I seven. For a time all went well, and we made good progress along the beach in the direction of City Point. But long before we got there his strength gave out, and he began to cry with weariness. I tried carrying him on the homeward trek, but that in turn exceeded my limited powers. I was upset about him, feeling responsible for his plight and yet not knowing what to do. Providentially, a kindly Irish policeman stopped and made inquiries. The upshot was that he carried the little fellow home, a matter of quite a few city blocks. I trudged on as best I could, being myself on the point of collapse. The incident, while devoid of serious consequences, quenched my desire for exploration and adventure for some time to come.

Although my mother never seemed to need religion and never went to church, she encouraged us to go to Sunday school, which involved a long walk to Boston (West Newton Street) and return. The church was one of two or three German Lutheran churches in Boston, all belonging to the Missouri Synod, the most conservative wing of the sect. This at least had the advantage that the service, conducted entirely in German, was strictly religious. In Sunday school we learned the Bible story, while the lengthy sermons dealt with major religious issues. The minister was an excellent preacher but unbending in his orthodoxy. I recall that he would occasionally repeat one or another of Luther's own prayers, invoking divine protection against the Turks, who in 1529 were actively besieging Vienna. However, we also sang the Reformer's greatest hymn: "Ein feste Burg ist unser Gott," as well as the countless beautiful hymns of Bach, Zinzendorf, and other devout Lutherans of the past. At Christmas there was naturally an appropriate service at church, when a huge tree, possibly thirty feet high, was erected and lighted with real candles, while the sexton and his aides stood by with wet sponges on long poles to extinguish immediately any unruly candle.

On April 6, 1908 the city of Chelsea, a neighbor of Boston, burned to the ground. It was a cold, windy, snowy day, but for all the discomfort, it was impossible to tear oneself away from the sight of the disaster. From the top of Dorchester Heights, the whole drama unfolded, the leaping flames and the clouds of smoke. Chelsea was a poor city of frame houses and small industry. The high wind made it impossible to save no matter how much fire equipment was brought into action. For this was still the day of horse-drawn equipment, with the pumping-engines fired by wood and coal. There was a fire station on Dorchester Avenue not far from our home, and we were always fascinated by the splendid horses, which were exercised daily in twos and threes along the avenue. There could be no greater thrill than to be on hand when the fire alarm sounded, the men slid down the brass pole from the floor above, the horses broke from their stalls and took their proper places, the harness, suspended from the ceiling, dropped on the horses and off they went at breakneck speed, while the boilers were being fired behind.

I remember the date of the Chelsea fire because I had already become much interested in history and a major disaster was not to be seen every day, and also because it followed roughly on my first academic achievement. In 1907 the tricentennial of the first English settlement in America, at Jamestown, Virginia, was to be celebrated. All over the country, schools were invited to submit essays in one of the many competitions. My grade, the fifth, was called on to write a composition on an imaginary trip to Italy. This was an assignment after my own

heart, for I loved geography and had studied our textbook over
and over again. One of my favorite rainy day occupations was
to trace on the map the places I should like to visit. I had
watched many a great liner arriving or leaving Boston Harbor
and could easily picture life aboard. Arrived in Italy, I touched
all the important places, described the scenery, reviewed the
art galleries, and in general produced a creditable minor
Baedeker. My essay was judged one of the best, and I was
obliged to read it in several classrooms before it was sent off to
Jamestown. There was one shadow on this pleasant episode,
however: My essay was tied for first place with that of another
boy who, among other things, had his ship sound a shrill whistle
as it got underway. This notion of the shrill whistle almost
broke my heart. Why had I not thought of this thrilling detail?
I was ready to yield first place to the boy who had had so impressive an inspiration. But apparently the judges were mildly
suspicious of this very phrase. Investigation revealed that the
boy had been helped by his father—the shrill whistle was
actually Dad's, not the son's. This ruled out my competitor's
effort, but I never really ceased wishing that I, too, had
equipped my essay with a shrill whistle. After all, great ships
could hardly depart without one.

My first literary effort led my teacher to suggest that I take
the examinations for admission to the regular six-year course
of the Boston Latin School, which a boy would normally take
at the end of the next (seventh) grade. Neither my mother nor
anyone else of our acquaintance knew anything of the Latin
School, although it was the oldest school in the country,
founded in 1635, one year before Harvard, for which it was
thought of as the preparatory school. In the early twentieth century, it was one of four central high schools of the Boston school
system, the other three being the English High School, the
Mechanic Arts High School, and the Commercial High School.
Only well-qualified boys were admitted, and even they were
quickly expelled and returned to their local high school if they
failed to meet high standards.

Originally located on the site of the present Boston city hall
on School Street, the Latin School had, over the centuries, made

several moves until in my day it was situated on Warren Avenue at the corner of Dartmouth. It was an elegant, well-lighted building, joined behind to a similar structure used by the English High School. Throughout the nineteenth century, it had remained a select school for boys, with only men as instructors, and in my time was still sending more graduates to Harvard than any other school, public or private. The roster of its graduates contained the names of many eminent leaders, in many walks of life. I need hardly say, though with due modesty, that I was deeply moved when in 1972 the Alumni Association of the school named me Boston Latin School Boy of the year. It was then sixty years since my graduation, during which I had never faltered in my devotion to the school and the principles it inculcated.

After this somewhat flowery tribute I regret to say that on first trying, I failed to pass the entrance examinations. This, I think, was chiefly because I took them a year earlier than was usual. Nonetheless, I felt so humiliated that for a week or ten days I could not bring myself to break the news of my failure to my mother. I did not go to the old school, but killed the time knocking around here and there and wondering how I might face the music. In the end I had no alternative, but was rather astounded that my mother took the matter less tragically than I had anticipated. The upshot of the incident was that I returned to the grammar school for another year. I liked the teachers and enjoyed the work. On completing the seventh grade I once again took the Latin School examinations and had no difficulty in passing them.

CHAPTER II

Education
of a Humanist

IN SEPTEMBER 1907, at the age of eleven, I entered the six-year course at the Boston Latin School. For years my schooling presented a real transportation problem since the school was at least three miles from my home. It meant crossing Dorchester Heights and going about six city blocks to the Dover Street Bridge, which crossed the Fort Point Channel of Boston Harbor and extensive railroad yards. Continuing on Dover Street one crossed Washington Street and after four or five short blocks Tremont Street, from which Warren Avenue ran as far as Columbus Avenue. In fair weather I would go by bicycle, following an entirely different and less populous route, going down the hill from our house to Columbia Road and Andrews Square, thence over a long stretch on Southampton Street over what at that time was a blasted heath. Southampton was eventually crossed by Albany Street which could be followed to Brookline or some parallel street, crossing Tremont and reaching Warren Avenue not far from the school.

Bicycling in cold or windy weather was not pleasant, and I often went to school on foot. Only in severe weather was I allowed to take the streetcar, which involved a five-cent fare each way. On the whole I liked to walk, for much of the pleasure of bicycling was taken away by the rough ride over the cobblestone streets. The only objection to walking was not the distance but the route which traversed some of the worst parts of South Boston. I was once beaten up by a gang of four or five boys at the corner of B Street and therefore preferred to take even substantial detours to avoid a repetition of the experience.

I think from my years in the Latin School that I benefited most from having mature, strong masters. A fatherless boy with a mother of strong personality would inevitably tend to have a feminine point of view. In early school years, children probably benefit most from the maternal understanding of women, but I think that in the critical years of adolescence it is important that pupils should be under the guidance and tutelage of teachers of their own sex. My mother's supreme virtue was consistency. We could predict her reaction with complete assurance in any situation, and this alone helped greatly to simplify life. In the Latin School I met with the same virtue, but in its masculine form. Corporal punishment being illegal, the masters maintained discipline by the strength of their personality and by the discreet use of the misdemeanor mark. They certainly managed to instill ideals of responsibility, hard work, and indeed all the manly virtues. Henry Pennypacker, the headmaster, was physically a real specimen, a man who enjoyed the reputation of having been a hammer-thrower in his college days. Not content with sitting in his office, he would appear unannounced in any class at any time and take the opportunity to speak intimately with the boys. I remember distinctly that at one of the regular Monday morning assemblies of the entire school, he announced in solemn words that recently a boy had come to his office emitting an unmistakable scent of perfume. It was hard for him to restrain his contempt. Never, he declared, did he want to smell on a boy any odor other than that of good yellow soap.

As for instruction, I would say that the Latin School in my day was distinctly old fashioned. I suppose it was modeled on English ideas. It was strictly classical, concentrating on Latin and Greek, ancient history, English composition and literature. The only foreign language taught was French, while mathematics was carried only through algebra. Science was mostly a dab of botany and chemistry, with emphasis on experimental physics. There was a great deal of learning by rote, with unremitting drill on grammar (French as well as Latin and Greek): conjugations, declensions, sentence by sentence translation. It took a lot of time and effort and it sounds terrible, but I am not sure that, in the long run, it was not a useful form of education. In my later teaching career, I have often been appalled by the ignorance of many students, some of whom came from high-grade schools. Clearly, they had no notion of grammar: They could not write an acceptable sentence or really appreciate great writing when they encountered it. In my own field, which was history, they would discourse sagely on major events and problems, while they quite obviously had only a scanty, muddled knowledge of the facts. Under the rigorous discipline of the older schooling, one knew what one knew. With a solid grounding, one could absorb new ideas and form judgments which rested on more than mere prejudice.

There would be no point in rehearsing the events of my school life, even when dealing with such eventful and changeable years as those of adolescence. I shall confine my remarks, then, to reminiscences of what were to me notable episodes.

In the lowest (sixth) class, I found myself under a legendary teacher, "Cudjo" Capen, who had then been teaching in the school for fifty-six years and, though he lived in Dedham, claimed never to have missed a day of school. Cudjo, who got his name from a Civil War novel entitled *Cudjo's Cave*, was eighty-five years old and used to assure us that he would live to be a hundred if allowed to teach. Actually he continued, I think, to the age of ninety-two, when the Boston School Committee belatedly passed a regulation requiring retirement at seventy. Needless to say, Cudjo died within a few months of his enforced retirement.

Capen was a benevolent old gentleman who always wore a Prince Albert frock. Every morning he stood ready to sharpen pencils with a curious, scimitarlike knife, and at the sound of the bell he would hobble down the corridor and return with a glass of cold water, which was evidently essential to his welfare. To tell the truth, he was too old to be teaching. We reached the point of declining *mensa, mensae* and conjugating *sum, es, est,* but without understanding what it was all about. On the other hand, for a lad of eleven a man of eighty-five was a truly venerable figure. With my historical proclivities, I realized that having been born in 1823, Capen was nearly a contemporary of Napoleon. At any rate, he saw the light in the very year of Lafayette's visit to Boston and the dedication of the Bunker Hill monument. Like myself, Capen was born in South Boston and claimed to have walked often to Harvard, from which he graduated in 1843. For me he was a living link with the past, and while I cannot remember that he taught me much, I loved and revered him.

In my second year I fell under the influence of a boy who, with his father, lodged in our home. He was not really a bad boy, but he was twice as sophisticated as I and tended to ridicule my scholastic and other efforts. The result was that my grades sank rapidly and would probably have had led to dismissal from school, had not the Latin teacher, Alaric Stone, intervened in typically drastic Latin School fashion. Standing at his classroom door during change of classes, he stopped me as I passed by and, taking me by the lapel of the coat, said sternly: "Langer, unless within the coming month, you raise your Latin grade from the present 73 to 90 I shall see to it that you are expelled from the school." He knew, of course, that I was basically a good student and that for some reason I had been slipping. His categorical threat was not to be taken lightly. At the end of the month my Latin grade had advanced miraculously to 93, and I remained in school.

By and large, my fellow students were a likeable lot. They came from all parts of greater Boston and the majority from reasonably well-to-do families. I have often regretted that I was not able to participate more freely in the school life. Not being able to afford the price of the school lunch, I ate my sandwiches and apple at my desk. I would have liked to join the Glee Club or take part in one of the sports, but I could not afford to stay for practice beyond the closing hours of 2 p.m. One afternoon a week I had to stay for military drill, at which I was not a notable success. It was squads right and squads left, but only the band interested me. In my final year, the bandmaster was a friend of mine, who strutted in front of the company twirling his baton, while I was consumed with envy.

About the middle years of my schooling, I have but few recollections except that I became engrossed in our history studies. The corridors of the school were lined with large sepia engravings of classical ruins. These I came to know intimately and to love, so my introduction to ancient history was natural. Each student had a Classical Dictionary, which gave in detail the involved biographies of all the ancient deities and the achievements of the classical heroes. Our instruction in history, as in other subjects, was more a matter of memorizing than anything else. Every week we had to learn by rote the contents of a mimeographed sheet dealing with a Greek or Roman institution. I cannot say that I felt the need to know that much about the *praetor* or the *quaestor*, but it was the teacher, my favorite teacher, Patrick Campbell, whom I shall never forget. A man of warm sympathy and lively humor, he could make anything interesting. I was not in the least surprised in later years when Campbell succeeded Pennypacker as principal of the school and eventually became superintendent of schools in Boston.

As far as I know, my grades in these years were consistently high, once my mother had gotten rid of the lodger and his objectionable son. This was true even of mathematics, though I had no aptitude for problems and often wished that men would not row diagonally across fast-flowing rivers, or other men take so much time in completing a set amount of work. My high standing must have somehow attracted the attention of the headmaster, for one day, while I was in the third class, he called me into his office and announced unceremoniously that if I could pass the preliminary examinations for admission to Harvard, he would have me skip the second class and become a member of the first or graduating class.

I must remark at this point that in those halcyon days College Entrance Examinations, carefully composed and scrupulously graded, did not exist. Harvard gave its own examinations in the required subjects, and it is probably safe to say that the professors did not devote their best thought or their most valuable hours to compiling what were, after all, only elementary tests. I knew nothing about Harvard, nor of what might be expected of me. I simply followed directions, took the streetcar, changed at Park Street to a Harvard Square line, located the old Jefferson Physics Laboratory and there took the tests, which I remember as rather simple and altogether fair. In short I passed.

Everyone, including Principal Pennypacker and myself, was delighted. I still treasure Pennypacker's note, handwritten in his bold style: "Because he stands accredited with twelve or more points in the Harvard College Examinations, William Leonard Langer is promoted to Class I, on trial."

It seemed at the time like a great idea, like appropriate recognition of capability beyond that required for the second class. Now, I am convinced that it was a very poor, a very mistaken idea. It certainly confused my education and I never quite recovered from the loss of a whole year's work. I had regularly won a modern or classical prize each year, receiving such treasures as Bulwer Lytton's *Last Days of Pompeii*, Creasy's *Ten Decisive Battles*, and Oliver Wendell Holmes' *Autocrat at the Breakfast Table*. (I loved them all, but none as ardently as Jane Porter's *Scottish Chiefs* which, despite its length, I read three or four times.) But now I was reduced to scrounging for even respectable grades. Besides, I lost all the companions of my school years and had to make an effort (none too successful) to break into a new circle of mostly older boys. When at the end of my senior year I was faced by the final examinations for Harvard, I was unable to do more than squeak by. It would probably have been pedagogically sounder to have given me more or harder assignments, and to have graded them more severely. To skip a class involves much more than added scholastic work for the student. He will almost invariably respond more favorably to additional assignments if allowed to stay with his own classmates.

I will wind up my review of my Latin School years with a reminiscence of my graduation with the class of 1912. My mother, naturally, sat among the guests, while I and my col-

leagues listened to the usual program. Eventually, we reached
the award of prizes. I remember feeling rather glum as the
various names were called and the fortunate recipients marched
up to receive their prizes. I had not the slightest reason to be
included. But at the very end the headmaster announced a
prize of which I had not even heard: It was a prize for the
student who had made the greatest progress in his final year,
and it amounted to eight five-dollar gold pieces. This prize was
awarded to me, in recognition of my having survived all the
tribulations of an out-of-course student. "Furthermore," said
Mr. Pennypacker, "Langer deserves special recognition as a
student who, during five years in the school, has not only not
missed a single day, but has never been tardy." I was surprised
by my own virtues, but most of all by the gleaming gold pieces
which, in terms of the values of that day, represented a substantial sum of money. My mother could not suppress her great
pride in my achievement. We never expected much praise from
her, for she always took the attitude that we were only meeting
the requirements of an impoverished family. I ought to remark,
though, that on one or two occasions I overheard her talking to
friends and was almost stunned by the glowing terms in which
she commended us.

By this time it had been decided, at least tacitly, that I
should go to Harvard. This was a great relief to me, because
at about this time the pastor of our church called on my mother
and explained to her that if she would allow me to train for the
ministry, the Lutheran Church would defray all the expenses of
my education. It was a tempting proposition, persuasively advanced. But my mother was not devout enough to see her son
committed to religious work for life. My religious feelings were
at that time much stronger, but I, too, found it impossible to
accept the idea of the ministry as a life work. Harvard seemed
much more alluring to us, especially as it did not involve leaving home.

In discussing my five years of school entirely in terms of my
Latin School experience, I have, naturally, been recording only
a segment of my life in the crucial years from eleven to seventeen. One of my great interests from early years was in music,

an interest which has been prominent in one way or another throughout my entire life. Eager as ever to encourage accomplishments as well as achievements, my mother found a violin teacher for my older brother, a short, passionate Polish youth who, so far as we could judge, really had an amazing technique and a real musical understanding. My brother was not an eager musical student, but he was induced to practice and became a reasonably competent amateur. Much later in life, he was still playing violin sonatas, with his wife at the piano.

I hope I am not arrogant when I say that music meant much more to me than to him. For a few dollars, my mother managed to buy an old square piano and to find me a genteel lady teacher. She sat doing her embroidery while I slaved away at "Purple Pansies Waltz" or some other gem of sheet music. I felt pretty unhappy about my lack of progress, so I was presently put in the hands of an elderly German gentleman in a frock coat, with the appropriate name of Lehrmann. I suppose he was, or had been, a competent musician, but his only interest was in having me play scales and Czerny exercises. Inscribing each assignment with the phrase "Mit Gott," he seemed to be invoking for me the support of the deity in conquering the keyboard technique. I begged him again and again to let me study a piece of real music, but his invariable reply was that it was useless until one had mastered technique. So surreptitiously I bought at a department store sale various pieces that sounded worthwhile. I worked in secret on the Anvil Chorus from *Trovatore*, on the lengthy introduction of *Wilhelm Tell*, and on kindred operatic gems which gave me at least qualified emotional satisfaction.

My musical efforts were necessarily hampered by the piano's age and situation—being in the unheated parlor room, it was ice cold during the winter months. When the keyboard became impossibly cold, I lit a Perfection oilstove and set it beside me. It helped, but not very much.

I cannot remember how long I "studied" under old Herr Lehrmann, but I well recall when my mother, unhappy over the situation, bought a new Henry Miller upright piano on the installment plan. This was very heaven, and I played and played even without instruction. Now, in old age, I grieve at all the wasted enthusiasm and effort, but I still cannot see where my mother could have found competent advice about our musical education. It is certainly a pity, if not a scandal, that when I graduated from the Latin School, I knew nothing of Bach, Handel, Haydn, Mozart, Beethoven, Chopin, and the other great masters. I may have heard their names but I was utterly ignorant of their music.

While we were still living in South Boston a certain Aborn Grand Opera Company produced, in English, a whole series of the well-known operas. They were given in Boston's attractive opera house, located on Huntington Avenue, close to where the Museum of Fine Arts has since been built. I believe that the price of the tickets was altogether reasonable, but what interested us most was that in the uttermost recesses of the second balcony seats could be obtained for twenty-five cents.

My mother was convinced that her older boys (and presumably she herself) could not afford to pass up this opportunity. So we went to opera weekly and heard very competent singers perform most of the customary operas. We were so high up on the balcony that we looked down on the singers' heads. In later life it always struck me as somewhat strange to be on the same level with them.

This operatic enterprise was not without its strenuous side. It involved a long walk, from the bottom of the Heights to Andrew Square and thence across an almost deserted wasteland, which was Southampton Street. This eventually connected with Massachusetts Avenue along which a very long walk, past Washington Street, Tremont Street and Columbus Avenue and another quarter of a mile brought us to the opera house. Operas, as everyone knows, are not distinguished by their brevity. It was often 11:00 p.m. when we emerged, but all aglow with the beauty of the performance and full of critical comment. It was a long and weary trudge home, but we were young and enthusiastic, and, if nothing else, accustomed to walking what now seems like unconscionable distances.

The decade preceding the outbreak of the First World War

was noteworthy for a number of inventions that have fundamentally changed human society. The automobile was making its way with the wealthy classes, though mechanical problems and the condition of the roads kept it from becoming common. The moving picture in one form or another may go back to the closing years of the previous century, but I saw an example only after entering the Latin School in 1907. Word spread in our class that on Dover Street there was a place where moving pictures were shown. The idea seemed preposterous, but the few pennies that I needed were somehow found, and I watched the screen in utter amazement as firemen fought a great blaze. It was primitive and jerky, but nevertheless immensely impressive, the rather crude forerunner of an art form that, even in the silent type, was to be highly perfected within twenty years.

Quite unforgettable to me was an even more incredible as well as ominous event: the great air meet at Squantum, just across Dorchester Bay in our full view. In 1911, less than ten years after the Wright Brothers' epochal flight at Kitty Hawk, many of the great pioneers of aviation assembled at Squantum. Among those present I think was one of the Wright Brothers, Graham-White, Santos-Dumont, Glenn Curtiss, and several others. During the meet one prize was awarded for a nonstop flight from Squantum to Worcester to Providence to Squantum, a total of less than 150 miles. Another great achievement was the flight over water to Boston Light and return, a distance of twenty miles. Since on their return to the Squantum field many of the fliers flew low over Dorchester Heights, we had marvelous views of them sitting on the wing of their biplane, tossed by the air currents on the hill.

Another great and spectacular event, though in no sense a human achievement, was the appearance in 1910 of Halley's Comet, which had been observed and recorded every seventy-six years since 240 B.C. In the course of my life I have seen three complete eclipses of the sun: one in Connecticut in the early twentys, one at Gloucester in the late thirties, and one at Mt. Desert, in Maine, in the late sixties. No one who has seen the sun gradually blotted out, the birds stop singing, everything become silent, and a purple haze cover the landscape would hesitate to describe the phenomenon as one of the most impressive in the universe. But a total eclipse is a matter of only seconds or at best minutes, while Halley's comet was with us for weeks. As I recall, it appeared hazy in the southern sky in late summer and increased in brilliance until late September or October, when it began to fade out again. It was the most beautiful spectacle I have ever seen. On every clear evening, and there were many in the New England autumn, it stood over Dorchester Bay, a huge ball of fire with a long and brilliant tail. I should very much like to see it again on its reappearance in 1986, but I fear that at my age this is probably a vain hope.

In all these years as we were growing up, my mother continued untiringly to carry the heavy burden of our support. It must be said, however, that she never pampered us. Wherever there were a few cents to be earned, we were pressed into service. On Saturday mornings we were required to take our cart to the city stables and bring back several loads of manure, with which she managed to cultivate her small and much-loved garden. This was hardly a congenial task. The one I dreaded most, however, was the periodic climb to the roof to reputty the leaky skylight. This involved placing a twelve-foot ladder on the uppermost stairway and climbing to the top, from which one could scramble up another few feet and struggle through the skylight. This happened to be located only about a foot from the side of the house, which meant a terrifying fifty-foot drop. For better or worse the job was done and we (my brother first) scrambled down feet first, found the ladder with directions from my mother, and so returned to the bosom of our happy home.

Our tenants were a quiet German couple on the third floor, and on the second Mrs. Wood, of Lancashire, and her consumptive son, Harry, a wool-comber. The mother, still quite illiterate, was a kind and patient soul. Harry occasionally suffered a severe hemorrhage in the middle of the night. Rudolph and I were then stirred out of our sleep and sent running a mile or so to summon the doctor, who quickly dressed, harnessed his horse and arrived in his gig in good time. He told Mrs. Wood that her son must eat a lot of spinach to recoup the losses of blood. But, she lamented, Harry detested spinach which, in her cuisine, was simply boiled in water and looked like a wet rag. My mother thereupon gave her a dish of delicious chopped spinach in cream which at once took Harry's fancy and drove his mother to hurry back and beg for more.

Among the longest lasting of our boarders was a man of late middle age, who had a rented room in a house opposite. He was much better educated than most and in every way more interesting, though his lameness tended to make him irritable in wet weather, and he was by nature argumentative and litigious. I do not know if he liked us, but he at least took an interest in us and at times would talk like a Dutch uncle to my older brother, who himself had a short temper and dark moods. The great thing about this Mr. Schaefer was that he owned a white bull terrier, with a black spot on his back. Since his owner was at work all day, Terry became, to all intents and purposes, our dog and a wonderful companion. Homely and ferocious-looking, he was one of the gentlest of animals and was rarely provoked by other dogs. But when he was, the bull dog in him came to light. He seized his opponent by the throat and would not let go. Men came hurrying with pails of cold water which they threw over the contestants and at times were obliged to build a little fire under them to break the stranglehold.

Terry was always prepared to run errands with us and had the sweet habit of invariably carrying a stick in his mouth. Sometimes he could not find a suitable one, and the poor dog would all but kill himself dragging a sizable branch or board. We loved him dearly, and I am sure that having him along helped protect us from trouble with hostile boys. On Saturday afternoons his master would take him to his lodging and give him a thorough scrubbing. He would appear at dinner time white as snow, with his hide showing a glowing pink under the white fur.

I am sure that, if I wracked my brains, I could recapture many more episodes of my boyhood years; but it will suffice if, after reviewing my Latin School years, I speak of our great and profitable enterprise, our newspaper business. So many boy-heroes in the novels of Horatio Alger and Oliver Optic had started in as newsboys and had made good, that we were all too eager to embark on a similar career. My brother Rudolph might have obtained a license two years before when he reached the age of ten. But he never wanted to become involved in new undertakings unless I was there to support him. So we had to wait until 1906, when I turned ten. Our applications for licenses went in and mine returned promptly, while my brother's was somewhat delayed. I was all for starting and finally offered to lend my badge to my brother, while I would operate illegally for a few days without the necessary credentials.

We started out for the Boston newspaper row on Washington Street between Milk and State Streets, only to find ourselves in an unruly throng of boys all trying to get the first bundles of papers off the presses and get the hottest news to the streets. Somehow we survived the pushing and hauling and swearing and were presently on Washington Street, each with twenty-five papers. All the nearby street corners had already been appropriated by others, so that eventually we had to go beyond Essex Street. I recall that on our way a gentleman stopped me in front of the old Adams House and asked me for a paper. I was completely flabbergasted by this sudden demand and appealed to my brother for help. He sold one of his papers while I still had my twenty-five under my arm. Eventually we reached Essex Street and beyond that point the pressure was less. My brother established himself on the corner of Washington and Beach Streets, and I went on to Kneeland Street, where a corner saloon seemed to hold promise of activity.

We did reasonably well on our first days, despite occasional challenges by other newsboys, who alleged a primary right to our corners. And then a strange episode occurred. A respectable-looking gentleman bought one of my papers and then engaged me in conversation. He thought, so he said, that a badge was required for selling newspapers. I replied in all innocence that I had a badge but had lent it to my brother pending the issuance of his badge. Without further argument he passed on, visited my brother at his stand and secured complete corroboration of my story.

A few days later my mother, to her great distress, received a summons for us both to appear in the South Boston Juvenile Court, where a hearing was set for the following day. With utmost trepidation we penetrated the sacred precincts. The judge listened gravely to the details of our wrongdoing and ended by fining me one cent for lending my badge to another, while he fined my brother one dollar for operating without proper credentials. I think this episode is worth recalling, if only to demonstrate the high degree of efficiency arrived at by the police and justice departments in those primitive times.

If my memory does not deceive me, we sold newspapers on Washington Street during the entire summers of 1906 and 1907. We would set out in the late forenoon, catch the early afternoon editions and, if the weather permitted, would stay on until eight or even nine in the evening to sell the baseball extras. It is hardly necessary to remark that in those days before radio the newspapers were the unchallenged source of news. Most of them sold for a penny, but I think the *Herald* fetched two cents and the high-toned *Transcript* (of which we sold mighty few) cost three cents. The Sunday editions were all ten cents.

Constantly on the alert to improve our position, we gradually worked our way up to Washington and Boylston Streets, one of the best spots in town. At that time one of the newspapers employed a mysterious Mr. Raffles, who carried a copy of the newspaper in question in his hand and each day moved about in an announced district of the city. The first person to recognize him then received a prize of a thousand dollars.

One day Mr. Raffles was slated to appear in Segal's, a large department store between Essex Street and Hayward Place, just opposite our newspaper territory. Naturally thousands of people foregathered to take part in the hunt. Since, in order to win the prize it was necessary for the finder also to have a copy of the newspaper in hand, we sold papers as fast as we could get them. Indeed, we did what is known as a land-office business and made a tidy sum of money without ourselves losing time in the search of Mr. Raffles.

In the autumn of 1907, when my older brother was entering the Mechanic Arts High School and I was embarking on the six-year Latin School course, it was clear that we could no longer continue our Washington Street activities, which, by the way, were extremely strenuous, considering that they involved a long walk from home and an equally lengthy trek in the evening after a long day on one's feet. We had, from the start, attempted to build up a clientele (what we correctly called a "route" while everyone else talked of our newspaper "rout"). In these efforts we had the support of our younger brother Walter, now seven years of age and both able and willing to do his share in local deliveries and collections. Walter was a quiet, unassuming youngster, too young to participate in the affairs of his elders. Rudolph, it seemed to me, always gave him rather short shrift, so that I could never avoid feeling protective toward him. Because of this it was something of a tragedy when, in a friendly tassle, I knocked him against the kitchen stove and caused a three-inch gash on his head. I was consumed with feelings of guilt and pity, and gladly went with him, every morning, to the outpatient department of the Carney Hospital, where his wound was dressed. Since then, and in fact throughout my life, I have continued to be devoted to him, as he is to me.

Having given up our Boston street sales, we rather quickly developed a substantial route. Indeed, we were able to afford delivery of the papers at our house by the Railroad News Company. They arrived around 6:00 or 6:30 in the morning, when we were all set to start off on delivery. I ought to interject here that newspaper delivery in those days was very different from what it is today. The paper had to be left at the door of whatever floor the customer lived on. If it was much delayed, we were taken to task. Nowadays we find it hard to secure delivery at all, and the newspaper may well be thrown from an automobile and remain on the lawn or the front steps until thoroughly soaked by rain. I recall one old gentleman who seemed to live for one edition after the other, and who was the only one of our many customers who subscribed to the *Transcript*. If, by ill luck, delivery of the papers to us was somewhat delayed and we could not meet his deadline even by special effort, we could be sure of a violent scolding followed by a threat to sever the connection. Looking back, I can see that he was far too wise a man to translate his words into action.

Before starting on our house-to-house delivery, we would leave a stack of papers at the corner grocery store at the foot of the hill, where men hurrying to work could take one and leave the money. The grocer, a not very amiable German, was nevertheless kind enough to let us keep our papers there and even to put weights on them to prevent them from blowing away.

Our business was definitely prospering, and every Saturday evening we would come home with a pocket full of coins collected from our far-flung customers, most of whom were commendably proper in meeting their obligations. But as we advanced in years, so our capabilities increased and our ambition mounted. At the foot of our hill ran the Bay View streetcar line to Boston. It was always crowded in the business hours, and as far as we could discover, the men had no chance to get a morning newspaper until they reached our stand. To meet this intolerable situation my brother and I both secured licenses to operate on the streetcars. We got aboard, worked our way through the strap-hanging throng, and sold a good many papers. To save time, we then jumped off the moving streetcar on to the cobblestone pavement and hurried back to our stand to await the next contingent. We became very adroit at this business, but it was in fact a risky procedure, the details of which my mother mercifully never learned. Strangely enough, neither of us had a mishap, not even a sprained ankle.

The newspaper business was truly profitable. My older brother dropped out of school after a couple of years, and took a full-time job in a seed and plant business. But he continued to help with the heavy Sunday morning assignment and, to all intents and purposes, Walter served as substitute. Personally, I was involved for six solid years, during which it was a source of great satisfaction to me that in our heyday we were able to earn as much as $15 a week, which was the accepted wage of the average workingman.

It was not, of course, all a matter of beer and skittles. My mother was positively heroic. On cold winter mornings she arose and brewed some coffee to get us going. Then she stirred us up, sleepy as could be, from the warm German featherbeds and almost before we knew it had us in warm underwear and clothing. We had a cup of coffee and were on deck when the newspapers arrived, but on really severe mornings we almost froze to death before returning home. I recall my mother having a hot kitchen stove and putting my numb feet into the warm oven, while tears streamed down my face and I could hardly eat my breakfast of rolled oats. How, under these circumstances, I managed to get to the Latin School by nine o'clock every day for five successive years is a question I have never been able to answer.

Sundays, far from being days of rest, were days to test the stoutest heart. The newspapers were not as voluminous then as they are in our own ludicrous times, but they consisted of five or six sections which were delivered separately and had to be assembled before delivery. This operation was performed on the floor of our front hall, where my mother, down on her knees, easily won the prize for speed and efficiency. Once assembled, the papers were too heavy to be carried in any quantity. We were forever tinkering with carts that would lighten the load. Time and again they broke down, but we somehow managed over the years, and they have left nothing worse than an unpleasant memory.

Some time in 1911, I think, a young fellow offered to buy our newspaper route. Although he could pay only $7, we decided to sell, as the demands of the job had become very onerous, and we speculated that other chances to dispose of the route were unlikely to be numerous. I must say, when it was gone, I felt for the first time in years like a free boy.

CHAPTER III

The Unknown Harvard

WHEN I began my career at Harvard in September 1912, I was as innocent as a newborn babe. Obviously, my family had no place in the roster of Harvard names. I had no relative or friend who had ever been to Harvard and had only the vaguest idea of how college work was conducted. I did receive from the college a copy of that lovely little booklet by Dean Le Baron Russell Briggs (the exact title now escapes me), which discussed what a college career meant and how Harvard men should conduct themselves. In addition I had, of course, the college catalogue, which I studied assiduously.

I discovered in the literature a number of intriguing items. First, a student might, by taking six courses each year rather than the usual four, complete the work for the degree in three years. Second, one could win honors by carefully planning one's courses to meet specific requirements.

I had a lively interest in the classics and in history, but after much consultation in the family it was decided that I had better choose modern languages as my principal field. I had had the normal number of years of French study, and while I had never systematically studied German, I had the advantage of hearing and speaking that language in the home. I could therefore begin German at a more advanced stage and, on graduation, would stand a better chance of finding a teaching position. I had long since decided that teaching was to be my métier and have always sympathized with those boys who, even in their senior year, are undecided as to their future.

I was much gratified to learn, from the catalogue, that an honors program in modern languages demanded further work in both Latin and Greek. Indeed, the program seemed tailored for my needs. I therefore enrolled in two successive years of French, a year of Greek, and a year of advanced Latin. I also selected a general survey course on the history of English literature and a half-course on solid geometry and calculus. I had no aptitude for mathematics, but it seemed to me that I should pursue the subject at least through calculus. The one flaw in my program was the lack of an introductory course in European history, or even in government. In my ignorance I counted on embarking upon the social sciences in my second or third year. As luck would have it, I could not fit them into my second year program either, and only then discovered that if these courses were taken after the second year, they would be given only half credit. Since I was working toward a three-year degree, I had to pass them up. How strange are the dispensations of fate. I, a future historian by profession, went through college without even the general survey course in history.

My mother's decision to allow me to enroll at Harvard was much criticized by our middle-class neighbors and even by our relatives. How could a woman, struggling to support a family, have such extravagant ideas? In that day even a high school education was exceptional, and the idea of going to Harvard seemed preposterous. The natural thing would have been for her sons, as we reached fourteen, to find some respectable job and earn an honest week's pay, leaving Harvard to the well-to-do. But my mother never wavered. Her lamented husband had preached to her that education was to be valued in the highest degree. I had been awarded one of the numerous Price Greenleaf scholarships, which covered the Harvard tuition ($150 per annum in those prelapsarian days) in return for two hours of work per week for a professor. This aid alone would lighten the financial burden.

It was of inestimable value to me that the subway had just been completed from Park Street to Harvard Square, thus greatly reducing the time consumed in travel. Nonetheless, it took me about an hour to go each way. I usually managed to make a change at Washington and Dover Street, which enabled me to run into a nearby modern Jewish bakery and get right from the great electric ovens a loaf of rye bread with caraway seeds, of which we were all exceedingly fond. This was at about 2:30 p.m., and I can still see "Mihel" with his twenty-foot shovel, going into the oven and trying various loaves in order to find one that was just done. It was, naturally, so hot that I could carry it only in my green book bag. But what a thrill, on arriving at home, to be served along with the bread a succulent slice of the pot roast that was usually simmering on the back of the stove, ready for any boy at any hour. (Bread has always been something of a problem for me. I could get no satisfaction out of any of the standard American types, most of which seemed like blotting paper. Consequently, I have gone to considerable trouble to find palatable bread. Light Jewish rye with caraway seeds is my favorite, but I am fond also of Italian and French breads, to say nothing of San Francisco sourdough, which I would certainly class with the best bread I have ever tasted.)

As I look back, I am again impressed by the traditional, not to say routine, teaching, even at an eminent institution like Harvard. Instruction in French continued to be primarily translation of set passages, naturally from the classics and of ever-increasing difficulty. There was some discussion of the great dramas as literature, but I cannot say that there was much reference to the classics in their historical setting. The Sun King or the French Revolution might be referred to now and again, but I certainly did not learn much French history. The courses in Latin and Greek were no different. We read the Latin authors through Horace and Lucullus and in Greek concentrated on Homer.

This all sounds like a dreary program, but the personality of most of the instructors far outweighed the routine nature of the work. I have the most pleasant memories of Rudolph Altrocchi, who taught French and later became a professor at the University of Illinois. He not only had an infectious enthusiasm for his subject, but such an agreeable, lively personality that he made almost any assignment interesting. I often walked across the Yard with him after class and discussed all kinds of personal and other problems as he sauntered along swinging his green bag.

The teachers of the Classics, too, were inspiring men, and I am sure brought out all that was amusing in Plautus and Terence, as well as the beauty of Horace and Catullus. But I think particularly of Kendall K. Smith who, I regret to say, was to die at an early age. He was a handsome man in his thirties, full of enthusiasm for Greek literature and culture, which he conveyed to his students. I was at a disadvantage in not having had more than beginning Greek in school, but I loved Homer, I admired Smith, and I enjoyed every bit of the work.

While it is not my intention to bore the reader with a play-by-play account of a college freshman's career, I must mention briefly my experience in the survey of English literature, if only as an illuminating example of my administrative innocence. I enjoyed this course very much, as the lectures were given every couple of weeks by different instructors. Kittredge on Chaucer and, especially, Nielsen on Shakespeare were nothing short of fascinating. I was somewhat puzzled, however, to find that by midyear the course had not advanced beyond Dryden and Pope. Already accustomed to mysterious arrangements, I proceeded to enroll in the mathematics half-course to replace the English literature. Imagine my astonishment when, a couple of weeks later, I received a note from the English instructor asking why I no longer handed in the book reviews. I explained that I assumed that, as a half-course, the work was completed. "Ah," he answered, "It is a half-course, but, as you should have noted, it extends through the entire year. You do a full year's work for a half-course credit."

I was glad to continue with the survey, though it never got much beyond Tennyson, leaving Browning, Meredith, Trollope, Hardy, Yeats, and others in limbo. All in all, I carried seven courses during the second semester of my freshman year. When, in compiling grades, the dean discovered this horror, he declared it impossible to have grades in more than six courses. In reply I argued vehemently that I had actually done the work and with creditable results. Finally, I had my way, but I imagine that I am the only Harvard student who ever took for credit seven courses at one time.

The mathematics course proved a real dud and brought me very low grades. The trouble was probably my ineptitude. I was not then and have never been much interested in abstract reasoning. But in this course my incompetence was at least matched by the ineptitude of the instructor. He was one of the country's greatest mathematicians and no doubt superb as a teacher of advanced students. Confronted with freshmen wrestling with what to him must have seemed transparently simple material, he constantly became confused and self-contradictory and left me in a thick, blue fog. Thenceforth, I never had the stomach to tackle another mathematics course or even an introduction to Aristotelian logic.

The work in German overshadowed all my freshman courses, since it was in this field that I hoped to score the greatest success. On the basis of my speaking knowledge, I enrolled in a third-year course on German literature in the nineteenth century. The instructor was William Guild Howard, a man hardly taller than a dwarf, with a neat, pointed red beard. He was not very inspiring, but he was, as I was to learn later, an accomplished scholar. The subject matter and the reading, extending from the dramas of Kleist through the Romantic literature and the realistic writing of the mid-century to the naturalistc movement of Sudermann and Hauptmann, was consistently stimulating, but two matters clouded my enjoyment. I knew nothing of German grammar, with all its conjugations and declensions. Hence, I was deeply embarrassed whenever the professor called on me to give the principal parts of a verb or the syntax of an involved sentence. This was bad enough, but I was positively dismayed to discover that literary German was very different from the simple, homely language used in the family. Not that my mother butchered the language by constantly mixing it with English. She spoke good German, but the vocabulary was limited and the ideas fairly simple.

By much reading I soon became proficient in dealing with even the more difficult and involved German writers. But I never entirely overcame my lack of easy familiarity with German grammar. I had a much better command of the Latin and French, even of the Greek. I knew that I should get a text and learn all the many forms and countless rules, but with six courses facing me in the autumn, I always felt somewhat handicapped.

My freshman grades were, except for mathematics, sufficiently high to win me a substantial scholarship for the second year. But in other respects, I could hardly say that I enjoyed college life. I could not enjoy or hate it, because I simply did not have it. In a sense, Harvard was still an elite institution, with a great many students coming from prominent families and select private schools. Many became close friends in the dormitories, the clubs, the playing fields, and the numerous dramatic and musical activities. I had lost my whole class in Latin School and knew only a few even of the Latin School boys at Harvard. I could not afford to live in a dormitory or take part in college activities, because I ate my homemade lunch in solitude between classes and spent at least two hours a day in commuting between home and Cambridge. The summer vacations during my Harvard years, and even before, were more of a nightmare than a lark, for some kind of paying job had to be found year after year, and the competition for such opportunities was intense. Usually I began hunting for a job several weeks before school closed and all examinations had been held.

My first summer job, while still in the Latin School, gave me a foretaste of the annual ordeal. I found employment with a photographer, an Armenian, whose chief business was to take panoramic views of Harvard football games and Harvard-Yale boat races, which he did sufficiently well to have a practical monopoly on official pictures. But his establishment was positively primitive, the attic of an old house on Dover Street, where the pictures were developed and printed in an airless, dark room.

I found this occupation tedious and, when the summer temperatures mounted to new highs, pretty exhausting. My mother urged me to set out early, while it was still reasonably cool. On my arrival at work I had at least twenty minutes before the work hour and was cooling myself in a shaded doorway when my employer, a good example of the heartless boss pictured in socialist literature, suddenly arrived on the scene. He gave me a merciless tongue-lashing for my indolence. Why was I not at work when the pressure for recent boat-race pictures was so great? Needless to say, he left me with a feeling of insuperable resentment. I told my story at home that evening, and my mother decided in a flash that, come what may, I should not continue in that job. Fortunately, there were no dire consequences. After some delay my older brother managed to get me a job as errand boy in the firm that employed him: the seed house of R. & J. Farquhar, two Scots gentlemen who had a six-story establishment on South Market Street and were so highly regarded that they enjoyed the patronage of many North Shore estates. My assignment was ill defined—primarily to deliver packages at Beacon Hill residences, to carry messages, and to make purchases. I learned to my surprise that the firm would obligingly buy and send to its farmer customers anything they needed, as listed in their orders. So I was now buying a bicycle at Iver-Johnson's, a summer hammock, a baby crib, or what not. In the course of my activities, I got to know old Boston in the premotorized age: Faneuil Hall Market, jammed early in the morning by wagons bringing in vegetables and other products, and later in the day, Commercial Street, Merchants' Row, and all other streets in the market area so congested by horse-drawn trucks as to be all but impassable.

The historian in me led me to love the old city and its many beauties. Sometimes I would be reprimanded for loitering on Beacon Hill, while making a delivery on Mt. Vernon or Chestnut Street and being distracted by the stately facade of the State House or the beautiful doorways of the elegant homes, most of which have now been taken over by clubs or business enterprises. Another irresistible temptation was to stop "briefly" on beautiful, winding Cornhill, lined with secondhand bookstores, each with stalls on the street filled with unbelievable bargains.

At lunch time my brother and I would ensconse ourselves

among the huge stacks of seed bags on the upper floors of the shop. One could arrange them as a cozy cubbyhole, altogether unfindable by others. We both loved the quiet and seclusion as we munched our sandwiches and drank our milk, with only the huge tomcats, who were kept to hunt the mice, as our companions.

My only sad recollection of Farquhar's is of the inescapable afternoon task of carrying packages to the North Station for dispatch on the crack Flying Fisherman to Beverly and the North Shore. Ordinarily they were not too heavy, nor was the weather intolerable. But there were days of oppressive heat and an excess of packages which I shall never forget. In those days nothing was known of synthetic fibres and light summer clothing. Wealthy men wore linen suits, which quickly wilted and looked terrible, however comfortable they might be. But ordinary mortals, definitely including myself, wore the usual woolen clothing, which on hot summer days must be experienced to be appreciated.

My second summer of work between Latin School and Harvard was marked by the greatest good fortune. Almost at once I secured a position as errand boy with two very Bostonian lawyers, at 60 State Street. They were genteel and considerate gentlemen, who paid $5.00 a week instead of the standard $3.50. Much of my work consisted of carrying messages or papers or copying correspondence on the old hand presses, which left the copy so wet that it generally had to be left to dry overnight. One episode of my "legal" assignment comes to mind whenever I see a plate of cherries on the table. I simply doted on them, though I rarely had a chance to indulge my appetite. But in early summer there would always be peddlars on State Street with large flat carts loaded with cherries. The price was fifteen cents per pound, or eight cents per half pound. I would have liked to take advantage of the bulk rate, but after one try I convinced myself that not even I could eat a whole pound of cherries. So I faced reality and bought the half pound, though pained by the financial loss involved.

I had hardly been with Hunneman and Balch for more than a few weeks when, through the Latin School, I was offered an opportunity to tutor a boy in Latin, at the incredible pay of $11 a week. I asked my employers to release me and was overjoyed to find that, far from being irritated, they shared my pleasure in my good fortune and wished me well.

My new employer was Dr. William Morrison, former Harvard star athlete and still connected professionally with the college's athletics. He was a kindly, elderly man, who inhabited one of the beautiful old houses that still existed in East Boston, as they did in South Boston. His son Gordon, the subject of my efforts, was a big, exuberant fellow, who could have made mince meat of me without trouble, but never had any intention of doing so. We became good friends and remained so as long as I did not make too much of an issue of tutoring. Gordon had a good mind and could easily do the assignments if the spirit moved him, which on hot summer evenings it rarely did. In any event, he squeaked by his examination, went on to Harvard, and at the time of his premature death had succeeded his father as physician to the Harvard teams. A truly likeable, lighthearted individual, he certainly served to counteract my own gravity.

My third summer of work, following my freshman year, was as disheartening as the preceding one had been encouraging. It seemed all but impossible to find suitable work, and at last in desperation I agreed to work for $7 a week for two rather young businessmen, Arthur and Samuel Feinberg, who, from their offices at 127 Federal Street, were carrying on a trade in cotton and wool waste. They were clearly alert and intelligent chaps, successful in business and very sure of themselves. Occasionally their wives would come to the office, dressed to kill and wearing very expensive jewelry.

My principal function was to receive and dispatch shipments of all kinds of waste and factory sweepings, which were stored in a huge warehouse on the East Boston docks. They gave me the keys with orders to hire some longshoremen and to weigh and load twenty or thirty bales on to freight cars which stood on the siding. It was a hot summer day, and I was baffled and scared when I reached the docks and saw at once that it would take at least three of me even to open the

huge doors of the warehouse. The problem, however, was immediately solved by a number of stevedores, who hurried over
and opened up for me. They all wanted the assigned job, which
paid something like fifty cents an hour. I picked a few of the
least ferocious looking, who promptly went to work. I was
amazed by the strength of these men who could handle heavy
bales without apparent difficulty, even when they had only
a hook instead of a hand to operate with. The job was soon
finished and the men paid off. With immense relief I got myself back to Federal Street, where I think my employers were
delighted to see me return alive.

I followed the same procedure repeatedly during the summer. Once I knew the ropes, I could act with greater confidence,
at times as needed giving the men a piece of my mind. But
things went very well. Big shipments came in and others went
out frequently. While the Feinbergs haggled over one-fourth of
a cent in the price of a pound of waste, I came to realize the
profits they were making when fifteen or twenty freight car-
loads were at issue. I worked entirely with the longshoremen
who, when there was no work, spent their time in gambling
and swearing, and when there was work all too frequently
carried their earnings directly to the nearest barroom. I think
they respected me, a boy of only seventeen, because I tried to
be scrupulously fair in allocating the work. For my part, I came
to have a liking for these hard-working men, who never got
beyond the margin of subsistence. As I write I still see before
me a bald, one-eyed fellow who on a hot summer day would
slave away in the oven which was our unventilated warehouse,
while the perspiration ran off his red, bottle nose in a steady
stream.

I had no reason to regret leaving the Feinbergs when the
new academic year approached. I thought they were decent
enough, though my job was a tough one for extremely modest
pay. Imagine my indignation then, when they tried their utmost
to keep me from returning to college. Look at us, they said, we
do well enough without a snooty education. As I stood firm
they finally offered me $15 a week and a chance for advance-
ment if I would stay. For me this was, of course, the last straw:
To think that I was worth $15 to them and that all summer they

had paid me $7 helped to explain their financial success, but seemed utterly outrageous.

I am sure that I had an easier adolescence than most children. For one thing, I do not recall ever having had one of the much discussed identity crises. From about the age of ten, I was convinced that I wanted to be a teacher at some level, and I never wavered in this resolution and never for a moment considered dropping out of school. But there were a few years —from around fourteen to sixteen—when I was often overcome by a sense of loneliness and self-pity. I convinced myself that I would probably not live beyond thirty-three, since my father had died at that age. I suspect that these minor attacks of depression were due to the failure of my overworked mother's health. On two occasions, in fairly rapid succession, she was in the hospital for surgery. The first time, in the Boston City Hospital, she was very unhappy. The nurses, she said, were negligent and gruff and made the ward patients feel that they should be thankful to be there at all. We were duly shocked to learn that a bag of oranges, which we had to leave with the head nurse, never reached our mother.

We were much too young to have medical opinions or even prejudices of our own, but my mother felt that her first operation had been a failure. Before long she was again stricken, and much more violently than before. She was taken to the Carney Hospital at the top of our hill, where the service was kind and efficient, and the Carmelite Sisters, who had charge of the hospital, were always ready with comfort or encouragement. I suppose my mother's condition was serious, for we were not allowed to visit her and could only wave to her from Thomas Park, the top of Dorchester Heights, whence we could see her and she us. On these occasions my Aunt Martha came and cared for the family with real love and concern. One day the doorbell rang, and one of the sisters announced that my mother would like to see us and would we come to the hospital at once. Something was obviously askew, and we were probably right in considering this a farewell meeting, especially since the sisters put themselves out to console us. I will not attempt to describe this sad occasion, except to say that we were all terrified at the thought of life without mother. Fortunately, she recovered from her second operation, and life soon returned to normal.

I can only guess, however, that these events made me pensive and troubled. I recall that when waiting to sell newspapers at a nearby button factory when the closing whistle blew, I would sit on the curb and watch the autumn clouds drift by, seeing in them all kinds of chariots and processions and wondering about life beyond the immediate concerns of the day. I began also in the crisp November evenings to steal out on one pretext or another and go to the so-called Cow Pasture, a huge strip of undeveloped land running from Thomas Park steeply down to the bottom of the heights. It was a wonderful stage from which to view the night sky, with its constellations and planets. I began to feel very small, very lonesome, very uncertain. During the winter I would walk along the beach, where huge ice blocks were piled up and where one could, if one wished, feel complete devastation.

This period of anxiety and actual fear came to a head in the summer of 1912 when I was earning fabulous sums for very congenial work tutoring. Every day I had to travel by streetcar to East Boston, which meant going through the tunnel under the Harbor. I grew to dread these trips, being sure that the tunnel would cave in and the sea engulf us. Similarly, as we passed over the Dover Street bridge across the Old Fort Channel, I was terrified each time lest the bridge break down and hurl us into the water. It is hard after many years to recapture and discuss these nameless and unwarranted terrors, but they were sufficiently realistic then to have remained in my memory these many years.

After entering college I was suddenly saved from prolonged despondency by becoming interested in (shall I say enamored of?) a young lady of about my own age. She, too, was of German extraction, though her family was more Anglicized than mine. Her parents, who were rather well-to-do and had an attractive home in Roslindale, rarely went to church, but they were members of the West Newton Street congregation, and we met through the Young People's Society, which staged occasional amateur plays and musicales.

Sophie, as I shall call her, was a good-looking young girl whom I naturally regarded as very beautiful. I may have been attracted at first by her looks, but soon came to appreciate her unfailing good humor and vivacity. I was thrilled when I was first permitted to accompany her after a church rehearsal to the Northampton Street station of the elevated railway, whence she could reach Forest Hills and from there catch a streetcar to her home. It sounds unspeakably old fashioned, but it was at least four months before I ventured to address her by her given name. That happened on a gala occasion when she accepted my invitation to a Latin School dance on Washington's Birthday, 1913. I walked all the way to the Boston Flower Market to buy her a fresh bunch of violets which, in those long gone days, had not yet been deprived of their fragrance. Since my partner happened to live at the opposite end of Greater Boston, I had a long trip to make before starting out with her. But nothing mattered beyond her high spirits and charm, her hair done up for the first time to replace the monstrous ribbon at the back of the head which young girls then wore. Dancing was just in the transition stage, the Hesitation, Lame Duck and other new-fangled steps replacing the good old waltz and two-step. But dances were still held in large halls (in this case the gymnasium of the Latin School) with considerable formality. Young men were expected to fill their partner's program with the names of other gentlemen.

This dance, during which we were together much longer than ever before, was the beginning of a closer companionship which continued uninterruptedly during the entire three years of my college life. We grew very fond of each other and often took long walks, sometimes in the company of other couples from our church society. Looking back from our hectic, sex-crazed days, it all seems unbelievably innocent. And by comparison with the present it certainly was, but one ought to remember that it was in keeping with other now antiquated ideas, such as that men owed respect to women, that to get a girl into trouble was unpardonable, and that to marry before one had the means to support a family was pure recklessness.

Having a girl in my life meant more than glowing happiness

and dreams of our next meeting and, be it added, time lost from studies in nonacademic thoughts. It was a new and wonderful experience. Consider that I had no sisters, that we had no friends with sisters our own age, and above all that any discussions of sex—in general or in particular—was firmly repressed in our family. Our education from primary school through college was strictly and unalterably masculine. While my views now are those of an old man, I felt then that we were missing something, and that we were utterly awkward in dealing with any woman or girl. I think the rage for sex education and the general looseness in sex relations today is dangerously excessive, and that it will lead to much instability, unhappiness, and misfortune. Yet, I think the attitudes prevalent in my youth were exaggerated in the other direction. Nothing that I can remember was ever said in school, much less in my home, about sexual differences and what they involved, nor was there any encouragement of uncomplicated companionship between boys and girls in their teens. I remember being first thrilled by a very attractive girl whom I always passed on Columbia Road as I bicycled home from school. I wanted so much to speak to her, but I never dared. The spell was only broken when, at a local dance, I saw her dancing superbly with an older man, which was more competition than I could face.

With this upbringing I disliked the idea of coeducation, feeling that constant association between the sexes robbed life of some of the charm of the unusual. But later in life, the presence of Radcliffe girls in my Harvard classes whether I liked it or not began to change my opinion. I discovered that boys and girls in the classes were no more and no less serious about their work than they had been when segregated; that there was very little distraction in the class; and that outside class the variation in the degree of intimacy was just about what it had always been. I repeat, however, that in my opinion the overemphasis on sex and the ever more insistent clamor for complete equality in every respect have tended to reduce social relations to a dead level of uniformity which is basically at variance with the arrangements of nature and the inescapable fact that there are two sexes which in certain fundamental characteristics are and probably will always remain different. I know that in my own case much of the attraction of Sophie was in her difference of viewpoint, interests, and reaction.

In our close-knit family, the emergence of a feminine factor made a great and regrettable change. I cannot, of course, speak with assurance of my mother's sexual interests. I doubt if I ever heard her speak of her husband in terms of passionate attachment, though her admiration for him was boundless. After his death she never remarried, making it fairly clear that her mission in life was to care for and educate us, whatever the price to herself. I suspect that at times she thought we ought to have some contact with girls, so she encouraged us to go to Sunday school and to join the Young People's Club. So long as we trudged off to church for a play rehearsal, she was quite content. But when, at about the same time, both Rudolph and I became interested in particular girls, she made no secret of her disapproval—not of anything we did, but because she had to share our affection with another female, with a girl who had contributed nothing to our welfare and yet might enjoy the fruits of her as well as of our own efforts. Naturally, the tension generated by this new situation became greater and greater as time went on. I know that my mother tried repeatedly to overcome her aversion, but she never succeeded. Eventually my brother lost patience and married unobtrusively, which caused a serious and lasting estrangement between him and his mother. I emerged somewhat better, but for years there was much unhappiness on both sides.

It was in this setting that, like so many humans before me, I thought I might find consolation in the Bible. Reading a chapter each night before going to sleep, I ultimately finished the Scriptures from cover to cover. The poetry and drama were very appealing, but I was surprised to find how much of the Old Testament was dry and uninteresting. Nonetheless, I think I was the better for wading through it.

During my second and third year at Harvard for various

reasons I grew in wisdom and understanding beyond simple growth in maturity. I continued Latin and French for a second year and contended with a number of advanced courses in German literature. I enrolled in several education courses to strengthen my record in the search for a teaching position. My mother had some compunctions about my choosing philosophy courses, being convinced that philosophy, while a noble subject, was only worthwhile for the idle well-to-do with no value for the practical affairs of life. I managed to overcome her reservations and actually took three half-courses in this abstruse subject. The science requirement led me to an astronomy course which only required two hours a week of laboratory work. I much enjoyed the descriptive part of the course and the late evening watches at the student observatory on Everett Street. But when it came to plotting orbits I lacked the necessary mathematics and ended in dismal failure. My grade, which I think was D, was the worst of my college career.

The social sciences, I regret to say, received but short shrift. I did take introductory economics, but I learned too late that my special love, history, was ruled out, since the full course (notorious for its difficulty) could count only as a half-course after the student's second year.

I would not say that my course work was of little value substantively, but I have always felt that, having entered college at sixteen with very little cultural background, I did not fully understand much of what I learned. My grades were consistently better than merely good; they were, in fact, mostly excellent. I must conclude, therefore, that I had intellectual ability and determination, and that there was every incentive to do well. But on many occasions I felt that I was operating in a blue fog and that the soul of the assignment was escaping me.

By way of compensation, however, I revelled in the personalities of many of my teachers. Professor Taussig's lectures in economics were strong, well organized, and crystal clear, helping me to enjoy a subject for which I felt no intrinsic attraction. Bliss Perry's course on lyric poetry was an unadulterated treat. I have never heard anyone, even Copeland, read aloud more effectively—which reminds me of Kuno Francke's half-course on Goethe's *Faust,* conducted almost entirely in German. To hear him recite this great tragic masterpiece in the original was never to be forgotten. Of my numerous other courses in German literature, only those of Professor Howard made a deep and lasting impression. I persuaded him, much against his will, to allow me to enroll in a graduate course in sixteenth-century German literature. He warned me that it would involve about 1,000 pages of reading in old German per month, but I waded in, read many of the tracts of Luther and Hutten, the controversial writings of Erasmus, the satires of Sebastian Brandt, and many of the numerous delightful farces of Hans Sachs, the Nürnberg shoemaker later immortalized by Wagner in his opera *Die Meistersinger.* In other specialized courses offered by Professor Howard, I came to love the neoclassical dramas of the great Austrian writer, Franz Grillparzer (all too little-known in the English-speaking world despite the admirable translations of my late friend, Dr. Arthur Burkhard), and the moving tragedies of Friedrich Hebbel, whom one might call a German Ibsen coming a generation before the famous Scandinavian dramatist. One would not describe Professor Howard as an inspiring person, but he certainly instilled in me high standards of scholarship and was always ready to discuss the problems that troubled me. Thus, many years before the tutorial system was instituted or discussed, I had as much tutorial instruction as I could absorb.

I think of my second year (1913–1914) as a mixture of good and bad. I felt insecure, and for a year or more was deeply religious. I went to church regularly and listened attentively to the long but excellent sermons of the pastor. During Lent I trudged again each Wednesday evening to hear the minister recount and interpret the story of Christ's passion. The doctrinal conflicts of the sixteenth century were more than theoretical for me. I think I was saved from dark despondency by the friendship of a somewhat older student, Bill Stuart, the son of our family physician and, I must say, a remarkably cultivated young man. He played the piano admirably, was widely read in American as well as European literature, followed the current theatrical scene, and freely expressed his opinions on almost any subject. He took his academic commitments lightly and held Harvard instruction in lower esteem than I did. Having arranged for my membership in the German Club, which at that time had rooms on the first floor of Grays, he was presently encouraging me to skip classes and spend the hour in the club over a stein of beer and a bowl of pretzels. I must admit that this was not an unqualified loss of time, for Stuart's conversation was not only instructive, but highly stimulating. I am sure that in many respects he widened my horizon. Nonetheless, he did contribute to my neglect of regular work, so that at the end of my second year I fell just short of the requirements for the best scholarships and had to borrow $300 from the University to enable me to return for my senior year.

The outstanding event of 1913–1914 was not, however, the course of my academic career, but the admission of my brother Rudolph to Harvard. He dropped out of high school before the end of his second year to work in the Farquhar seed house where he remained for six full years. I need hardly add that his periodically increased wage was important for the family finances. Yet, Rudolph became restless, and my going to college enhanced his desire to do likewise.

Luckily my mother's brother, who lived in Chicago, had in 1908 paid us a visit for two or three days. Rudolph discussed his problem with his uncle, who suggested that to become an electrical engineer he could do no better then to enroll in a course of the American Correspondence School, which I believe was somehow connected with the University of Chicago. The enrollment was made, and my brother was soon receiving assignments and corrected papers in the mail. I cannot imagine anyone more thrilled or enthusiastic. He did very well even as the work became more difficult and exacting. Too tired in the evening to study, he took to awakening at 4:30 a.m. and working until breakfast. He had the small bedroom to himself and in the cold winter months slept with a Perfection Oil Heater at his bedside, ready to be lit and properly equipped for brewing a cup of coffee.

I had no idea that correspondence schools were anything but second-rate institutions. This one, however, was dead serious: the work carefully planned, all principles adequately explained, papers returned with the fullest and most scrupulous comments or corrections. I was amazed to see Rudolph's design of complicated cogwheels and elaborate electrical connections. I was even more astounded by his persistence in the pursuit of his objective. Year in year out, for three or four years, he was at his desk. No effort seemed too much for him.

It was highly embarrassing for me when Rudolph eventually began to talk of getting admitted to Harvard on the strength of his demonstrated achievement. The idea was so irregular that I winced at the very thought. But ultimately I was persuaded to go to Dean Hurlburt with my story and my proposal. He was a kindly, patient man, but his answer was a categorical negative. "Surely, Mr. Langer," he said, "you must know that a full high school education is required for entrance to Harvard." I did know, and I felt pretty hopeless. On the other hand, I was greatly impressed with the work Rudolph was doing, and with the pertinacity and determination he demonstrated every day of his life.

After a decent interval, I returned to Dean Hurlburt with specimens of Rudolph's work and pleaded that he be given a chance. Finally, the dean made a suggestion which, I have no doubt, he expected to end the matter. "This is what I'll do," he explained; "I'll have your brother take the entrance examinations, and then we shall see what he can do."

In May 1913, Rudolph took the examinations and, to the family's surprise and the dean's consternation, passed them all with respectable grades. What now was to be done? The dean had another bright idea: "I'll allow him to enroll, but only as a special student and with no commitment of any kind on the part of the university. He cannot be accepted as a candidate for any of the usual degrees."

The rest of this amazing story, this eloquent demonstration of Harvard's lack of indifference, can be briefly told. My brother's grades in his freshman year were all A's and obliged the harassed dean to capitulate. Rudolph became a student in regular standing and a member of the class of 1918. His high achievement remained unbroken during his entire course, no matter what the subject or the teacher. He was elected to Phi Beta Kappa in his junior year, and unless I am quite mistaken, graduated in 1918 at the head of his class, with the astonishing record of something like fifteen A's and one B and a string of valuable scholarships.

Since this is the story of my life, not of his, I will say simply that his great ability and capacity for sustained hard work stood him in good stead until his death in 1968. After the First World War, he continued his studies in mathematics in the Harvard Graduate School. He was awarded the Ph.D. degree in 1924 and spent an additional year of study at Göttingen. In 1927 he became professor of mathematics and eventually chairman of the Mathematics Department at the University of Wisconsin. He played a prominent role in Wisconsin faculty affairs and in 1961 crowned his career by founding and directing the U.S. Army Mathematics Research Center, which attained world renown for the quality of its staff and the importance of its basic research. My brother died, perhaps mercifully, in 1968, a year or so before the center was bombed and largely destroyed by fanatic students who had mistakenly convinced themselves that it was there that the plans for the nefarious Vietnam War were being drafted and developed.

With a second son in college it became difficult to continue living on Dorchester Heights, and my mother sold the house at a modest profit. I think she did so regretfully, not only for nostalgic reasons but because for seventeen years the two upper flats, steadily rented, had covered the entire costs of the house and enabled us to live rent free.

We then proceeded to house-hunt in Cambridge. It was not easy even then, at least not in the vicinity of the university, but it was far from today's frantic situation. Despite the subway terminal, Harvard Square was still a cozy town center, taken over by small shops, of which Leavitt and Peirce, Max Keezer, Hazen's Coffee Shop, and Billings and Stover were the chief ornaments. Across the street the Harvard Coop occupied a Greek temple, reverently approached by a flight of stairs. Next to it was the Harvard Trust Company and College House, the largest and cheapest of the dormitories. On the other side of the Coop was a deep vacant lot which served conveniently as a receptacle for discarded newspapers and other trash. The lesser streets around the Square were still unpaved. Palmer Street was a mere alley, and Church Street the headquarters of plumbers, painters, roofers, and other essential workers.

The Yard was not yet walled with dormitories, but was largely disrupted by construction of the huge Widener Library, completed and dedicated at commencement, 1915. In the early months of my Harvard years, the old Gore Library was still in use, with books being constantly shipped out to other buildings to relieve the congestion. When it was torn down to make room for Widener, the books were stored here, there, and everywhere. During my three years, the general reading room was on the second floor of Massachusetts Hall, while the main books repository was far away, in Randall Hall, at the corner of Divinity Avenue and Kirkland Street.

One of the great hopes for the splendid modern Widener Library was that it would once again make possible the consolidation of the numerous special libraries, and that it would suffice for a century. It was once described by Professor Gaetano Salvemini, an eminent Italian scholar, as the greatest scholars' library in the world. He stoutly maintained that when a book he needed was not in the library catalogue, it would be ordered from Paris and delivered in Cambridge in less time than it would have taken to withdraw it from the Bibliothèque Nationale. Whether or not this was an exaggeration, it is safe to say that there are hundreds of thousands of Harvard alumni and guest scholars who would gladly praise the riches, the convenience, and the fine services of this great institution.

A few more words about the Cambridge of those days: From Massachusetts Avenue to the Charles River was a conglomeration of old frame houses, most of which were later demolished to make way for the undergraduate houses. On the other side of Boylston Street were the subway and streetcar barns which, to use a convenient botanical term, have been marcescent, that is, dying but never quite dead, for these many years. I think I am right in saying that the Charles River was still tidal and that coal barges still unloaded at docks where

Eliot House now stands. The Anderson bridge was not completed until 1915. The thundering herds of cattle, coming up
Kirkland Street from Somerville and marching through the
Square, crossed the new bridge several times a week finally to
meet their fate in the Watertown slaughter houses. In summer
it was impossible to approach the river, which was the privileged domain of mosquitoes. These pests would pursue a
rash intruder in large swarms for the better part of a mile. Add
to this that at almost any time of year the westerly winds would
waft the stench of the slaughter houses over the entire Harvard
area. Pollution is not really a modern invention.

As a separate item, I might say that the huge elm under
which Washington took command of the Colonial Army in 1775
still stood in the middle of the street at the junction of Garden
and Mason. It was an impressive old giant, obviously approaching its final days. Eventually a great gale (I think the hurricane
of 1938) wrecked it to such an extent that it had to be taken
down, to the sorrow of the sentimentalists, but to the joy of an
increasing number of motorists.

Having examined various houses in the general area of the
university, the Langers were smitten by a nice old one-family
house at the corner of Mt. Auburn and Hilliard Street. Overgrown with wisteria and buried in shrubbery, it looked like the
perfect haven of rest. And the price was reasonable—$4,800.
Yet, after we all sat and pondered and calculated, we had to
agree with mother that we could not afford a house that brought
no income. Regretfully we settled for a two-family house
where Carver Street meets Hammond Street. This turned out
to be a very satisfactory solution. There were two five-room
flats and on the third floor a couple of large rooms which had
been adapted for light housekeeping. The flats had central
heating, though the system was less than 100 percent efficient.
The adjoining vacant lot gave the living room a very attractive
southwest exposure. There was no electricity, but my brother
Walter, who had dropped out of school to work for an electric
company and had then enrolled in a night course at the Franklin
Institute, eventually passed the state electricians examination.
With this in hand he proceeded, in his spare time, to electrify
the entire house to the satisfaction of the city inspectors. Of

course, electric light was a great boon, as was the family's first bona fide bathroom. But we still preferred the kindly, warm light of the kerosene lamp. Until late at night we would sit around the dining room table, a boy on each of three sides and the fourth appropriated by my mother who, now that she no longer had boarders or lodgers, could devote time to reading. My brother's mathematics were soon beyond her reach, though she would often listen attentively as he explained the difficulties that confronted him. German and English literature were of course more congenial to her. She read a great many novels in both languages, freely expressed her critical opinions, and never hesitated to query the judgments of critics in her areas of competence. For a woman with only a grade school education, her interest and understanding were truly astounding.

My summer jobs were, as the reader knows, rich in variety. In 1914 I was fortunate in finding, without much trouble, a position on the night force of the National Shawmut Bank, located on Milk Street, across from the Central Post Office and not far from newspaper row on Washington Street. Our group consisted of about twenty men, working either from 8:00 p.m. to 4:00 a.m. or from midnight until 8 a.m.—at least in theory. Our job was to run the checks that came in all night from New England banks through the adding machines, only two or three of which, incidentally, were electrified. On being hired I was told that it would occasionally happen that by 4 a.m. the accounts would not quite balance, in which case one would have to stay another thirty or forty minutes until all was in the clear. I have never been more cruelly deceived, for many checks were hard to read. Vermont farmers commonly wrote 3 and 9 much alike. So there were often disparities and many checks had to be rerun, so that only six or eight mornings in the whole summer was I able to leave at 4 a.m. Very commonly it was 5 a.m. and on some occasions 5:30 or even 5:45. It was tiresome work under a cranky and exacting supervisor, and I was weary as I trudged home and to bed. One of my problems was to wake up in time to keep a Saturday afternoon appointment to play tennis with my sweetheart. We met in Franklin Park, which had several grass tennis courts, but required the players to bring the nets. We jumped and ran around, and though we always enjoyed being together, not much was to be said for our tennis.

All this was dwarfed when on August 1, 1914 the First World War broke out in Europe, initially with Great Britain, France, and Russia against Germany and Austria-Hungary. Like most people I had not the foggiest notion of what it was all about. I recall that one of my fellow workers, a Hungarian by birth, explained to me for the first time the conflict of nationalities in the Habsburg Empire and made a point of the trade rivalry between Britain and Germany which had led Britain and her friends to annihilate German power once and for all.

My sympathies, naturally enough, were initially with the Germans, though I quickly became interested in the entire problem of European politics and began reading avidly in Morton Fullerton's *Problems of Power* and kindred works. In the early weeks of the war the victory of the Germans seemed inevitable, however, and it was generally believed that the conflict would be over by Christmas. The German armies, having violated the neutrality of Belgium, were wheeling in a great enveloping circle around Paris, and it seemed impossible to stop them. So I was dispatched approximately every hour to newspaper row to read and report the latest news of General Kluck's spectacular advance. As we now know, the German high command, alarmed by the Russian attack on East Prussia, dispatched several divisions to bolster that front. The resulting gap in the German lines in the West was exploited by the French command who, summoning all its forces and sending men in taxis from Paris to the front, managed to insert a wedge into the German lines and compel their retreat in the decisive battle of the Marne. Before the autumn was over, the war in France had become one of position, a trench warfare, which, with variations, continued for several years. Meanwhile college had reopened, I had thrown up my job, and had resumed the congenial life of a student.

CHAPTER IV

Debut of a Teacher

THOUGH THE LAST of my three years at Harvard was spent within an eight to ten minutes walk of the Yard, it was too late for me to participate in college activities and, while still living at home, to establish closer contacts. My one close friend was Harold Kurth, who was to go on to the Medical School and become a practicing physician in Lawrence. Being of German extraction, he enjoyed many of the German literature courses, which we took together.

The early months of 1915 were exceptionally busy for me, because I was obliged to write and submit an original essay in my field of concentration. In those days men who went out for honors were regarded as rather queer. The program then was so tough that anything like the present award of honors to 75 percent of the graduating class would have been regarded as pure fantasy. The required courses and high grades were in themselves a considerable burden. But the final paper and examination were enough to test even staunch souls. After much searching I hit upon a subject in German literature that proved definitely rewarding: a comparative study of the historical dramas of Schiller and those of Ernst von Wildenbruch, a now forgotten but quite prolific dramatist whose patriotic plays glorifying the Hohenzollerns were extremely popular in the 1870s and 1880s. The job involved a great amount of close reading and note taking, to say nothing of the preparation of the ultimate product—an essay of some 100 handwritten pages.

My dissertation evidently found favor in the appropriate circles, and I was summoned to an oral examination. This was attended by five or six professors (including even Kittredge) and continued for two hours. In the discussion of sixteenth-century German literature it emerged that I had actually read Sebastian Brandt's *Narrenschiff* (Ship of Fools). This led to further probing, and eventually Kittredge asked whether I knew anything of the history of this fascinating book in England. No one knows the limits of my field of knowledge better than I, but, as luck would have it, I could answer this question accurately and at some length. Kittredge made no effort to conceal his surprise and suggested that the examination be closed, to which the examinee as well as the examiners agreed wholeheartedly.

My grades were never as consistently high as those of my brother Rudolph and included two D's for the mathematics and astronomy courses, where I was helpless without trigonometry. But they were mostly A's and B+'s, and I had, moreover, completed the four-year course in three years. Naturally, I looked forward to the award of Phi Beta Kappa. But I was to be deeply disappointed: I was not included in the new list and was given to understand that those two low marks made me ineligible. I can hardly remember a time when I was more indignant nor when I expressed my sentiments more freely, but to no avail. Years later, when I was a young professor at Harvard, one of my colleagues, who was very active in Phi Beta Kappa affairs, came to me and reported that the governing board of the fraternity recognized that an egregious mistake had been made, and that the regulations had now been changed to take account of more than mere course grades. He begged me to accept the honorary membership that had now been voted me. I still felt so hot about the matter that I refused, but since he was very persuasive and I derived no satisfaction from nursing a grudge, I finally accepted. But I could never overcome my initial resentment, never wore a key, and never attended a Phi Beta Kappa function. I doubt if the organization suffered irreparably from my obstinate attitude.

I was more than a little irked when in May 1914, in the

midst of my agonizing over my honors thesis, I received a call from the Student Employment Office saying that a Dr. Phillips in the Museum of Comparative Zoology needed someone to read an article on ornithology in the *Journal für Ornithologie*. This proved to be the prelude to a long and pleasant association that filled a substantial segment of my life.

The circumstances were rather unusual, as I learned after meeting Dr. John C. Phillips, the curator of birds in the museum. He was a wealthy man, with a splendid estate and farm overlooking Wenham Lake on the North Shore. He had become deeply interested in the American wood or Carolina duck, a beautiful bird somewhat like the Chinese Mandarin duck, but less showy and flamboyant. In Audubon's day the wood duck had been common in our southern states, and not uncommon even in the northern part of its range in New York state and New England. It was good eating and consequently had been hunted to the verge of extinction. Conservationists of that early day had secured legislation protecting this attractive bird throughout the year on pain of severe penalty, but the question remained: Could the wood duck still be saved from complete extinction, and could it possibly be revived as an American species?

Dr. Phillips had secured several pairs of this beautiful bird and had bred them on his Wenham farm with some success. At this point he discovered that Dr. Heinrich Heinroth, the chief ornithologist of the Berlin Zoological Gardens, had had the very same idea. He had obtained several specimens, had done everything conceivable to create the proper environment for them, and had bred them even more successfully than his American colleague. In an unusually long article in the *Journal für Ornithologie* he had analyzed the problem and described the procedures by which he had reached success.

It was of the utmost importance to Dr. Phillips to read this article, but he knew no German. This is where I entered the picture. I sat next to him and looked at the text. It was written in a highly professional jargon, interspersed with many symbols. I was dumbfounded. After vain efforts I had to confess that I did not know what all these ornithological terms and symbols meant. To which Phillips replied: "Forget about all that. I know the professional terms and symbols. What I need is to understand the sentence structure and the meaning." So much I could certainly provide him, and he was very pleased. The article was indispensable for further work in this field.

As a matter of interest, I might mention that I have been informed by the Audubon Society that at present, after sixty years, the wood duck has indeed responded to protection. It is now widespread in Massachusetts and breeds in suitable localities. For about six weeks in the autumn it can be legally hunted, though the daily bag may contain not more than two wood ducks.

At the end of our initial session, Dr. Phillips made some inquiries about my status and interests, and eventually asked whether I would be available to work with him that summer. He had, so he said, quite an accumulation of German and other foreign language materials which he would be delighted to have me survey. He offered me $12.50 a week to start, and suggested that the hours from 10:00 a.m. to 4:00 p.m. would be quite ample for such exacting work.

Well, I could not envisage a more attractive and welcome graduation gift. I had had no time to go job-hunting, and here I had a most congenial assignment offered me. The Museum of Comparative Zoology (commonly called the Agassiz Museum after its founder) was only two blocks away from my home, and its library was quite deserted in summer. To be sure, it was not air conditioned and could be quite uncomfortable on a hot, sultry day, especially since the director, old Dr. Henshaw, was a stickler for formality and would allow no one, not even Dr. Phillips, to work in his shirtsleeves. I suppose if this work were being done today researchers would be sitting around in running pants and sandals. How the female staff would be clothed I will leave to the reader's imagination.

At the very time when Dr. Phillips was assuring me of an attractive summer job, I also had the great good fortune to secure a permanent teaching job, toward which all my plans and efforts had been bent. I had registered with a Boston teaching agency, which arranged an interview for me with Dr.

Daniel Abercrombie, the headmaster of Worcester Academy, one of the old private boarding schools. Abercrombie was looking for a teacher of modern languages, primarily German, and was attracted not only by my college record, but by my good speaking knowledge of the language. Only my age (I was nineteen) gave him pause, for his school, well known as a "football school," had many brawny boys on its roster. In the end I suppose he reckoned that where I had in the past overcome many obstacles, I would somehow hold my own. He was certainly taking a chance, for it was nothing exceptional for the students to harry a new teacher out of the school if he seemed a likely victim. I saw two Spanish teachers harassed into flight until Abercrombie came upon a huskie who had spent many years at sea. This newcomer sat around in his rooms with his bare feet on his desk and let it be generally known that he was prepared to break any insolent student in two. Of course, I could not boast such prowess. Mrs. Abercrombie told me later that she thought her husband had gone mad when he came home and described the new teacher of German whom he had just engaged. Happily I did not know, in June 1915, what situation I was to confront in September.

Frankly, I thought as little as I could of what Fate might have in store for me, and enjoyed my new summer job to the utmost. Dr. Phillips turned out to be a veritable prince of men, kind, patient, generous. I may as well say now that the summer of 1915 was only the first of seven summers I worked with him, the one exception being the summer of 1918, when we were both in military service in France.

The reader need not fear a detailed review of our researches. At first I did various odd jobs, became acquainted with the literature and the library, and gradually studied particular genera and species of wild ducks, using Tommaso Salvadori's great catalogue of the birds in the British Museum as a guide. Of course, I had no field experience and, in fact, never developed any desire to become an ornithologist. But Phillips had traveled and shot in all parts of the world. His knowledge and judgment were simply superb. So I increasingly drifted into researches in the literature while he added the stamp of his experience. Despite his wealth and leisure, he was a serious scholar as well as traveler. On even the hottest summer days, he would arrive in his splendid Pierce-Arrow car from his Wenham estate and work with me cheek by jowl until late afternoon when, on his departure, I would walk down to the Harvard boathouses on the now fortunately regulated river and row for an hour or so before going home. Starting with a wherry I passed to more advanced compromise boats and ended as an accomplished oarsman in the single-seated shell. It was exhilarating exercise, and I eventually came to know the river from the Basin to Watertown so intimately that on starting out I could equally well turn in the one direction or the other. As a piquant detail I might add that on returning to the boathouse and storing my shell, I, like most other oarsmen, took a plunge in the Charles, the mere thought of which makes one shudder in these days of pollution.

Phillips and I worked so harmoniously and efficiently together that he raised my salary annually until it reached $50 a week. Furthermore, larger and larger vistas opened before him, and he ended by planning a grand monograph on all the ducks of the world. Since the species of ducks are exceedingly numerous and are found in all parts of the globe, from the far North to the far South, in the highest Andes and in the smallest island groups of the Pacific, this was a formidable undertaking. In this monumental treatise we discussed every known species of duck, reviewing classification and nomenclature, mapping distribution, analyzing feeding habits, describing courtship and breeding practices, longevity, behavior in captivity, and any other items, such as its historical role, that might apply.

Nonetheless, it was eventually completed and published in 1923–1925 in four beautiful quarto volumes, each with a frontispiece by the well-known painter Frank Benson and richly illustrated by master bird-artists such as Louis Agassiz Fuertes and Major Alan Brooks. The limited edition of 400 copies which sold at $50 per volume quickly became a collector's item.

It stands to reason that, working on such a project over many years, I acquired a good knowledge of the world's geography. There were literally thousands of locations to be identified and countless environmental situations to be studied. I even had a delightful touch of historical research, since a number of species played more than a routine part in human life. The beautiful Egyptian goose (really a duck) was, I believe, the first bird to be pictured in the Egyptian tomb-paintings. My wife and I saw large numbers of them on the sandspits of the upper Nile in our East African journeys in 1972 and readily agreed with the ancient Egyptians in regarding it as a most unusually attractive creature, somewhat larger than most ducks, and distinguished by a long, graceful neck.

I think of the Eider duck as another species with a long history. Its down has been prized by northern peoples for untold centuries, hence it was important for us to learn as much as we could about it. This gave me an excuse for reading the literature of Arctic exploration, the scientific appendices of which frequently contained highly valuable information. Among other ducks, I also loved the little-known torrent ducks found on the cascade streams in the Andes at altitudes of 13,000 feet.

But the steamer duck of southern South America, locally known as "the racehorse" or "loggerhead," presented the greatest challenge. This duck is common in the Falkland Islands, on the Atlantic and Pacific coasts of South America, on Tierra del Fuego, and throughout the Magellan Straits. Since the later sixteenth century explorers and naturalists, including Darwin, had been puzzled because while some of these birds flew like other ducks, many appeared to be flightless, racing over the water by churning it up like a side-wheeler at speeds up to eight miles an hour. Were there two species or only one?

In the hope of settling this controversial issue, Phillips sent special observers to the area to collect specimens and all other available information. He even suggested that I go with them and get a taste of field experience. But I had no intention of becoming an ornithologist and was unwilling to abandon my historical studies for a prolonged absence.

On the return of his mission, Phillips examined many specimens and concluded that, while a definitive statement was still impossible, there were probably two species or varieties of steamer duck, a large, gray, heavy type with remarkably short wings and therefore flightless, and a smaller, reddish variety whose wings were larger than those of the flightless variety, and who were fully capable of flight.

Writing now, more than fifty years later, I wondered whether further progress had been made in this problem, or, indeed, whether a definitive solution had been found. My good friend and colleague, the eminent naturalist, Professor Ernst Mayr, referred me to the extended and, he thought, conclusive discussion in Robert C. Murphy's book *Oceanic Birds of South America*, especially Volume II, 951–975 (1936). After examining over a hundred specimens taken from all parts of the bird's range, of all ages, all seasons and both sexes, Murphy decided that there were actually three varieties: a flightless type found only on the Falkland Islands; a flightless type found on the coast of Chile as far north as Chiloe Island, but not on the Patagonian coast; and a third, flying type, which intermingles with the flightless variety throughout the range but is rare in the Falklands, where it has probably been more hunted for food than the unpalatable flightless variety. It seems that now most, but not all, naturalists have accepted these findings, ending what was one of the weirdest problems in the history of ornithology, the problem of what one writer has called "these troublesome birds." My only excuse for raising the issue here is my personal curiosity and interest in a question that baffled not only Darwin, but many lesser naturalists.

I shall always look back on my summers with Dr. Phillips not only as seasonal employment, but also as excellent research experience and a source of useful knowledge of world geography. But most important was the close professional association with one of the finest gentlemen I have ever known. With deep regret I must close this paragraph by relating that Phillips met his death on a shooting expedition at the early age of sixty.

My ornithological activities were, so to speak, placid interludes in the development of my teaching career. In September 1915 I put the ducks on the shelf and set out for Worcester. It was the first time that I was to live away from home, and my soul was filled with nameless anxieties.

Worcester Academy was even then over a century old. It had originally been built on a substantial hill on the outskirts of the city, but had long since been engulfed in lower-middle class housing. The original building, Davis Hall, was a semi-Gothic, turreted structure of the early nineteenth century. Other buildings had been added, such as administrative offices, classrooms, dormitories, dining hall, and most recently a fine gymnasium and swimming pool. The playing fields were about a quarter of a mile from the school.

The total enrollment of the academy was only about 200, from ages ten to twenty, with the older boys preponderating. A substantial number of these were graduates of rural high schools who required an additional year of schooling before being admitted to the leading colleges. Wealthy Latin American families seemed to have developed a great liking for the school, for there were always a dozen or fifteen Latin American boys, some in rather questionable ways more sophisticated than their fellow students. The faculty numbered about twenty, mostly men in early middle age, including several bachelors. Whether married or not, however, the teachers lived in the dormitories and had specific responsibility for discipline at any and all hours. Indeed, they were under discipline themselves, for they were allowed to smoke only in a special smoking room, where most foregathered after lunch to show their devotion to neckties and to engage in conversation about politics or sports.

Dr. Abercrombie had been headmaster for thirty-seven years and lived in a separate house on the campus. A small, serious man, he was the typical educator of the old school. No matter what the size or age of a boy, Abercrombie could cow him with a few words by taking him by the lapel of his coat and waving his finger at him. Not that Abercrombie was a Dickensian type—far from it. He was generally kind and sympathetic and was highly respected by both teachers and boys. He seemed to have taken a great liking to me and spoke before the whole school of my wide knowledge and maturity of thought. Actually, I was always tortured by a feeling of ignorance, not only of things but of social relations.

The terms of my contract were, I suppose, not far from the norm for those days. My salary was to be $900 per annum, from which I was to deduct $5 per week for board and $4 for laundry and miscellaneous items. I was given a rather pleasant corner room on the third floor of old Davis Hall, with full responsibility for what went on there and with the further assignment to preside at evening study for the younger boys every few weeks. My teaching was to be entirely in the German field, since an older, Dartmouth man was doing a highly successful job as teacher of French and coach in baseball, swimming, and diving.

I liked my colleagues at Worcester. They were a pleasant and always helpful group who gave me the feeling of having sympathetic backing. I was genuinely frightened when I saw some of the students moving about the campus. Among them were the football stars who contributed heavily to the school's reputation by generally defeating the freshman teams of Harvard and other major universities. As luck would have it, a few of these boys appeared in my advanced German class and quickly indicated their intention of giving me a rough time. Being all but defenseless I at once adopted a policy of conciliation and peace. I stopped the class and said I was perfectly aware that I was no physical match for my students. If they chose to raise hell I could not stop them. But I was ready to help them prepare for the College Entrance Examinations, and they could always rely on finding me reasonable. Thereupon, one brawny fellow, even now I remember that his name was Warburton, got up and announced to the class, which numbered only about fifteen: "Come on, let's stop the fooling and get down to work." No one queried his authority, and it was never again necessary for me to make an issue of discipline. No doubt word of these amazing events seeped down to my more elementary and hence younger classes, for I had not the slightest trouble from them. This was true as well of the evening study hour for younger boys, where nothing more than the throwing of a penny across the room ever disturbed the peace.

I cannot say that I enjoyed my teaching at Worcester. In the first place, I had not sufficiently mastered the elements of German grammar to be able to rattle off lists of prepositions taking the dative, etc. Frankly, I found the teaching of first-year German tedious and unrewarding. The second-year German class was somewhat better, since we then read simple stories and essays as well as continuing with grammar and composition. Only in the third year did we arrive at the great classic dramas of Schiller and Lessing, and only then did I have an opportunity to discuss German literature. All in all, the teaching of languages in the days of my youth was a deadly, discouraging business. I studied Latin for seven years without being able to read it fluently, much less speak it. After five years of French, I was indeed able to read the language with considerable ease, though I would say that it requires more than average competence to read the novels of Balzac and some of the other realistic writers. As for speaking, it has always required at least several days in France before my tongue would loosen, and I cannot honestly say that I ever became fluent.

Daily life at the academy was interrupted in the morning by compulsory attendance at chapel, where I first learned the well-known English hymns. Then came lunch during which, as at dinner later, each teacher had a table of eleven boys. They were usually hungry and boisterous and left the teacher but little time for satisfying his own wants. Some generous bequest had made it possible to have ice cream for dessert three times a week, on Sundays, Wednesdays, and Fridays. My heart always sank when one member of my table was absent, for I was then required to cut the two-quart block of ice cream into exactly eleven equal parts. When possible, I would facilitate my task by omitting my own portion.

During most of the afternoon, the boys were busied with athletics and those teachers who had no coaching responsibilities could relax by taking walks in the country or even quietly reading a book. But from 5:00 to 6:00 p.m., the boys were required to attend yet another class, supposedly to keep them out of mischief when they returned from the playing field. I thought this a wretched and altogether mistaken idea, for the youngsters returned so exhausted by physical exertion, that even big fellows would sometimes fall asleep. The evening hours were officially study hours. In fact, they were the time of greatest mischief. Unpopular boys were harassed by having their rooms "stacked," and a large variety of other pranks were played. The floor teacher was constantly jumping up, rushing to the scene of disturbance, trying to isolate the innocent, looking for ringleaders, etc. At ten o'clock all students but the seniors, who enjoyed another half hour of grace, were required to have their lights out. Actually, it was not until 10:30 that the floor began to quiet down, and only by 11:00 could one count with assurance on the continuance of peace.

It was inevitable, I suppose, that I should suffer from loneliness while at the academy. I sent home practically the whole of my monthly salary to help with family finances while Rudolph was in college. My brother Walter also did his share, during his military service and after. He had returned to school in 1915 and in 1917 graduated from the Rindge Technical School in Cambridge. At the same time he passed the entrance examinations for Harvard. But the United States had already intervened in the European War, and Walter enlisted secretly in the Signal Corps at the very outset. He served for some months in France, and on his return home at once entered Harvard while at the same time taking a night job at the Hood Rubber Company. Since he had been rather badly gassed, he was finally classed as 56 percent disabled and received his tuition and $100 a month from the government for four years. This enabled him to contribute substantially to the family budget.

With only about $10 a month at my disposal, I was not in a position to cut many capers, even had there been any available. I went home by interurban streetcar about once a month, but no longer saw much of my former sweetheart. Somehow we had drifted apart after I left home. I think my college education tended to open a gap in our relations, and it is, of course, possible that she had become interested in someone else. For a few years I maintained a tenuous relationship with one of her close friends, of whom I became fond. During the war we corresponded regularly, which meant much to me. But after my return home, we, too, drifted apart. Neither of us had felt really in love with the other, but I remember her as a lively and interesting companion, who for a few years gave me the feminine friendship which I chronically lacked.

Among the faculty members at the academy I formed one close and invaluable friendship. Charles W. Bradlee, Jr., the son of a minister in Malden, came to the school at the same time as I, but he was ten years older and had years of experience as a teacher of shop work. He was a portly man, who set himself high standards. In fact, he always went to church on Sunday in frock coat and silk hat, carrying a cane. Since church-going involved a fairly long walk through a rather seedy neighborhood, this demonstration called for some degree of courage. But Bradlee could and did carry it off. Evidently, his imposing personality was all the protection he needed.

Bradlee was unmarried and had charge of the dormitory floor below mine. He never had the slightest trouble with the boys, who simply adored him, even when he took them to task for some slight delinquency. For me his friendship was a god-send. When I had trouble on my floor, I could always look to him for support. Not that he intervened in my behalf. He would have regarded this as the worst thing to do. But he would discuss the situation and the boys involved with me, and lead me to see for myself what would be the most effective course of action.

Our nocturnal walks and talks are among my pleasant memories of these years. At 11:00 p.m., when the dormitory seemed to have finally quieted down, we would slip out and walk down the hill to the center of Worcester for coffee and a doughnut in one of the all-night dairy lunches. Bradlee's interests were definitely intellectual. He read the *Atlantic Monthly* regularly and kept himself well posted on the affairs of the world. Furthermore, he was genuinely concerned with ethical and other philosophical problems and even though he had had no training in these fields, his thoughts were always worth listening to, especially when they led to debate.

I suppose that in our enlightened day my relationship with Bradlee would be regarded as having definitely homosexual overtones: I do not believe it for a minute. I would say most emphatically that never in the years I was associated with him was there ever even the faintest suggestion of anything sexual. I have never known of a man of greater integrity, and I might add that he went on from Worcester Academy to become principal of Lawrenceville Academy and ultimately of a private school which he himself founded in Syracuse.

Speaking of homosexuality, I think the ultraliberalism of our time has led to a great exaggeration of its prevalence and role. My life, at least until I was twenty-five, was spent almost entirely among men and boys. And yet I can recall only two occasions when homosexual advances were made to me, and they were never pressed after they were energetically repulsed. During my more than two years at Worcester Academy only two boys were expelled for having homosexual relations. I can hardly believe that among soldiers in the field homosexuality was rare, considering that most of the time we were sleeping cheek by jowl on the floor of a barn or ruined building. But I can affirm that, even as a sergeant, it never came to my attention, so that it must have been very sub rosa, certainly never paraded as seems now to be the fashion. Of course, if every close association and attachment between members of the same sex is to be classed as homosexual, I am sure that it is common and widespread. Indeed, I think the world could well stand more of it.

Since I had no athletic responsibilities, my afternoons were usually free, and I thought that I might resume my musical studies. There was in Worcester a small conservatory directed by a Swede named Hultman. He agreed to give me lessons and made great efforts to develop my sight reading, as well as giving me music by Grieg, Chopin, and other classical composers for practice. At the academy there was one good grand piano reserved for students who were seriously studying music. This instrument was locked in the tower room of the gymnasium, and thus completely protected against abuse. I made the fullest use I could of this opportunity, but my stay at the academy was too brief to ensure much progress, and, what was sadder, I had to convince myself that despite my really intense love of music, I had but a modest performance capability. If devotion to music had any relationship to musical endowment, I might have been among the great players of my time.

Not only in music did I try to exploit the time at my disposal. It had soon become clear to me that I could not and would not spend my life teaching foreign languages at the elementary level. The war in Europe, of which I understood so little, whetted my appetite. I tried hard to study the background of the war and to read over the entire field of modern European history. I recently discovered a diary which I had kept in the first half of 1917, the very existence of which I had forgotten. This has come to me as quite a revelation. It shows a serious young man, deeply dissatisfied and restless, religiously devout, with a longing to advance, like Goethe, to human perfection. Again and again, I refer to the feeling of having a great mission, without knowing what it might be. Appended to the diary is a list of books I read (often well before breakfast in the morning) during the six months. In addition to various works of poetry or fiction, it included books on church history, philosophy, history and biography, and art—an impressive list under any circumstances.

Somehow I learned that, as a college graduate, I might enroll in an advanced course or seminar at Clark University, which was located at the other end of the city. I made inquiries and presently found myself one of four or five members of the seminar conducted by Professor George H. Blakeslee, a specialist in international relations and an editor, or *the* editor of the *Journal of Race Relations.* Race relations in those days meant international relations, as, for example, relations between the British and Teutonic peoples. Blakeslee's journal was the forerunner of the much more famous and influential review *Foreign Affairs.* I soon learned that Blakeslee was a member of a scholarly group, known as "The Inquiry," which was studying specific problems likely to confront the United States at a future peace conference. I was assigned (because of my fluent command of German) the analysis of the German colonies in the Pacific and to report on the German administration. This was a new world to me, and I soon became immersed in the limited literature on the Pacific islands. I did manage to complete a report which Blakeslee, a kindly soul, was good enough to commend, but I enlisted in the Army in December 1917 before I could do much more scholarly work. I was glad, however, to have had this opportunity to do research in depth on a historical and political problem. Later, I was to become a colleague of Professor Blakeslee and to enjoy a further association with him.

During my two years at the academy, three events of major importance occurred which left a lasting impression on my mind. In chronological order they were the first great polio epidemic of the autumn of 1916; the hotly contested presidential election between the incumbent, Woodrow Wilson, and Charles Evans Hughes in November 1916; and the intervention of the United States in the Great War in April 1917.

Poliomyelitis or infantile paralysis was a little-known disease usually ending in serious paralysis if not death. Therapeutic methods, highly developed in our day, were as yet unknown. In 1916 the first epidemic put fear into the hearts of all parents. Some stayed at the seashore or in the mountains to forestall contact with other children. Even adults avoided theaters and other aggregations of humans.

When the academy opened in September, terror of polio was already rampant. Abercrombie decided on strict quarantine. The gates were closed, and for two months no one, either teacher or student, was permitted to leave. Whether it was this enforced isolation or just plain luck, no one at the academy contracted the dread disease, and the quarantine could be safely discontinued when the cold weather ended the epidemic.

For me, who in later life was to spend much time and effort in the study of the psychological effects of great epidemics (notably the Black Death of 1348–1349), the great fear of 1916 was unforgettable. The oppressive dread under which parents lived day and night, the danger that the disease might strike any child without warning, the prospect of a loved youngster spending his life as a cripple, all are still vivid in my mind. People became depressed and unsociable, and many of the ordinary activities of life were in abeyance. Some major diseases, such as smallpox, were already quite well understood and controlled. But of polio little more was known in 1916 than of the plague in 1348, so the situation was roughly analogous: The many advances and inventions of mankind in the intervening centuries were of little avail.

The crucial election of November 1916 hinged largely on the issue of intervention in the war against the Central Powers. Initially, the country, long accustomed to the luxury of isolation, took but a moderate interest in Europe. There was much pro-British and pro-French sentiment in the Northeast and the South, but the Middle West was correspondingly inclined to sympathize with the Germans, who were surrounded by powerful enemies on all sides and yet more than holding their own. Leaving aside the business aspects of the situation (the sale of munitions to the Allied powers, the financing of the war, etc.) which were certainly not unimportant, I think sentiment and psychological involvement on the part of the American public was due chiefly to the well-organized, relentless, and highly effective British propaganda, of which very little, indeed, was known at the time, but of which a great deal has since been revealed by the British themselves. Secondly, Americans were naturally outraged by the torpedoing and sinking of the liner *Lusitania* (May 7, 1915) with the loss of over 1,000 lives, including over 100 Americans. Since 1915 much has been learned of the *Lusitania* case: the use of a supposedly unarmed merchantman to transport huge quantities of munitions, the warnings of the German consulate in New York against sailing aboard her, the strange confusions in sailing directions, etc. At the time, however, the attack on the liner appeared as a dastardly, barbaric act.

The *Lusitania* episode led to a strong demand for intervention in the war against Germany, but President Wilson, despite his sympathies with Britain and the pressure of business and academic groups, still hoped to keep the country out of war. He repeatedly warned the German government and finally, following the sinking of the *Arabic* in August, extracted from Berlin an assurance that thenceforth no liners would be sunk without warning and without provision for the safety of noncombatants.

In the November election, then, much was made of Wilson's keeping the country out of war. Nevertheless, the country was so wrought up by the agitation of Theodore Roosevelt and other prominent leaders that Mr. Hughes, the governor of New York, piled up a huge vote. For a couple of days the outcome of the election was uncertain, and, in the preradio age, vast crowds collected at the offices of the newspapers to read the bulletins posted as new information came in.

The academy teachers as well as students shared in the general excitement and were as eager as others to read the bulletins. Perhaps it would have been a good idea to proclaim a holiday and permit the entire school to demonstrate its public spirit by going downtown on the crucial evening when the final returns were to become known. In fact, only the teachers were granted this privilege, on condition that provision be made for supervision of the dormitories. As the youngest member of the staff, I was one of the victims left with a four-story dormitory to keep in order. Of course, I failed abysmally. While I was on one floor, all hell broke loose on the others and I spent the evening rushing up and down stairs hoping to catch some of the malefactors red-handed. My success was negligible until it occurred to me that, like the boys, I might operate in my stocking feet. I pounced on some of the ringleaders, who then charged me with having taken an unfair advantage. Actually, we were all in the same boat: While most of the faculty were participating in the demonstrations and excitement downtown, we had been cruelly discriminated against. In the end I was given some credit for having outwitted even the keenest brains of the student body.

This is hardly the place for a detailed discussion of the forces and events which culminated in the American declaration of war against Germany. By 1917 the great conflict was entering upon the decisive phase. As we now know, the Allied powers, unable to break the deadlock on the western front and faced with the paralysis of revolutionary Russia, were near the end of their tether, and the United States was obliged to decide whether to allow the Germans to dominate Europe or throw its weight in men and resources on the side of the hard-pressed Allies. The Germans, for their part, saw victory in the offing. If they could effectively block the arrival of men and supplies in England, they could probably defeat their enemies before the United States could effectively intervene. This seemed to them the only sensible solution. They therefore repudiated their previous commitments and on January 31, 1917 announced the initiation of unrestricted submarine warfare. The United States at once severed relations and, after several further incidents, declared war on April 6, 1917.

By this time my sympathies, like those of many Americans, had shifted in favor of intervention. Whatever the rights and wrongs of the contending parties (and they are still a matter of dispute), Americans, guided by British propaganda, had come to think of the Germans as Huns, as brutal aggressors who, if they were successful in Europe, would soon make their pressures felt in the New World. The American public had become increasingly convinced that the United States had a direct interest in saving Britain and France from destruction. I learn from my diary that I was much impressed, as the war went on, by the eloquent addresses of President Wilson, whose "Peace without Victory" was generally misunderstood. Actually Wilson did his utmost to mediate a compromise peace, recognizing that a punitive peace would leave a legacy of hate and revenge that would ruin all prospect of converting the German people to democracy. German submarine warfare ruined all such hopes: How could any trust be placed in a government that made and broke promises without compunction and that treated neutrals and neutral rights with complete contempt?

The United States declared war on Germany during the spring vacation at the academy. I was back at my Cambridge home while the school was temporarily closed because of a serious epidemic of German measles. On a beautiful evening in early May, I was dining with my old college friend, Harold Kurth, at Jake Wirth's, a well-known and much-frequented Boylston Street restaurant. I well recall that we reviewed the whole situation over a mug of beer. We had been reading about the war for two years and were familiar with the horrors of trench warfare, but we were agreed that the Germans had made themselves impossible and that there was no alternative to our shouldering the burden. In my diary for April 5, 1917, I had already noted that while I knew and feared the current warfare, I was not terrified and would do my part. Like most soldiers, I was convinced that I would return from the fray, if only to fulfill the great mission to which I felt destined. I hated being in the rank and file and thought for a time of enrolling in the Officer Training Corps, but as yet there was nothing to be done. I completed the school year at Worcester and spent the summer as usual in ornithological researches. When I returned to the academy in September, it was only half-heartedly. I knew that I would get into the conflict, if only because I felt that I could not afford not to play a role, however modest, in so stupendous a historical event. (In my own words to Harry Kurth: "We must run the gamut of all of life's possibilities.") It was known that by December 15 compulsory military service (the draft) would be inaugurated. I did not want to be taken; I wanted to act voluntarily. After much soul-searching, my mother, who was entirely American in her sympathies, agreed that I should enlist, which I did before the December deadline.

A few more words may be desirable to explain my mother's attitude. No one could have been more patriotic. She felt that only in this country would it have been possible for her to raise her family as she did and to give her children an advanced education. Germany, she would argue, meant nothing to us, while we had a distinct, major obligation to this, the country of our birth. My diary reflected all too well the agony and heartbreak with which she faced the prospect of her three sons being drawn into the holocaust. Naturally, she hoped that we could avoid service in the trenches. My brother Rudolph was, in fact, appointed to the Bureau of Censorship, where his ability to read intercepted German letters, even in the Gothic script, was much valued. I think I was more anxious than he to see action at the front, but even so it seemed that as a college graduate with language qualifications, I could and should do more than shoulder a rifle. I might have enlisted in the Officer Training Corps at Plattsburgh, as many college men did. But that would have delayed everything for months, and besides, I had no compelling desire to command. Under the circumstances it seemed a great stroke of luck to read in the newspaper that the colonel of the 23rd Engineer Regiment (a road-building unit) badly needed someone with foreign language skill and invited qualified persons to apply. This I did without delay and in short order received a telegram from the colonel (which I still have) instructing me to report to the recruiting station in Scollay Square and show the commanding officer the telegram addressed to me. The thought of my serving as an interpreter did much to cushion the blow of enlistment as far as my mother was concerned, and I myself reckoned that the 23rd Engineers would presumably be building roads in France, not in Florida. So all seemed to be going swimmingly.

That my mother's attitude was not shared by all German-Americans was sadly demonstrated by the reaction of my Aunt Martha and Uncle Walter, who had no children themselves and were thus less directly affected. They had always been good to us, and we were very fond of them. Deep, therefore, was our chagrin and sadness when they energetically opposed our participation in the war unless obliged to do so after being drafted. My aunt spent practically her entire life in this country, and I would say it was a very pleasant life. Yet, she was forever dreaming of Germany and even in old age saw more virtue in Hitler than she was prepared to confess to us. As for my uncle, he was not even a German, but a German-Swiss; yet he was as deeply involved emotionally as anyone I ever met. He refused to have anything more to do with us until his death years later. After that my more soft-hearted aunt was only too ready for a reconciliation. Nonetheless, we always carefully avoided discussions of politics and especially of international affairs. She never became a real American. Even when she died in ripe old age, her love was still with Germany, where everything was so much better than here. I suppose it must be a real hardship for any person to have to live and work in a country for which they have never developed a genuine devotion.

CHAPTER V

Bullets and Books

FOR A STRANGE REASON I am really quite perplexed about how to recount my fifteen months service in the Army. In the course of my enlistment as a private, I was promoted to the rank of sergeant (and ultimately to that of master engineer, junior grade, a rank that has long since been abolished). As right guide of the company, I was marching beside the captain in the days after the Armistice, when he suggested that an appropriate way of spending the funds in the company's account would be to present each member of the company, on his discharge, with a little book recounting the company's experience, a book which he hoped I would write. The proposition was not unattractive to a budding historian and was accepted. The book was written in great haste, rushed to a job printer on our arrival in New York, and completed in record time to be presented to the men. Entitled *With 'E' of the First Gas*, it was a unique souvenir. I always had a secret love for it, not because I regarded it as a masterpiece, nor even because I believe it was the first published narrative of the experiences of an American unit, but because it was my first historiographical effort, an eyewitness account of an experience shared by many.

Since only 400 copies of the book were printed (and a very credible job the harassed printer did), there were just a few copies available for some of the larger libraries. In forty years it was a collectors' item, if any collector had enough interest to inquire about it. And in 1965 my good friend and distinguished publisher, Alfred A. Knopf, celebrated the fiftieth anniversary of his firm by republishing *With 'E'* under a new title: *Gas and Flame in World War I*, for which I wrote a new introduction, telling in detail how it came to be written. Like all Knopf books, it was beautifully printed on excellent paper in a distinguished binding. Thenceforth, it was available in the trade, and I could look with real pride on a pioneer effort made under most trying circumstances. On the other hand, I am now embarrassed to have this little book stand in the way of my recollections. Since I have not the slightest intention of retelling my experiences as a military man, I will try to draw a distinction between the trials and tribulations of the company, and my personal impressions and reflections.

I must, however, introduce the subject by relating how the best-laid plans of mice and men gang aft agley. The recruiting officers were uninterested in my telegram. I was herded along with other recruits, and after some weeks in Camp Dix (New Jersey), I found myself assigned to Company E of the 30th Engineers, who were lodged in the fine brick barracks of Fort Myer, opposite the city of Washington. Time and again, I waved my telegram before the eyes of the authorities without eliciting even a trace of concern. On my last effort the captain at Fort Myer convinced me that my case was hopeless and persuaded me that his company, which was part of the new Chemical Warfare Service and was presently renamed the First Gas Regiment, was an excellent organization, containing a number of college-bred men as well as a contingent of the regular army.

I never regretted ending up not only in an engineer regiment, but as a common soldier in a regiment devoted to the new chemical warfare, whatever that might mean. The regiment consisted of only six companies, volunteers from every part of the country. There were men of all ages, though mostly young, and from all walks of life—college graduates, businessmen, artisans, and artists. Most were attracted by the slogan "Early Service Overseas," and utterly impatient of the old-fashioned drill and parading that went on around Washington. It seemed a pity that some experienced instructors could not have been sent from the other side, for no one in our company, not even the officers, knew anything of the equipment or operation of "chemical warfare." Hence, we had to wait impatiently for six months before we finally embarked for overseas.

The United States Army did not compare favorably with the British or the Frencch. Most of the officers had had only a few months training. They did not know much and could not always avoid revealing their lack of assurance. Most objectionable were many of the lieutenants, who tried to make up by firmness and even harshness for what they lacked in experience in dealing with men. A few were well liked, but for personal, not professional, reasons. The men themselves insisted that they were free men and resented discipline and orders. It was the sergeants who felt the brunt of the problem, for they were left to carry out the orders decided upon by the officers. Promoted myself to the rank of sergeant on our arrival in France, I speak on this matter feelingly and from experience. I was far from being a giant and had to learn the proper proportion of tact and firmness to be employed in any situation. I had to learn, too, that the plain English language can be pretty ineffectual. Orders given without the proper ingredient of profanity failed to register completely. I became quite a master of the expletive and, indeed, was unable to rid myself of overly strong language for several years after the war.

I do not mean to imply that army life was hell for the men. The many soldier songs and their popularity even today testify to their healthily good spirits. Soldiers singing as they tramped in rain and mud with heavy packs, usually in the muck of drainage ditches while great army trucks slithered along on the narrow roads, occasionally grumbled, as even Napoleon's *grognards* were reputed to have done. But there was always a good deal of companionship, especially at the front, and only the queerest ducks were unable to find some congenial soul. I recall that one of my most interesting comrades was a Columbia-trained engineer employed by the Pennsylvania Railroad. He was a taciturn loner, yet a man of many interests. In fact, he was the only man I ever knew who could explain the doctrinal differences between the innumerable Protestant sects, a strange hobby, it must be confessed, and not one that would appeal to many people.

Of general army life it is hardly necessary to speak here. It varied greatly as between barracks life near Washington, where food and lodging were good and where weekly passes to the capital provided many additional attractions, and life overseas, especially at the front line. In France we generally slept on barn floors, or in bunks of straw mattresses laid on a network of wire. In the action zone an attempt was occasionally made to provide hot coffee, but basically the soldiers lived on cold corned beef, canned tomatoes, or Campbell's baked beans. Though all of this was nourishing food, it became insufferably monotonous. The mess sergeant did what he could to dress things up and was more than delighted when, in the Argonne, we occasionally captured a store of German dried soups, which were superb, and once we came upon a soldier garden in which the cabbages and carrots were just ready for harvesting. If for no other reason, the field kitchen must be remembered for the resulting cabbage soup, which was even better than that at the Ritz Carlton.

We arrived in France at the end of July 1918 after a ten-day voyage on the *President Grant*, the largest of a convoy of some dozen transports which made the passage with 90,000 men, protected by cruisers and destroyers. Fortunately it was summer, so that the unbelievable congestion and lack of proper ventilation could be tolerated if one could find a nook somewhere on deck. I was so anxious to see Europe that the sight of the French villages and countryside and even the sound of the Breton dialect, which bore no resemblance to any French I knew, gave me a great thrill. It took us four days to make the train trip from Brest, where we disembarked, to the vicinity of American headquarters at Chaumont. We were quartered in a village named Choignes, some five kilometers from Chaumont, where the troops far outnumbered the inhabitants. My hopes of perfecting my spoken French were quickly blasted when I found that French peasants, while not unfriendly, were so reserved that there was rarely an opportunity to talk with them.

Overseas pay for American soldiers was generous. Since there was not much opportunity to spend money at the front, most men agreed to salary deductions for government insurance and family allowances. There was in every outfit, however, a group of gamblers, most of whom were content to lose their month's pay to the company shark in a night of reckless gambling. Alcohol, too, provided an outlet for superfluous funds, and there were the inevitable prostitutes who appeared outside the villages and were ready to pursue their profession in the shrubbery for any who had the inclination and the wherewithal to indulge their passions.

Soon after arriving at Choignes serious training for service at the front finally began. To the disgust of the men, the instructors were Englishmen, and "Limeys" were generally despised until, at the front, their dash and courage came to be appreciated. Our job, as it turned out, was not very complicated. The six companies of the regiment were to be broken up into platoons for operational purposes. They were to be sent to spots where enemy machine gun nests or artillery positions made advance impossible. These positions were to be liquidated by the use of concentrated gas, flame, or smoke attack. We had two weapons, of which the most dangerous and laborious turned out to be least useful: the gas projector, an eight-inch pipe closed at one end. In series of twenty they were to be set in a triangular trench, hooked up electrically, and set off by an exploder. Using phosgene gas they would theoretically so inundate an area that it would become untenable.

There were several troubles with the gas projector. For one thing, they had a range of only a few hundred feet, which meant that the required trench would have to be dug at night almost within earshot of the enemy. Then the heavy projector, filled with gas, woud have to be carried on the backs of men, frequently over considerable distances from the base store. And finally, we rarely needed so heavy a concentration of gas, and the projector crew was always in acute danger of being wiped out by enemy machine gunners.

A much lighter and more effective weapon was the Stokes Mortar, a three-inch tube with a firing pin inside the closed end. Both mortar and ammunition were easily portable, could be set up in almost no time, and could be adjusted for proper elevation. Its range, though not great, was superior to that of the projector. It was operated by the gunman allowing a bomb of thermite (flame) or gas to slide down from the muzzle, striking the firing pin and flying out again. The one danger was that the operator might not be able to withdraw his hands quickly enough to avoid serious wounds. But this rarely occurred.

The platoons, each under command of a lieutenant, were freely and frequently shifted along the front, wherever the advance ran upon unusual resistance. Thus, the organization was far more mobile than were other troops. I once calculated that in our two months at the front, my unit worked with some ten or twelve different American divisions, seeing more differing conditions and problems than could reasonably be expected.

Although the first two companies of the regiment had arrived in France in time for the battle of Chateau-Thierry, the remaining companies participated only in the St. Mihiel drive in September and in the great Argonne offensive in October. Our billets, just behind the lines of the St. Mihiel salient, were idyllically located in a dense forest with an abundance of blackberry bushes loaded with ripe fruit. For a couple of days, we devoured blackberries by the pailful, but even this luxury was not enough to quell the impatience of the men who, as the phrase went, "were hell bent to get at the Boche."

My enthusiasm was somewhat dampened, however, when I first found myself in the labyrinth of trenches and communication trenches at Limey, with the Germans at Thiaucourt not far away. Every dwelling in the area had been long since demolished, and German shells were falling lazily all around. Some exploded, others were duds, but they made me feel that one could not possibly survive more than twenty-four hours in this atmosphere of continuous destruction. Fortunately all soldiers are convinced that they, personally, will be spared, as most of the Americans, who were only at the front for a matter of months, were.

The assault on the St. Mihiel salient was a natural initial operation for the relatively inexperienced and but superficially trained American forces. It was lightly held by German divisions which, judging from the age of the droves of Germans that surrendered, must have been reserve troops. Large numbers of

American troops and hundreds of artillery pieces had been concentrated for the attack. There were so many of us that, at the zero hour, we hardly had enough room in the trenches. I can remember struggling in the rain and mud through Marine formations which were about to go over the top. The advance was so rapid that our unit never succeeded in carrying up ammunition in time. The sky was illuminated by artillery fire and primitive airplanes were swooping low over the field, which was strewn with equipment of all sorts, much of it discarded by the Marines as impediments to a fierce bayonet attack. Soon German prisoners came in, dispirited and weary. I talked to a number of them, and without exception they said that they were glad to be captured and hoped the Americans would soon bring the war to an end.

The operations in the Argonne were more difficult, prolonged, and on a much larger scale. Our unit was based at Les Islettes ("Lazy Lizzie," according to the boys), about halfway between Ste. Menehould and Clermont on the main road from Paris to Verdun. This front had been stabilized for almost four years, the broken, wooded terrain obstructing operations. As a result, a broad belt of destruction, called "La fille morte line" ran through the forest from west to east. Nothing was left of the trees but a few charred stumps, and the entire terrain was churned up by bomb craters, some of great diameter and depth.

Since the roads northward were few, narrow, and precipitous, the American forces spent many nights bringing up supplies and equipment. The trucks were slow and not very reliable, while the artillery was still largely horse or mule drawn. In the dark every little crossroad was so jammed with traffic of all sorts that a solution of the problem seemed impossible. Only when enemy shells started to fall near the crossroads did everything clear up as if by miracle.

In the initial American advance, things went smoothly. Our own unit soon found itself in Varennes, where, as I explained to my comrades, King Louis XVI had been stopped and turned back during the attempted flight of the Court during the French Revolution. For a well-deserved rest, we were sent back to La Grange aux Bois, a village not far from Les Islettes and quite near Ste. Menehould. There, we found to our joy that it was possible to buy fresh French bread daily, and the best Camembert cheese that I have ever tasted. Furthermore, there was a British unit stationed in the village, and the two forces, after some initial vituperation and threats, had come to fraternize to their mutual pleasure.

Back in the line, we suffered considerably from the rain and the cold, sleeping in wet blankets on the ground. Night after night, we toiled up the road from the village of St. Juvin to the close proximity of St. Georges, which was still in German hands. I must interject a tribute here to an elderly man, a Knight of Columbus, who every morning crawled through the brush to give us chocolate and candy. In less exposed positions, the women of the Salvation Army were always on hand to serve hot coffee (Java) and doughnuts.

We dug in twenty gas projectors preparatory to a heavy gas attack which was to open the American offensive on the night of October 31. It was hardly a noiseless operation, and it was therefore not surprising that the enemy should have watched us carefully by sending up Véry lights that illuminated all activity.

The upshot was that they greeted the American offensive with a terrific machine gun barrage followed by the most ferocious artillery attack imaginable. I, as sergeant, had to take refuge with twenty men in the ditch along the road, where we used our ponchos to keep out the hail of mud that descended with every shot. It was the worst night of my life, and I was greatly relieved when, after some hours of bombardment, I was able to bring my contingent back to St. Juvin, mostly by crawling on hands and knees, with the loss of only one man.

This Halloween show was the last major German effort and came only eleven days before the Armistice. Thenceforth the American advance was rapid and I think all of us felt that we had seen enough of "Service Overseas." Nothing could have been more pathetic than the thousands of refugees, with carts and bundles crowding the roads back to their former homes. Everywhere, the Americans were hailed as victors, and, indeed, there can be little doubt that it was the intervention of the United States that brought the Allied victory. By mid-1918 the

Russians were already out of the war, and the Germans were bringing divisions from the East to bolster the Western Front against further attack. The British and French were barely able to hold their own against the ferocious assaults of the German forces. They were, one might say, literally on their last legs. It was at this point that American troops began to appear in the line in large numbers. They had been slow in preparing, and their intervention was indeed a last-minute affair.

The impression one got from the final fighting in the Argonne and elsewhere was of utter confusion, which under other circumstances would have cost us dear. But the American troops were young and fresh, and they were thrown into the battle in such numbers, supported by such immense artillery firepower that the Germans, however valiantly they might resist, could not hope to hold the line. Ludendorff, then, after the initial assaults in October, was quite right in his judgment. His great mistake was to reverse himself later and call for more and more resistance. The sole effect of his desperate counsel was to raise havoc in German politics and hasten the collapse which had become inescapable.

A few days before the Armistice (November 11), while defeated Germany was sinking into revolution, our unit was withdrawn from the line and lodged temporarily in the ruins of one of the large French estates on the road to Verdun. It was cold and rainy, and we felt completely isolated while rumors of an armistice were proliferating. Actually, it was only on the next day that a courier arrived, slithering through the mud on a motorcycle, to announce the glad news and bring us the Paris papers with their flaming headlines: "La guerre est gagnée."

We were presently moved to the ruined stone barracks at Verdun, scene of perhaps the most stupendous battle in history. Our quarters had little furnishing beyond wire bunks, while the cold east wind roared through the open windows. I remember being deeply moved by a visit to the centers of the battlefield, around Douaumont, but by this time all of us had had our fill of war. According to rumor, our regiment was to be one of the first to return home, and, strange though it may seem, rumor proved correct. We presently entrained for a very tedious and uncomfortable journey across France to Brest. There the rain was pouring, as it is apt to do on the Breton coast. We were housed in tents and had to pick our way to the mess hall on duckboards that were mostly underwater. A more disheartening and uncomfortable ten days it would be hard to imagine, though personally I came off much better than my comrades. I had already contracted to record the experiences of the company, for which Corporal Robert B. MacMullin, a Massachusetts Institute of Technology man, had prepared an excellent introductory chapter on the techniques of gas and flame warfare. We enlivened our text further by including a few maps and postcards which we had salvaged in German dugouts. All was ready for the printer on our arrival in New York.

The voyage home on the passenger liner *Celtic* made up for the ordeal we had suffered at Brest. There was ample room and good food, and the weather, even in January, was so sunny and pleasant that most afternoons the band played on deck. When we reached New York, MacMullin and I were able to arrange for the printing and binding of our little book, which was distributed to the men on their discharge at Lakehurst, New Jersey, the headquarters of the Chemical Warfare Service, before the end of January.

The First World War, without a doubt the greatest manmade catastrophe in history up to that time, was originally expected to be over in a few months and actually continued and spread for four years. The loss of millions of lives, the material destruction, the political breakdown of the European system, the ideological crisis, all these facts of the great conflict boggled the imagination and now, looking back after some sixty years and a second and greater World War, one can hardly escape the conclusion that this first gigantic contest, if it did not originate many of the major problems of the later twentieth century, at least gave them increased impetus and in many cases provided the setting for their fruition.

Possibly even greater than the social costs, were the burden of individual misery and the loss of a whole generation of young men on whom the future would normally have depended. Countless families lost their sons or only recovered them after years of captivity and silence. The disruption of life and the loss of private property were incalculable. When the American soldiers returned from abroad, they were cured of the yearning for danger and conflict. The United States had entered the war when most of the damage had been done. Its intervention clinched the victory, but at relatively small cost in men and material. Even so, most returning soldiers felt that they had seen enough, and that no such cataclysm should be permitted to occur again, if humanly possible.

And yet the Great War, as in fact any war can, benefited some individuals. Many men enlist primarily to get away from intolerable personal entanglements or domestic strife. Such was certainly not my case, but honesty obliges me to admit that I eagerly welcomed the opportunity to give up a perfectly good teaching position, which did not at all appeal to me. My great passion was the study of history, and my one great regret was that in planning a three-year college course, it had proved impossible to enroll in the introductory course in European history. In normal times the financial situation of my family would never have permitted me to give up my position at Worcester Academy and return to academic study. But from my army pay I was able not only to continue to contribute to the family finances, but to save a substantial sum of money. I do not remember my overseas pay as a sergeant, but it was substantial. And then, in the last couple of months, the promotion to master engineer came as the swelling act of the drama. The captain of the company, a well-meaning but not very effectual officer, confided in me that he deeply regretted his failure in not sending me to an officers' school in France. The rank of master engineer was, therefore, intended as a solatium. In any event, the compensation was better than the title, for the master engineer had but ill-defined functions, no discernable responsibility, and no effective master. Yet the pay was blissfully high and added a good deal to my total funds.

On my return home in February 1919, I found affairs in a sorry state. My brother Rudolph, utterly unable to reconcile my mother to his interest in his girlfriend of several years, was married quietly in New York, to the great distress of my mother.

Furthermore, my brother Walter, as eager as anyone to get into the fray, had surreptitiously enlisted in a Signal Corps Company and had gone to France, where he and I tried in vain to establish personal contact. Since he was not discharged from the Army until August 1919, I found my mother entirely alone and quite miserable. She was even disturbed and apprehensive that during the war I, like most soldiers, had corresponded with a girlfriend at home, and that occasionally I would go out in the evening to call on Paula, who had written me loyally and regularly during my months in the Army.

On one subject, however, my mother and I were in complete agreement—that I should use what money I had, to be supplemented by my summer pay, to return to Harvard and enter the Graduate School of Arts and Sciences to study history. Incredible though it may seem, Harvard at that time had a generous policy specifying that if one had once paid tuition of $150, one would never afterward have to pay more. Since my graduation in 1915, tuition had already been raised from $150 to $250, but this ominous development left me entirely unmoved as I registered as a first-year graduate student in history.

During the war Harvard had temporarily adopted a three-semester system. I was overjoyed to find that the third semester was to begin late in February, so that I would be able to get into harness at once. But unfortunately, very few courses began in the third semester, and I had to ransack the catalogue to work out a program. I finally found four courses of which two at least were historical. Most helpful and enjoyable to me was Professor Merriman's "England and France in the Seventeenth and Eighteenth Century." Merriman was a superb lecturer, at least in the narrative type of history. This particular course was just what I needed—political and military, with an occasional dash of economics, thrilling in substance, and excellent as a general background.

I was less happy about the course offered by Harold J. Laski, a brilliant young English scholar who, one might say, was then the toast of the academic profession and was later, after his return to England, to become the influential mentor of the Labour Party. Far beyond most scholars in the depth of his

knowledge, he loved to display it and simply doted on controversy, which allowed him to demolish one or more victims.
As I remember it, Laski offered a course on modern English
history, than which no historical subject could be more interesting or important. But he was an avowed radical with heavy
Marxist leanings. It would have been understandable had he
concentrated on the Industrial Revolution, which transformed
English society and was eventually to affect human life on the
entire planet. But Laski preferred to lecture on and discuss
chiefly the origins and development of the British Labour
movement which, though imporatnt, was far from being the
whole story.

Even as a student in Laski's course I felt somewhat estranged
by what seemed to me his intellectual arrogance. In discussion
he tended to call on certain students, few in number, whom he
could depend on to support or even reinforce his views. One
seemingly insignificant episode soured me even more. When, in
May, I asked him what books I might profitably read during the
summer, he replied without a moment's hesitation: "Read
Lecky's *History of England in the 18th Century* [a matter of
six substantial volumes] and Graham Wallas's *Life of Francis
Place*." Now the point is not that these books were not worth
reading. They were then and have remained first-rate works.
But they were far too advanced and specialized for the average
student, who, furthermore, was not likely to have the time for
so formidable an assignment. My case, indeed, was worse than
the average, for in summer I spent the day working with Dr.
Phillips on the history of ducks. On warm summer evenings I
soon grew sleepy when faced with serious reading. Nonetheless,
I saw the Laski recommendation through—I read Lecky from
the first cover to the last; I learned a great deal from him and
came to appreciate what really superior historical writing involves. As for Graham Wallas, his biography of Place, published
around 1900, has become a classic. It is a beautifully written as
well as a thoughtful story of the London britches manufacturer
who was a pioneer labor organizer and champion of reform. But
even Wallas would have meant more to me some years later. I
find that now in my old age, I read him with greater pleasure
and appreciation than ever before.

I am not going to burden the reader with a detailed account of the further four years of my graduate training. In most respects, no doubt, it did not greatly differ from that of any budding historian studying at a major university. It completely overshadowed my college years. I was studying a subject every aspect of which aroused my interest and stimulated my thought. I made many lifelong friends among my colleagues as well as among my teachers.

The requirements for the Ph.D. degree called for at least two years of additional course work. With four courses a year there was ample opportunity to study the histories of various major powers, which for me meant the entire area from France and Italy through Central Europe to Poland, Russia, the Balkans, and the entire Byzantine and Ottoman empires. In addition there were courses on methodology, political theory, and other ancillary subjects. Every student was required to take one year of seminar work, which represented systematic training in research and writing. I found this work so rewarding that I enrolled in a seminar every year for three years. In what time remained, I audited lecture courses and did as much reading as I could.

The Harvard History Department was already one of the largest and most influential in the university. It included scholars of great eminence in many fields. Channing and Hart were still on the scene, and Morison, Schlesinger, and Merk were already shining lights in the American field. Ferguson in ancient history, Haskins in medieval, Merriman in early European, Lord in the Slavic fields, and Coolidge in modern diplomatic history constituted a veritable galaxy of great scholars as well as great teachers. Widener Library was without a peer in its scholarly holdings and was a paradise for the bookworm.

My first seminar, consisting of three students besides myself, was directed by Robert Howard Lord, a comparatively young scholar, who in 1908 had taken his doctorate with a (handwritten) dissertation on the second partition of Poland, a splendid piece of work using Polish materials, which was published in the Harvard Historical Studies and over sixty years later was translated and published by Polish scholars. I stupidly offered to prepare the first seminar report, on the Alvensleben

Convention of 1863, an agreement for common action by Germany and Russia against the insurrection in Russia's Polish provinces. I wish I could remember what the trouble with my report was, but I recall with gratitude Professor Lord's asking me to come to his study after the meeting. There he explained to me that he recognized all the work I had put into the paper, but then proceeded to explain to me frankly that I had gone about it in quite the wrong way. I have never forgotten this episode and in my later career always followed Lord's practice of outspoken criticism to save the student from misapprehensions that might eventually cost him dear. After all, as I often told myself, the teacher's function is to teach, not to praise. In any event I have been eternally grateful to Lord for setting me straight before I could possibly go far astray.

I am happy to say that my initial misconceptions were not so grievous as to blind Lord to the other qualities of the report. This is the only conclusion that I can draw from his inviting me to take over, a couple of months later, when the assistant in Lord's large undergraduate course was obliged to withdraw on account of illness. I was delighted until I realized what was involved: not only the grading of occasional tests and examinations, but the reading of over 100 term essays. This in itself was a stupendous task, particularly for me, whose knowledge of nineteenth-century European history was still, shall we say, somewhat superficial. I did what I could to equip myself and was much gratified when, on reviewing some of the more doubtful gradings, Lord came to much the same conclusion as I had reached. Not only that, but he asked me to continue as his assistant in the following year, and I was automatically carried over in this position to the second semester of the course, which was conducted by Professor Archibald Cary Coolidge.

Despite our professional association over two years, Professor Lord remained a reserved man, and I think was felt to be so by most students. He had, in 1918–1919, been a member of "The Inquiry," the commission of experts studying the problems of an eventual peace. With his knowledge of Polish, Lord naturally was assigned that problem. It is hardly too much to say that his recommendations were pro-Polish without reservation. The generosity with which the Polish eastern frontiers were drawn had much to do with the Polish-Russian War of 1919–1920, which ended in the forced abandonment of the extreme nationalist hopes of the Poles. Even more fateful was the decision to award the new Polish state a corridor to the sea through East Prussia, leaving the Germans only a narrow connection to Danzig, which was declared a free city under League of Nations auspices. It may well be that the consequences of some of his recommendations may have preyed on Lord's mind. He became a Roman Catholic convert and soon resigned from his Harvard professorship to become an ordained parish priest.

Lord had been a stellar student of Professor Archibald Cary Coolidge, that remarkable man who, though he published relatively little, had a profound influence on the course of European history studies in the United States. Abandoning a diplomatic career, Coolidge had, as far back as the early 1890s, begun to preach the importance of Russia and the desirability of studying the Slavic languages. At an early date, he had also seen the importance of Near Eastern history, to say nothing of Asian and Latin American history. It was only natural that, in the days of Theodore Roosevelt and Mahan, he should have become engrossed in problems of international relations. In 1908 he published a volume of essays entitled *The United States as a World Power,* a remarkably prescient book which he hoped to follow with other volumes on France and possibly Germany.

Coolidge never married and hence was not as distracted by family affairs as many other scholars. Furthermore, while for many years he was financially comfortable without having the substantial fortune that ultimately came to him, he devoted what funds he could afford to the purchase of books in European and world history. By 1900 he had already become involved in the affairs of the college library which, among other problems, was plagued by lack of space. The story of Coolidge's role in building up the Harvard collections and of his contribution to the planning and construction of the Widener Library has been recently told from the records by William Bentinck-Smith in a beautiful volume entitled *Building a Great Library:*

the Coolidge Years at Harvard (Cambridge, 1976). It is the story of a great, imaginative, yet modest man.

Coolidge, too, was a member of "The Inquiry" and was concerned primarily with the knotty and hopelessly entangled affairs of the moribund Habsburg Empire. He could not possibly compete in influence with Masaryk and Beneš, nor could he resist all the pressures which threatened to leave Austria a little rump state forbidden by the peace treaties from joining Germany proper. But he did fight for a fair application of the principle of nationality and managed to save a major portion of the German-speaking Burgenland for the new Austrian Republic. He was gratified by this minor victory, but probably a bit amused when, in 1923, Calvin Coolidge succeeded Warren Harding as President of the United States, and people of consequence in Central European affairs, who had never heard of Calvin Coolidge, congratulated themselves that the well-informed and fair-minded Archibald C. Coolidge was to take over the reins of the American government.

I attended Coolidge's seminar in 1920–1921, when the making of the various peace treaties absorbed the attention of all who were interested in international relations. The exceedingly harsh treatment meted out to the Germans in the dictated Treaty of Versailles (June 1919), which obliged them to acknowledge sole responsibility for the outbreak of the great conflict, immediately evoked much criticism. That the Germans, still suffering under a rigid food blockade and so completely disarmed as to be at the mercy of their opponents, accepted sole responsibility (the famous Article 231 of the Treaty of Versailles) did not mean that they even remotely acknowledged it. On the contrary, they regarded it as an unheard-of affront to their national pride. They never forgot this cruel indignity and, in the sequel, turned to Hitler in large numbers partly in the hope that he would wipe out this stain on their honor.

Because of Article 231 in particular, the Germans immediately began to publish documents and memoirs to prove their innocence of the charges levelled against them, or at least to expose the transgressions of their opponents. Within a few years the first of some fifty volumes of German Foreign Office documents, covering the period from 1871 to 1914, began to appear. Though even this vast agglomeration of evidence could only be an extensive selection of archive records, the work was done by competent historians and was, on the whole, recognized as an honest source by members of the historical guild in all countries.

Professor Coolidge, an expert in matters of foreign policy, was deeply interested in the international controversy that now developed, which was soon dubbed the *Kriegsschuldfrage* or *War Guilt Question*. As an historian he was particularly interested in the background and causes of the war, and himself published an excellent little study of the Triple Alliance. It went without saying that the members of his seminar were assigned problems in this area, particularly in the period prior to 1890 which was already covered by the official German publication (*Die Grosse Politik der Europäischen Kabinette*). It was fascinating research, constantly stimulated by the publication of important apologia and by occasional efforts at repudiation by French and British writers. Actually some of the most influential and impressive contributions on the side of the victors, if they did not accept the German thesis, showed real understanding of it and in several cases denounced the methods and results of the peace making in no uncertain terms.

I never heard Coolidge express a definite opinion on these matters, but we seminarians learned from him the importance in historical work of appreciating the needs and aspirations of all the participants, and particularly of taking into account the human equation and the tremendous strain under which statesmen were obliged to act in time of crisis. I am sure that Coolidge, if obliged to pronounce himself, would have said that all the major powers shared responsibility for the situation that culminated in 1914. The relative share of each might be debated, but the effort to pin sole responsibility on the defeated party was not only a gross injustice, but an unpardonable stupidity which was to cost the world dear. In general, these were also the sentiments of his students. Though by nature and education more understanding of things German than British, French or Russian, I had been entirely soured by the German leadership's unrestricted submarine policy that brought the United States into the war, and I think I could view the policies and activities of the Allied powers with the same detachment for which I strived in analyzing those of others.

In the last fifty years, mountains of documentary and other source materials have appeared, some of it from the German side distinctly damaging to German war aims in 1914–1918. Moreover, the French and British governments could not afford to leave the entire field to the huge German collection. They were obliged to publish selections of their own Foreign Office archives, and these, too, were commendably scrupulous and well balanced. In the course of reviewing and utilizing this material, I have been eternally grateful for the training in understanding and justice that I owe to Professor Coolidge.

During my graduate studies, while I much enjoyed the excellent lectures of men who were good teachers as well as good scholars, financial considerations regrettably deprived me of much time that I would have liked to devote to reading. Since until 1922 I had been working with Dr. Phillips, I had little energy for serious summer reading, especially in those great historical classics, with which I was not nearly as conversant as I should have liked to be. I may as well say here that while I always enjoyed teaching and made great efforts to keep abreast of the new literature in the fields for which I was responsible, I was always torn between using spare time for more general reading (and I loved reading in fields altogether foreign to my own work) and my passion for research and writing. Even as a graduate student, I could not resist the preparation of essays in competition for the Toppan Prize, which I won twice, first with a paper on "Bismarck and the Ems Telegram," and again with a study of German relations with Britain and Russia in 1898–1901. This was a crucial period, during which some people thought that a German-British alliance might have been possible. It was on this subject that I decided to write my doctoral dissertation, which I began in the autumn of 1921.

In order to enable me to go abroad for travel and archival study, I had been awarded a Bayard Cutting Fellowship of $1,200, which in those days of galloping inflation in Central

Europe, was ample for my purposes. But I had, in the interval, fallen in love with Susanne Knauth, the sister-in-law of one of my former Worcester Academy colleagues, who was convinced that in many respects we were ideally suited to each other. He had urged me to call on the young lady, who was about to begin her senior year at Radcliffe College.

My prospective wife was the second of three sisters in a family, which, like my own, was of German extraction. Her father, who had died before I knew him, was a prosperous New York corporation lawyer and an excellent amateur cellist. He held a substantial interest in the private bank of Knauth, Nachod and Kühne, which had moved to New York after the German Revolution of 1848–1849, but still retained connections with the Leipzig bank. Her mother also came from well-to-do parentage, her father having owned a substantial textile plant in Chemnitz.

The Knauth family had an almost indescribably beautiful summer estate on Lake George, just above the village of Bolton opposite the tip of Tongue Mountain. Next to this estate was that of a deceased brother, who had prospered in the banking business. He had fathered five sons, roughly the ages of their girl cousins, with whom, one might say, they grew up. Both families were not only financially well off, but highly cultivated. My future mother-in-law had sold the New York house after her husband's death and had purchased a splendid, stone Dutch residence in Kingston, New York. The oldest sister, who had married my friend, had an unusually beautiful soprano voice and sang German lieder as I have never heard any woman except Lotte Lehmann sing them. The youngest daughter was an exceptional beauty of the Botticelli type. She had recently married a young lawyer from Amherst College. The third daughter, on whom I called, impressed me as unusually serious. Her great passion was music, and she was energetically study-ing the cello. She also took courses in theory and composition with "Doc" Davison, the great Harvard luminary in music at that time. She admitted to me that Davison had told her even as a freshman that for all her love of music, she lacked the natural endowment to go far in it. Since he raised no objection, however, she continued to enroll in his courses. I would say that even if she was not a great musician, she had a thorough grounding in the history and structure of the art. Since all I had was the love of music, her knowledge and appreciation were alone enough to draw us together. She encouraged me by occasionally giving me her ticket to a Boston Symphony concert or to a performance of the Budapest String Quartet.

I was invited to spend a week at Lake George in the summer of 1920 and came away with the conviction that there could not be a more beautiful place in all the world. For one thing, as a thorough city boy, I had never before seen a mountain, nor smelled the marvelous fragrance of hemlock and other evergreen woods. The house stood on an eminence, looking straight over the lake to Tongue Mountain and beyond. It was the day before outboard motors and speedboats, and all was placid and silent. We did some canoeing along the shores of the lake and, of course, took full advantage of the swimming. I know that now, fifty years later, the town of Lake George (ten miles from Bolton) is a veritable tourist and souvenir trap, and that even Bolton is no longer a sleepy village—all the more reason to recall with gratitude when one could enjoy the majesty of mountain nature in peace.

I am not sure that my wife-to-be was really interested in marriage. She was by temperament a scholar, if there ever was one, deeply engrossed in philosophy and especially logic, as well as whole-heartedly devoted to music. I think that she liked and admired me for having done so much with so little. At any rate, we had many common interests and got along very well with each other, though I was less addicted than she to long tramps in the woods and mountains. Eventually, her mother and sisters talked her into marriage as the only sensible course for a young woman and assured her that the conjugal life would soon awake other than purely bookish interests.

We were married early in September 1921 on the eve of my departure for Europe. My brother Walter, who was the proud owner of a 1917 Dodge, insisted that my mother and I join him in the drive to Lake George. We started a day in advance to make sure of my being on hand at the crucial moment. The car did not behave very well and called forth all the mechanical skill my brother could command. None of the roads was in good condition, and in southwestern Vermont, which we had to cross, they were simply primitive—unpaved, dusty, and full of potholes. On arriving at our destination, I asked the Irish chauffeur to inspect the car to see if we had missed any loose bolts. "Gosh, Mister," he reported, "it's a miracle you didn't drop all your guts in the road."

The wedding, in beautiful surroundings and in perfect weather, went off without a hitch. Among the gifts was a substantial check from my mother-in-law which allowed us to do certain things in Europe that would not otherwise have been possible on my traveling fellowship. After a short stay in the Adirondacks, we embarked on the *Rotterdam*, a comfortable old steamer that took eight days to make the passage to Plymouth and that did just enough rolling and pitching to remind me of the power of the elements.

CHAPTER VI

To Europe and Back

I WILL PERMIT myself only the briefest summary of a ten months stay in Europe, which for me, a budding historian, was full of new and interesting experiences. Our first stop was in London, where we lodged for ten days in a Russell Square pension. We explored the old City and especially the Minories, where there were wonderful secondhand bookstores. The double-decker buses were ideal for visiting all the famous sites before we began the weeks of peregrinations by train. There was still very little automobile traffic, especially in the country-side. In the railroad coach one studied the guidebook, decided where next to stop, and chose the name of a suitable hotel. There was no need to scramble for a taxi at the station, for every hotel had a carriage or omnibus waiting, and there was no difficulty whatever in having body and baggage taken to the hostelry. I might interject here that, much as we loved England, we found the food in the average hotel or restaurant badly cooked and very monotonous.

The September and October weather while we were in England was exceptionally beautiful, which added greatly to our pleasure. We visited Oxford and Cambridge and a good many of the cathedral towns. Each of the great churches had something distinctive to recommend it, but I remember as most beautiful Durham Cathedral on its bluff with the river winding around it, and Ely, with its quiet closes and the swans lazily drifting on the moat.

Toward the end of October, we cut short our delightful English tour and went on to Leipzig, where for a few days we visited my wife's relatives and again poked about in the antiquarian bookshops for which the city was world famous. Due to the inflation of German currency, I was able to buy a fine set of the entire fifty volumes of Leopold von Ranke's works for $14.50, delivered to Cambridge, Massachusetts. Needless to say, nothing quite as amazing has happened to me again.

Our prime objective was Vienna, where I planned to spend the winter in archival study before visiting Italy and France in the spring. We arrived there on November 2 in the midst of an early snowstorm. To our surprise and consternation, we were unable to secure a hotel room and finally had to appeal to Thomas Cook and Son for help. They obligingly sent out a runner to see if he could find a room in a private home. To our immense relief he returned in an hour or two after securing lodgings in Leopoldstadt. The room, when we reached it, was large but gloomy, with several layers of curtains and a set of shutters over the window, mostly, I suppose, to keep out the cold.

Professor Coolidge had given me a letter of introduction to Professor Alfred Francis Pribram, one of the senior historians at the University of Vienna, who had published, from the archives, *The Secret Treaties of Austria-Hungary*, the English translation of which Coolidge had arranged. Pribram spent most of his time in his heated study in the Foreign Office (Ballhausplatz), a splendid palace made famous by the Congress of Vienna. He was a small, kindly man, who was shocked by our experience of the previous day. His wife, he said, owned most, if not all, of the Hotel Imperial and could certainly have helped us find a room. Hearing that our existing accommodations were unattractive he suggested that we might like to live with his family in their "cottage," or single residence, in Döbling on the outskirts of the city. This cottage turned out to be an attractive house with surrounding grounds, located in the XIXth District, that is, in the outer ring of suburbs surrounding the old "inner" city. We accepted his kind offer with gratitude and truly enjoyed our association with the Pribram family. When, in the following year, the professor came to Boston to deliver Lowell lectures and found the Faculty Club noisy and restless, he lived for several weeks with us in our apartment. I recall his strange and alarming habit of strolling about the rooms and every now and then tossing a couple of aspirins down his throat. Nonetheless, he survived to reach the mideighties.

Pribram said while there would be no difficulty about my working in the Austrian Archives, they were unfortunately closed for the period after 1895, so that it would be impossible for me to pursue the topic of Anglo-German relations at the turn of the century. I had to make a quick decision and concluded that the best course would be to study the making of the Franco-Russian Alliance in the years 1891–1894. The French government had recently published key documents relating to this strange compact between the radical, republican regime in Paris and the unqualified despot Tsar Alexander III. My wife and I worked assiduously for several months reading the Austrian ambassaadorial reports from St. Petersburg and Paris. Happily, these documents had been written in impeccable manuscript by embassy secretaries, which made them easy to read. We found much interesting material which gave my dissertation, as eventually published, a certain basic value.

We had no conception of what life in Vienna would be like. All that remained of the venerable Habsburg Empire was the little Austrian Republic, mostly agricultural, and the top-heavy capital, which was securely in the hands of the Social Democrats. Social conditions were appalling, for fuel and food could be secured only with the greatest difficulty and at fantastically inflated prices. We were able, from time to time, to buy 100 pounds of cannel coal, but it was impossible to heat our large tile stove with the small lumps we could add from time to time. For the rest, the Pribram house was entirely unheated, except for one room in which the stove was lighted for the reception of company. As the really cold weather set in, the plumbing froze, and since the water pipes were in the walls, the choice had to be made between tearing down the house, or resorting to the public toilet facilities, a block away. The decision fell on the latter, so all winter we arose in a frigid room, hurried into essential clothing, and fled to the public lavatories.

For us money was no problem as the exchange generally hovered around 5,000 crowns to the dollar. We could afford to eat in good restaurants and to lounge in the most elegant coffee houses. Since the archives closed when darkness set in, we had a chronic problem of how to avoid freezing, for which the coffee houses provided a solution. Then, too, I went to the home of Mrs. Mitrofanov, widow of the late Russian historian, and spent some time reading Russian with her. About the only Russian book we could buy in Vienna was Miliukov's history of the first Russian revolution of 1905, which was really too advanced for me.

Our salvation from cold lay chiefly in the theaters and operas, for dramatic and musical life continued in Vienna as though nothing had happened. It was not unusual to find listed in the Sunday edition of the *Neue Freie Presse* some twenty performances scheduled for the ensuing week. There were operas, theaters, and concerts of all kinds, great and small. Since we could get the best seats in the house for the equivalent of fifty cents or less, we became habitués of the Burgtheater, where we saw most of Shakespeare's plays in excellent German translation, all the beautiful dramas of Vienna's own Franz Grillparzer, and many of the French and other European classics. In the splendid opera house, from the seats that had replaced the old imperial loge, we heard all the Wagner operas and also a good selection of other German and Italian operas. These performances, of the highest grade, were in themselves an education, and I would say that they were worth the hardships of life in Vienna in the critical postwar period.

In addition to work at the archives, I decided to enroll at the university and hear the lectures of some of the great authorities. Even allowing for the abnormal conditions of the time, I came to consider the Viennese university training greatly inferior to that of Harvard. Hans Uebersberger was a world authority on Russian history, yet I learned nothing from his lectures that I had not heard from Robert Howard Lord. In the catalogue there was not a single course on French,

British, or United States history. The instructors (*Dozenten*) received no stipend beyond what the students paid them. They were for the most part in such dire straits that they had to rely for one square meal a day on the lunch provided by American relief. Under the circumstances, no fewer than four of them tried to attract students by offering courses on the history of socialism, a case of blatant but understandable duplication.

Professor Pribram and most of his colleagues paid very little attention to their university responsibilities. They usually lectured on a subject on which they were writing a book, without reference to its larger interest or importance. Pribram, who was an excellent lecturer, spent the day working in the archives, and then, on his way home, from five to six, stopped at the university and lectured on Napoleon's foreign policy from 1807 to 1812, a very detailed and interesting topic, but obviously a bit specialized. Although the university was entirely unheated, he had a large audience of students muffled in their overcoats. But they seemed to mean nothing to him as individuals. When, after the lecture, a student had the temerity to stop the professor to ask a question or seek advice, Pribram regarded it as inexcusable effrontery.

The chaotic conditions of the university gave us an excuse to plan an escape. Since all work was suspended from December 10 to February 1, my wife and I decided to flee the cold, the somber skies, and the everlasting snowstorms for refuge in Italy. The more we thought of it and the more we realized the benefit to us of the depressed Austrian currency, the more we concluded that we might as well be hanged for a sheep as for a lamb. We would go all the way, to Greece and even to Constantinople, returning refreshed for a second bout with Viennese miseries.

The first leg of our odyssey was a night train ride to Trieste. Despite the lateness of the hour, the train was so crowded that we had to stand in the corridor during most of the long trip. In compensation we had gorgeous views of the snow-covered Alps and the forests flooded with moonlight. At the Yugoslav frontier, a pompous official came through the car collecting either one dinar or three Italian lire. We had nothing but Austrian currency, which we offered him in generous amounts, but he treated the venerable crowns as now mere trash and insisted that we pay on his terms or leave the train. As we were clearly terrified by the prospect of a night in an Alpine station, a kind passenger offered to provide us the necessary lire in exchange for crowns. We vowed eternal gratitude, only to learn next morning at Trieste that we had been properly fleeced. This, I suppose, has been the fate of travelers since the beginning of time.

We embarked on a steamer of the Lloyd Triestino Line, on which both the food and accommodations were definitely below average. But the weather grew steadily warmer as we advanced southward through the Adriatic. After stops at Bari and Brindisi, we steamed along the Albanian coast, past the Ionian Isles, most alluring in the fine winter light, and through the Gulf and Canal of Corinth to Piraeus and Athens. At Piraeus King Constantine, recently restored to the throne, came out to the ship to greet his mother, Queen Sophia, who was one of our fellow passengers. The trading community, which was Venizelist almost to a man, gathered about in small boats and watched the proceedings in glum silence, which was reciprocated by the King.

Athens fifty years ago was, I imagine, less than one quater its present size and population. The train from Piraeus to the capital passed through what seemed like wasteland. We spent an entire day in Athens. It was my wife's birthday (December 20) and as beautifully sunny and warm as a day in June. We devoted most of our stay to the Acropolis, which I have seen several times since, but never in the sublime quiet of our first visit without droves of restless tourists.

A night's voyage took us from Piraeus to the Dardanelles, where the terrible scars of the recent fighting and the wrecks of sunken warships were still much in evidence. But the approach to Constantinople in the early morning was another matter. Among the cities I have seen, I would say that only New York and San Francisco can rival Constantinople for natural location, and I would prefer to New York's skyscrapers the gleaming domes and graceful minarets of St. Sophia and the other great mosques.

We stayed at a modest hotel, but, in reaction to the poor food we had had for a week, we decided to splurge and have one grand meal at the Tokatlian, the best hotel in town. Used as I was to inflation, I was shocked, after dessert, to be handed a bill for more than seven American dollars, which was more money than I had on my person. I explained to the waiter that I could run across the street and secure more funds on the basis of my letter of credit. When I noted his dissatisfaction, I offered to leave my gold watch with him as security. "No, sir," he replied, "You will leave your wife," which was what I had to do.

Constantinople was in turmoil. The victorious nationalists of Kemal Pasha had not yet taken over and the city was still under control of three commissioners (British, Italian, American). There were thousands on thousands of refugees from the defeated White Russian armies in South Russia. Many of them were destitute, while the more fortunate found employment of a menial kind. The congestion everywhere was great, and on the one bridge which spanned the Golden Horn, it was almost impossible to thread one's way through the medley of tooting automobiles, the caravans of camels, the flocks of sheep, and the innumerable hamals or porters, who carried anything short of a piano on their backs.

Of course, we reveled in all the great sites, including the impressive walls, but above all we were fascinated by the beauties of the Bosporus, which we explored as far as Bebek, where friends of my wife in the diplomatic service had a charming home, just below Robert College. The weather was uniformly beautiful, and nothing marred our enjoyment until we tried to leave. Exit from the city required the permits of all three high commissioners. Since we were in the midst of the extended Christmas holidays, no one showed much inclination to transact business. The Italian commission especially refused to be bothered, although we had passage on an Italian ship back to Trieste. Finally, the American authorities raised their voices and produced action. We were rushed to the dock, into a rowboat and out to the steamer, which got under way the moment we stepped on deck. The steamer had waited, we soon learned, because we constituted two of a total of seven passengers.

Our return voyage was uneventful, except that we were late in arriving in Venice and had to hire a gondolier, who literally raced through all kinds of back canals to get us to the railroad station on time. He deserved to win, but just could not make it, so we had a layover of a night at the hotel opposite the railway station. We arrived in Vienna in time for the opening of the next semester at the university, and I, of course, resumed my research in the archives. We had not been missed, though we had had a most rewarding and enjoyable look at the Mediterranean world.

The second lap of our Vienna sojourn was more or less a repetition of the first. Constantly hoping that the weather would improve, we were just as consistently disappointed. At the end of March, when my work at the archives was completed, we decided to bid farewell to the beautiful city where, despite all discomforts, we had reveled in music and theater, and again seek solace in the South. Only one intervening episode must be mentioned. One of the shop windows displayed a good-looking violin and bow for sale at 50,000 crowns. Since in American money this was only about $10, my wife persuaded me that it would be downright folly to pass up such a bargain. I have never regretted buying it. It is a rather fine Stradivarius-type fiddle of French, late eighteenth-century manufacture. But, just as great oaks from little acorns grow, a little fiddle may produce much music. Why not, having the instrument, take a few lessons, which would be very cheap? Having the time, and no dearth of interest, I succumbed to the temptation and began to take lessons from the organist of the Karlskirche. The time was far too short and my abilities too limited to produce any impressive results, but the teacher was not only an enthusiastic musician, but a Viennese heart and soul. The great events of the city's past were as vivid to him as though they had just occurred. Under his guidance we had to review the entire siege of Vienna by the Turks in 1683: Here were the bastions and the connecting earthworks; here the Turks tried to tunnel under the walls, only to be met by the Austrians burrowing in the other direction; here was the gate on which the last desperate and futile assault was made. It was fitting instruction for a young historian, and I have always fondly remembered this genial musician and devoted Viennese patriot.

Like so many Germans of the past, we set out for Italy, the land of felicity, "wo die Zitronen blühn." In Venice, we found the weather so damp and raw that we hurried on to Florence and then to Rome, in the desperate hope of finding a little sunshine. Even Naples, world renowned for the softness of its climate, was not much better. As a last resort we embarked on a ship for Palermo, where we arrived the next morning after a stormy passage. In Palermo, too, though it was warm, it was raining. We were already sinking into hopeless dejection, when suddenly the weather cleared and we were at last in brilliant sunshine. And what a view and what a location, with the Conca d'Oro stretching away along the shore! We spent several days in this heavenly place and even bargained with one of the coachmen to drive us up to Monreale for a reasonable fee. I have not been to Sicily since, and perhaps I imagine the present situation to be worse than it actually is, but I picture a procession of touring buses from all over the world, chugging up the hill to Monreale and distracting one from contemplation of the priceless mosaics in the cathedral. Early in 1922 conditions in Europe, and especially in Italy, made for few tourists, and mass transportation was still unknown.

From Palermo we went on to Girgenti (Agrigento) where the Hotel des Temples was completely walled in against bandit raids at night. The temples were a superb sight, as later, at Siracusa, were the Latomia in which the Athenian captives in the Peloponnesian War were confined. At Taormina we stopped only long enough for a marvellous meal of Mediterranean fish and a positively fantastic view of the sun setting behind the cloud of smoke that hung over Aetna.

By this time the weather in northern Italy had finally improved, and at Salerno we hired a coach and made the long but fabulous drive to Amalfi and thence around the end of the peninsula to Sorrento on the lovely Bay of Naples. Those who have been privileged to see these charming places need no description, and those less fortunate could never capture the beauty through even the most eloquent description.

In fact, narratives of other people's travels are apt to be tiresome if not irritating. I will say simply, then, that we saw the monuments of Rome and were enchanted by Florence and its many art treasures. I had a letter of introduction to Mr. Bernard Berenson from his brother-in-law, Professor Ralph Barton Perry. Berenson received us most cordially, showed us about his villa, *I Tatti*, and its marvelous library of art books, and entertained us at lunch with disquisitions about Italian primitives. I must say, I never felt more ignorant. I knew little of art history, except possibly the Renaissance, and was unable to comment on, much less challenge Berenson, whose notions, as everyone knows, were strongly held. But I have often, in retrospect, wished I had been equipped to profit more from this visit. It reminds me, too, of my near-meeting with Sigmund Freud in Vienna. Freud was just then emerging into world fame, and Pribram, who was a personal friend of his, kept saying: "I must have you meet Freud." The name meant very little to me, and I have always been diffident about taking people's time without some specific purpose. I never pressed Pribram, and nothing came of his notion. Actually, looking back, I have no idea what I would have said to Freud, had I met him, so I am at least innocent of having wasted his time.

Going north we stopped at Padua to see the gorgeous and deeply moving Giotto murals, and then back to Venice, which now showed itself at its best. How glad I am to have seen it before the current crisis. A little vaporetto plied the Grand Canal from end to end, making countless stops on either bank. Beyond that, no power boat of any kind was permitted in the city. Gondolas were expensive, and we soon discovered that the way to see Venice is on one's own legs. Otherwise, one misses the charming little streets and passages, and the many lively and colorful squares. When some years later (in 1933), I again visited Venice, I was appalled by the motor boats that were racing up and down the Grand Canal, lashing the foundations of the palaces on either side in an unending wake. Even then, it seemed unlikely that the old buildings could long survive this treatment. One wonders how such boating could even have been allowed.

By this time we were well aware that our first baby was on the way, so we omitted a much desired visit to the Italian lakes and stopped only at Milan. We admired the great cathedral and climbed to its roof, but were sadly disappointed by Leonardo's *Last Supper*, which was then in urgent need of cleaning and renovation.

Although Italy was in the very throes of the Fascist agitation, one did not get the impression of any major crisis. Here and there, groups of enthusiasts sang the *Giovinezza* as they paraded through the square, and on the train from Pisa to Genoa crowds of youngsters several times forced stops and took over the engineer's job. They evidently knew enough to run the train to the next station. We reached Genoa with many interruptions but no mishaps, and a week's voyage in summer conditions brought us home in mid-June.

During our absence my mother had sold the Carver Street house at a substantial profit, and had bought a new two-family house in a developing area below Walden Street. We lived there with her until the birth of our son Leonard (August 30, 1922), after which we took an apartment on Newport Road, near Massachusetts Avenue not far from Porter Square. My mother, though at first reduced to tears at the thought of having become a grandmother, was soon reconciled to the new situation. She got along reasonably well with my wife, whose background and knowledge she respected, and developed a deep and lasting affection for the baby, who in later years often stayed with her for extended periods.

I cannot but think of my last year of graduate study as one of the busiest of my life. I served as an instructor in the introductory European history course, which involved much reading and grading, and many conferences. I also felt that I must complete my dissertation within the academic year so as to be in the market for a regular teaching position. The situation was somewhat complicated by Professor Pribram's visit and by my relations with Professor Coolidge, who liked to have me drop into his elegant office in Widener almost every day to discuss new books in the international field and the great question of responsibility for the recent war. He was deeply involved with a group of New York businessmen, politicans, and publishers who were concerned lest the United States, having rejected membership in the League of Nations, return to isolationism. This Council on Foreign Relations, which was thought of as the counterpart of the British Institute of International Affairs, proposed to publish a quarterly devoted to the nonpartisan study not only of American policy, but of world affairs in general. Coolidge had been named as the editor of *Foreign Affairs*, which in the five remaining years of his life he made into one of the most authoritative and respected organs of international affairs. He often discussed his editorial ideas and problems with me, and I especially recall his determination to enroll responsible Soviet authorities, if possible, among the contributors.

My friends were often amused by the ingenuity with which I solved at least one of my problems when my wife was out. While writing at my desk, I tied my swivel chair to the rocker in which the baby was secured. Whenever he became restless, I would wiggle my chair which would gently rock his and, since he was a model child, would persuade him not to distract his father from his important task.

I had a great deal of material on the Franco-Russian alliance from the Vienna archives, in addition to a great stack of notes taken from my readings. To write a full-length doctoral dissertation in history within a year, even with all the material at hand, is generally recognized as an impressive feat. I certainly slaved at it and somehow managed, by the April 1 deadline, to have a completed document of several hundred pages. I was completely floored to find that, because of the quotations in foreign languages, the cost of typing the thesis came to $275. Nowadays, it would be easy to recover this sum either from departmental funds or from any one of several foundations. But not in 1922, and in a way I am glad of it, for

I promptly decided that if I intended to do much writing, I must learn to compose on the typewriter. This I did, becoming in time sufficiently proficient to think just as well at the keyboard as with a pen in hand. Furthermore, I was always able to make a carbon copy, which was of some value. I never claimed to do a professional job, but then, so long as a typesetter could read the text, nothing more was required. Later, with the advent of corrasable paper, it was so easy to correct errors that in correspondence, at least, I could make my letters look almost professional. I never succeeded in working effectively with a research assistant, although I employed several young women in succession. They were all perfectly competent, but I could never write history from notes taken by someone else, and I found it trying to direct the work of an assistant when I wanted to get on with my own. Consequently, I never had a secretary except when one was made available to me in an official capacity, and even then her services were pretty much confined to taking dictation and typing letters.

I passed my final examinations for the doctorate without, I felt, much distinction, since I had not been able to find the time to prepare properly. An eminent French historian, Henri Hauser, who was visiting at Harvard, sat in on the examination and confided to one of my friends, that my replies to questions had revealed *lacunes* in my historical knowledge. Actually, he completely ignored the terms of my candidacy and queried me about matters far removed from my field. I felt rather unhappy, too, about my dissertation. It was a good, sound factual study, but lacked the larger philosophical reflections that I felt the subject required. I therefore made no effort to have it published until I had had a chance to put more work on it. Since the ensuing years were much preoccupied with teaching and other obligations, it was to be a long time before I could consider it finished. It must have been 1927 before I submitted it for publication in the Harvard Historical Studies and had it accepted. Even then the little printer in Vermont, who offered to do the job much cheaper than the university press, took forever to complete the assignment, though he did a remarkably good job. The upshot was that my first historical study saw the light only in 1929.

With the attainment of the Ph.D., I had at last reached my immediate goal—preparation for teaching European history at an advanced grade. It is hard to believe, but prior to the First World War, European history had not been prominent in our universities. Beyond an introductory survey, there might have been a course on English history or on the French Revolution, but relatively little attention was given to Central or Eastern Europe, and even less, I should say, to the comparative study of the European nations. Economic history had become quite fashionable, but the emphasis was on the general history, and far more attention was understandably given to developments in the United States than to Europe.

It was the World War which had stirred interest in European history and revealed its importance to the future of this country. Consequently many institutions were intent on expanding their offerings. I was offered positions by no less than five universities, large and small, and finally decided for perhaps the smallest of all: Clark University in Worcester, with only a few hundred students and a faculty of thirty to thirty-five. I had several good reasons for making this choice: Worcester was only forty miles from Cambridge, and I could, therefore, continue to use the unrivaled resources of Widener Library and maintain close contact with my mother, who was now living alone. Moreover, George Blakeslee, whom I already knew, was chairman of the History Department which, with only four professors, made no effort to cover the entire field. In most institutions a newly appointed Ph.D. would be expected to work chiefly in the survey courses. At Clark I was to give annually a course on European history between 1815–1914, with which I was already familiar, and in addition in successive years a course on modern French history, on German and Central European history, and on Russian and Near Eastern history. In other words, the opportunities to expand were much greater than elsewhere and, I might add, the beginning salary, normally $2,000, was $2,300.

I never for a moment regretted choosing Clark University. Blakeslee was a most considerate chairman, and my colleagues, Alfred L. P. Dennis and James B. Hedges, were congenial in every respect. While the preparation of a new major course each year involved a stupendous amount of reading and, I suppose, may have explained the headaches from which I often suffered, I had complete freedom in organizing my work. We bought a small cottage on the outskirts of Worcester, near Tatnuck, and I arranged to go to the university three days a week. By concentrating my work, I found some time to continue revising my dissertation and even to publish a few articles on the Franco-Russian alliance and on the French occupation of Tunisia in 1881.

There were few distractions in Worcester. Even the arrival of a second son in 1925 did not greatly affect the regimen of our lives. My wife enrolled as a graduate student in philosophy at Radcliffe and usually went to Cambridge by train once a week to attend lectures in modern logic by Henry Sheffer and a seminar by Alfred North Whitehead. On such days we were able to secure the services of neighboring girls to take care of the children, and I would drive down at 10:30 p.m. to the terminus of the streetcar line to meet my wife returning from Cambridge. Then on Friday afternoons, we would generally motor to Cambridge and spend the weekend at my mother's, if we were not immersed in library work.

There were of course no superhighways. One traveled to Boston over the old post road, two lanes wide, fantastically winding and passing from one end to the other of every intervening town. It took at least two hours to make the trip, much of which was spent behind truck traffic, which at that time made only about ten miles per hour and on every one of the numerous hills was obliged to slow to three miles. Cars and roads were not much good either. One could rarely make the trip without at least one flat tire, so we generally carried two spares. In winter the roads were badly plowed, if at all. Skidding was an ever-present danger, and on raw nights no matter how warmly dressed, one might well have frozen to death in the unheated vehicles. But we were young and, after all, did not suffer more than other people. Since we could combine a visit to my mother with a solid day's work in the library, there was nothing more we could ask.

My mother had again sold her house and was now living in

a new and attractive single cottage on a hill in Lexington. At last provided with a pretty garden, she, too, was more at peace with the world than she had been for some time—which did not mean that, whenever I appeared, she did not expect me to do what chores there were, such as mowing the lawn, trimming the edges, setting up beanpoles, etc. My most memorable experience was the construction of an asparagus bed. The pamphlet of the Department of Agriculture, which was gospel to my mother, spoke of planting the roots in a two-foot deep trench. I began to do this, only to discover that like much of New England, the Lexington land was basically a granite quarry. After herculean labors I had a ten-foot trench completed and planted the roots. The first spring there were a few shoots and thereafter quantities of them, from April to June. All told, Mother's little garden supplied the family with an abundance of vegetables, berries, and fruit. A little sour-cherry tree that I planted, so that she might bake cherry pie for the boys, soon deluged us with cherries. The birds ate thousands of them, and I grew to like them eaten from the tree, but there were still far too many for pies or any other purposes.

To add to my labors in these days was the bibliographical work for *Foreign Affairs*. Coolidge had decided that, appended to each number of the journal, there should be a list of books on all or any aspect of international affairs, in any civilized language. It was not to be a simple list of titles, which is never of much value, but a more or less critical analysis of each title —something about the standing of the author, the character of the book, the nature of its sources, the author's viewpoint or conclusion. This rather formidable task was at first performed by Harry Elmer Barnes, who resigned after a couple of years. Barnes, who was to play a continuing role in my professional career for some time, claimed that Coolidge appointed me his successor at his (Barnes's) recommendation. I never found out whether this was so. It did not seem important, and I have never been inquisitive about personal affairs. I became slightly irked years later, however, when Barnes posed as my patron and protector, who had launched me on a successful career. He never claimed, so far as I know, to have written any of my books. But even his assertion of having floated me in *Foreign Affairs* always struck me as a little ridiculous. I knew Coolidge far better than he did and was in much closer contact with him. It was most unlikely that Coolidge should have relied on Barnes for an opinion on a young scholar whom he himself had trained.

My relations with Barnes over the years were chequered and at times infuriating. Without knowing it at the time, I was his successor at Clark, where he had resigned after a row with the president. He was then professor at Smith College for many years, as a historian, I suppose, though his interests always ran to the sociological. Some years older than myself, he had taken his Ph.D. at Columbia. I once heard him deliver a speech and was astonished at the moderation of his style and the mildness of his manner. But given a pen and paper, he was an entirely different man: alert, well informed, contentious, ferociously vituperative. Yet Barnes was, by nature, a kind and generous soul and, I am sure, was motivated by genuine moral indignation in all his conflicts.

Barnes was among the first historians to attack the peace settlements, especially the Versailles Treaty. He not only rejected the notion of Germany's sole responsibility for causing the war, but devoted much time and effort to exposing the devious policies of the British, French, and Russians. While not maintaining that Germany and Austria-Hungary were innocent victims of encircling powers, he certainly assigned the major share of the responsibility to the Allied powers and considered Woodrow Wilson and Colonel House the dupes of British machinations.

I cannot remember just how I first came in contact with Barnes. Our relations were almost exclusively by correspondence. I think he wrote me first congratulating me on a book review I had published and, thereafter, saw to it that other books of the same tenor were sent me for review. As the Germans began to publish their Foreign Office documents and more and more "revelations" flooded the market, a veritable battle developed over the *Kriegsschuldfrage*. I would say that the most uncompromising diehard on the anti-German side was Professor Charles H. Hazen of Columbia, who was Barnes' bête noire but found more qualified support in men such as Professor Bernadotte E. Schmitt of the University of Chicago, who had been a Rhodes scholar and was inclined to be Anglophile. On the pro-German side was Barnes' colleague at Smith, Professor Sidney B. Fay, who eventually, in 1930, published the two-volume *The Origins of the World War*, perhaps the most influential work in the entire controversy. Fay's book, which Coolidge had hoped to see published in his lifetime, set off a new explosion of controversy, during which some very harsh things were said. His book was followed soon after by another two-volume work, *The Coming of the War* by Bernadotte Schmitt, in which every effort was made to vindicate the policies of the Allies and particularly of England. Although Schmitt and I had been friends for years—somewhat to Barnes' irritation—I felt impelled to publish in the New York *Herald-Tribune*, a most devastating critique of his book, in which I found a number of mistranslations and even more misinterpretations of the sources. I will say that Schmitt took the criticism in a scholarly spirit, and we remained friends until his death years later.

With the publication of the Fay and Schmitt volumes, and the translation from the French of the judicious study by Pierre Renouvin on *The Immediate Causes of the War,* the dispute over responsibilities began to peter out. In the last analysis, most scholars competent in the field, like Coolidge, took a middle position, rejecting the notion of Germany's sole responsibility, but also finding much to criticize in German policy, especially during the July crisis of 1914, as well as recognizing the important role of Russia and the weaknesses or errors of Britain and France. In this country attention focused on the congressional investigations into the influence of munition manufacturers and bankers on the formulation of the American interventionist policy, while in Europe the rise of the Nazi party and the spectacular career of Adolf Hitler turned men's thoughts to the Second World War, which was emerging from the mistakes of the First.

In the summer of 1926, I took over Professor Schmitt's work

for a term at the University of Chicago, leaving my family at
Lake George for the eight weeks of my absence. My program
at Chicago was light, consisting of European history from
1870 to 1914 and a seminar on the problems of the postwar
period. I found to my surprise that while most of the students
were graduate students, mainly from smaller Midwestern institutions, the instruction was not expected to be on a level
much above that of the Harvard undergraduate. I found that
I had more time than usual and tried hard to progress with the
revision of my Franco-Russian alliance. I even ventured to
embark on a novel, which had been in my mind for some time.
I thought I had an excellent, timely theme: A beautiful French
girl of the oldest aristocracy and the purest nationalistic attitude falls in love with a young deputy of progressive views.
He is a doughty champion of international cooperation as the
only antidote to war, and consequently devotes himself to the
new League of Nations. The developing tension would make
an interesting story, I was sure, but I was not clear what forms
it would take beyond the first chapter, when I realized that
fiction was not my dish. I have always thought that while I had
an excellent historical imagination and could easily think myself into past problems and situations, I was not made either
for creative art or for strictly abstract speculation.

On my return to the East, I took on an additional assignment. Even before going to Chicago, I had been invited to come
to Harvard for the autumn term of 1926 to replace Professor
Lord, who was on leave. This meant motoring to and from
Cambridge three times a week under the then trying conditions of travel, but I naturally enjoyed being back in Cambridge,
where I had hoped for some sort of appointment immediately
upon receiving my Ph.D. Something might have come of that,
had I not indiscreetly advertised my opposition to the new
tutorial system, which was so dear to President Lowell. It
seemed to me then, and seems to me still, that discussion of
historical problems, except on the most elementary level, with
students who have had only one or two courses to operate with,
was a pretty unprofitable use of time, leaving most of the
students as well as the tutors dissatisfied. Of course, it may well

be that I simply lacked the knack of arousing interest and stimulating thought by this method. At any rate, preference in making appointments was certainly shown to young scholars who had been to English universities and were therefore conversant with the tutorial system.

All this was now water over the dam. My assignment to Lord's work was in line with my own specialization, and I had no great difficulty in fitting it in with my work at Clark. The first term ended in January 1927 when, to my complete surprise, I received an invitation to return to Harvard as an assistant professor to replace Lord, who had now resigned to prepare himself for the Catholic priesthood. I was to teach the first semester of the course on nineteenth-century European history, conduct a graduate seminar, and be responsible for four or five tutees. My initial salary was to be $3,500. I also hoped to succeed to Lord's course on Russian history and had, since 1919, spent considerable effort in studying the language, but these hopes were dashed when, at the very time of my appointment, the History Department invited Dr. Michael Karpovich, formerly of the Imperial Russian Embassy in Washington, to take over this field. It proved an excellent choice, for Karpovich was a trained historian, an effective teacher, and a most lovable character. His role in developing Russian studies in this country was considerable.

Despite my lack of faith in the tutorial system, I accepted this wonderful offer with alacrity. We sold our Worcester house with some difficulty, but in the summer succeeded in finding temporary quarters on Hammond Street, not far from where I had lived on Carver Street. There followed a long and futile search for an appropriate home in Cambridge. I insisted on something reasonably close to Harvard Square because I was permanently soured on any arrangements that involved substantial travel to my work. In the end we decided to purchase land at the corner of Raymond Street and Huron Avenue, in an area formerly part of Gray Gardens and then being developed. We engaged an excellent architect and had him design an early American house with simple lines and oiled clapboard siding. It turned out very well, except that it should have been somewhat larger. But it had a fine living room, a generous master bedroom, and two other bedrooms, plus a large attic room with dormer windows and open rafters, in which bookshelves housed most of our library. The house had four good fireplaces, which was twice as many as were really needed, for those in the dining room and master bedroom were but rarely used. On the other hand, the living room fireplace was a joy throughout the winter, and the third-story fireplace was in constant use. It is interesting to note that at this late date domestic heating by oil was still so underdeveloped that after experimenting with it in Worcester, I returned to a coal system in the new house, only to switch once more to oil a few years later when the stoking problem became too much for me.

CHAPTER VII

The "Compleat" Scholar: Return to Europe

IT STANDS to reason that these building operations could not have been undertaken on available funds or even on the expectancy of the future. But it so happened that my wife, at the age of thirty, fell heir to a substantial legacy which, together with a mortgage, gave us the wherewithal and the courage to embark on so expensive an enterprise.

Chance was presently to play an even greater and more decisive role in my career. A few weeks after the opening of college in September 1927, Professor Coolidge went to bed with an obscure ailment which at first did not appear serious. But it resisted all efforts at relief. Coolidge began to lose strength and became bedridden, and in January 1928 he died, at the early age of sixty. This was one of the most severe blows I have ever experienced. I was utterly devoted to him and visited him frequently in his Beacon Street home. He discussed with me in detail problems connected with *Foreign Affairs* and related matters, and I could see him constantly sinking and eventually losing heart. He was not only a great scholar, but one of the most imaginative persons I have ever known. A plaque in the entrance to Widener Library pays tribute to his untiring devotion to that great repository of knowledge, and *Foreign Affairs*, which has now passed its fiftieth anniversary, is a monument to his breadth of interest.

Among other bequests, Coolidge left the university $300,000 with which to found a professorship in history in his memory. Since he died only a few weeks before he was to take up his regular lecture course and seminar, there was no time for the usual thoroughgoing search for a first holder of the Coolidge Professorship. His field and mine were identical, so I was called upon to step in temporarily. Thus, for the first time, the two halves of the course on nineteenth-century history were given by the same man, and a young man at that. By the end of the academic year, the department had still been unable to decide on a new appointment, and I continued with the double assignment. I had the reputation even then of being a good lecturer and teacher. All seemed to be going satisfactorily, and the department was content to let sleeping dogs lie. Despite worldwide efforts to find an eminent Coolidge Professor, the administration gave up in despair. In 1931 I was given tenure as an associate professor and in 1936 was promoted, to my immense satisfaction, to the rank of full professor and first incumbent of the Coolidge Professorship.

The additional work assigned me on Coolidge's death forced the department to change its original plans. I was soon relieved of all tutorial work. Although I had never had more than a few of the ablest students, with whom I enjoyed working, I had never convinced myself that so much institutionalizing was necessary. I sometimes said that as a student I had gotten as much tutorial stimulation and support by sauntering through the Yard with my professors as later students got through scheduled assignments and hours. The tutorial system has, in fact, been so repeatedly changed or at least modified that a real solution has not and cannot be found.

One of Coolidge's great interests had been the Near Eastern Question, which for centuries had plagued the relationships of the European powers. He had inspired me with the same interest, and when the department began to bemoan the loss of Coolidge's course, I offered to take over. For a long time the subject was treated as a half-course, dealing particularly with the international relations of the marcescent Ottoman Empire. It was indeed a most useful discipline, for European history looked quite different when viewed from Constantinople rather than from London, Paris, or even Vienna. After all, the Turkish armies had twice stood at the gates of Vienna, and Turkish pashas had ruled most of Hungary and all of the Balkans for centuries. I was fascinated by the clash of cultures, even as far back as the first Ottoman conquests. I began to study the origins of the Ottoman Turks and even induced my colleague, Robert P. Blake, to explore the Armenian and Georgian sources for whatever light they might throw. Together we published an article on the subject in the *American Historical Review* in 1932 which, if it served no other purpose, provoked more competent European Orientalists, such as Mehmed Fuad, the dean of Turkish historians, and Paul Wittek, to attack the problem anew. Over the past forty years, they and other scholars have added greatly to our knowledge, but I think I am not exaggerating when I say that the fundamental argument of our paper still holds true.

As I studied the Near Eastern Question over the years, I saw more and more clearly that the relations of the West and East depended in the first instance on conditions in the different countries, particularly on the strength or weakness of the Ottoman Power. I studied, as well as I could from Western sources, the internal history of the Sultanate and presently extended my course to a full year. In the period following the Second World War and the establishment of the Center for Middle Eastern Studies, this whole complex of problems became more and more important, and I shared the course with my colleague Richard N. Frye, the Iranian expert, and with Robert L. Wolff, whose specialized knowledge of early Russian history and especially of the entire Balkan area added immeasurably to the richness of the course.

My regular offering at Harvard was a large undergraduate course in two parts: Continental Europe from 1815–1870, and the same for the period 1870–1914. I repeated this course to a much smaller class at Radcliffe. It sounds monotonous, though it was not, for it was being continually revised and at times fundamentally reorganized, not only in the light of new data, but with reference to changing emphases and interpretations.

I had taken over the main conception from Coolidge, though I gradually enlarged on it. Neither he nor I ever offered a course on the history of one country, excepting the Ottoman Empire (which was a world of its own), and for one or two years a history of modern Germany (really of Central Europe) pending the appointment of a specialist in that area. Our great objective was to view the history of the continent in all its interrelationships, ideological and cultural, as well as political and military. No doubt something is lost by this procedure, such as the continuity of certain forces and factors. But much more gained in the broad sweep of international problems and policies, and especially in the interaction of economic forces and the movement of ideas. With this comparative approach in mind, I found the subject eternally refreshing, while students frequently expressed their surprise at learning how apparently minor events and problems reacted on the whole continental structure. How futile it would be, for example, to discuss the outbreak of the World War without reference to the spread of nationalist ideas to the Balkans and the hostility of little Serbia to a major power, Austria-Hungary!

Even more important than my undergraduate course, was the seminar, which generally numbered eight to ten men, with an occasional Radcliffe student added. I realized then, and I realize now, that to many students I must have appeared a veritable martinet, for the seminar was conducted along rigid lines, each of which aimed at a particular objective. Since my own seminars as a student had always met from 4:00–6:00 p.m., which is perhaps the low point of the human intellect during the day, I always scheduled my own seminar from 8:00–10:00 p.m., when minds were more alert. Furthermore, to get away from the barren atmosphere of the classroom, I invited my students to my home. We met in the roomy attic study, with comfortable chairs and books readily available. After the formal part of the meeting, my wife would bring up refreshments. Over a stein of beer or a cup of hot chocolate, the conversation would turn to some general topic, either historical or contemporary, and the discussion, which was often provocative and stimulating, would continue until 11:00 p.m. or beyond. My son, whose bedroom door the students passed as they thundered downstairs, asked me one time why he so often dreamed of elephants on seminar nights.

As the course was organized, each student was allowed an hour to present his report orally, to give him practice in lecturing. After this presentation, I called on each student at random to criticize his colleague on any score—organization, source material, reasoning, and even style. Since each student knew that he was going to have to express an opinion, close attention by all was guaranteed. I took no part in the discussion until all the students had had their say, when I would offer my own comments and also criticize the critics. By the end of the semester, each student would then submit a written essay on the subject of his report which was limited to thirty double-space typewritten pages plus a bibliographical note on the books that had been found important. The written reports, of course, represented the crowning effort, and they were scrutinized from every conceivable point of view. Typographical errors were treated exactly like manuscript errors. Students were warned that in their later career editorial and typographical corrections on manuscripts would turn out to be a tragically expensive matter.

The rigidity of my seminar procedure was due largely to my impatience at sitting in meetings where wretched reports were put off with milk-and-water comments. My objective was to teach young historians to be professional and to do a really professional job. They knew in advance what to expect, but they came, nonetheless, and the great majority proved successful and even eminent in their later careers. It would be presumptuous to maintain that their professional future hinged only on my seminar training. Many of them, if not most, were young people of outstanding ability, well worth the drastic training to which they were subjected. I am not boasting but simply reporting what a number of them, now in high positions in our leading universities, have told me: that the exacting standards set in their student days had guided them throughout life.

Something must be said of the subject matter of the seminar.

It was usually, though not always, centered on the diplomatic history of the period from 1870–1945. This may seem strange in view of my previous remarks on considering history-in-the-large. But the explanation is simple: First, students are naturally unable to criticize each other's reports if the reports are on widely differing periods and subjects. By working on fairly closely related topics, they all became acquainted with the main source materials and their relative value. Secondly, the American student cannot, like European students, step around the corner and work in the unpublished archives dealing with abstruse subjects. He can do effective work only if he has a wealth of source material at his disposal. In this country this is most true of diplomatic history where the published sources are if anything too voluminous for large-scale studies. It has often happened that advanced students have used seminar reports as the basis for more extensive and intensive study in preparation for their doctoral dissertation. Some have then used their dissertations as foundations for yet further and wider studies prior to publication in book form.

Before closing this discussion of graduate instruction, I want to say that I have never attempted to influence students in any way in the choice of subjects for their dissertation or later contributions. I always remembered that when, as a student, I went to Europe, the first question I was asked in Germany was "Wessen Schüler sind Sie?" (Whose student are you?) I soon discovered that many European professors were deeply offended if their students failed to follow in their footsteps. It took real courage on the part of young scholars to strike out on their own. I am proud to say that a substantial number of my students have followed their own, quite different interests and that they have produced works of great interest and originality.

I always think of the 1930s as a bright period in my career. I was young, energetic, enthusiastic, and reveling in all the opportunities with which Fate had favored me. My brother Walter, who had graduated from Harvard in 1923, despite demands made on him by outside work of various kinds, began to suffer frequently from respiratory difficulties, resulting, presumably, from his war services. He had enrolled in the Graduate

School as a student of psychology and in 1925 had accepted a position in Silver City, New Mexico, where he presently designed and built a most attractive school in the Spanish style, for the care of problem boys. Back in Cambridge on business in the summer of 1928, he persuaded me to put aside my books for a few weeks and drive back to New Mexico with him. It was quite a thrilling experience to see something of my own country. We drove into the Deep South and crossed the Mississippi at Greenville, proceeding through the desert country to see Carlsbad Caverns, which were then still devoid of elevators and all other tourist comforts. Silver City was a typical mining town, and for a few days we enjoyed life on the range. But Walter was still recruiting boys for his school and again seduced me into joining him on an extended tour of the West Coast. Starting from San Diego we drove north to Los Angeles and San Francisco, where there was as yet no Golden Gate Bridge and no Bay Bridge. We crossed the Bay to Berkeley by ferry and found the town to be still a rather attractive academic community. Eventually, business took Walter north to Seattle, and thence to Cheyenne where I left him and returned to Cambridge by train.

This stark outline cannot, of course, reflect the thrills of so many new sights and experiences. For the first time I realized the magnitude of the country and its endless variety, the grandeur of its mountains, the desolation of its deserts, the immensity of its trees and forests. To take the time for this trip was certainly well worthwhile, and I have always retained vivid memories of it.

By the time my *Franco-Russian Alliance, 1890–1894* appeared in the Harvard Historical Studies (1929), I had long since lost interest in the subject. I had always been rather unhappy that, because the evidence was lacking on some important points, a definitive statement was impossible. I was, therefore, gratified and astonished by the uniformly favorable reviews it received on both sides of the Atlantic. Note was made that here was a detailed analysis of an important topic in the history of diplomacy without the usual references to the question of responsibility for the World War. I was complimented for the breadth and depth of my scholarship as well as for what George Peabody Gooch, the editor of the *Contemporary Review* and a leading authority on modern diplomatic history, called my "serene impartiality" in analyzing the policies of the various powers. "It is a masterpiece of presentation and interpretation," he wrote me in a letter. On the French side, the most outstanding authority, Professor Pierre Renouvin of the Sorbonne, while complaining that I, like most foreigners, simply could not understand the depth of French feeling about Alsace-Lorraine and the effect of that feeling on French foreign policy, nevertheless declared the book "very interesting," opening up, in many respects, new viewpoints. In short, I had nothing to complain of and felt that at least I had gotten off to a good start. In fact, my fame soon spread to even remote regions. A professor at the University of Ufa in Bashkiria, wrote me in 1933 begging for a copy, since it was impossible for Soviet scholars to buy or induce their libraries to buy expensive foreign books.

My professional activities had by now expanded considerably. For many years (in fact, until 1933) I provided the quarterly bibliographies for *Foreign Affairs*. In 1925 I was elected a member of the Council on Foreign Relations and thenceforth took an active interest in its activities. The council moved from time to time to larger quarters until eventually it found an appropriate home in Pratt House, where it is still located. Hamilton Fish Armstrong, who had been managing editor of *Foreign Affairs*, succeeded Coolidge as editor on the latter's death. He and I worked well together and became fast friends over the forty-odd years before his death. In those days I went to New York often to attend study groups at the council or consult with publishers. The usual procedure was to leave at midnight on the Owl, the crack nonstop sleeping car train to New York, which arrived at eight next morning and returned by the same route the next evening.

It was Armstrong's idea that the bibliographies should be reevaluated after ten years, and a selection published in book form. I undertook this job with Armstrong's unstinting help and the able assistance of Ruth Savord, the librarian of the council.

The volume appeared in 1933, and similar summary volumes have since been published at intervals, culminating in a valuable volume of analytic reviews by experts, published on the occasion of the fiftieth anniversary of *Foreign Affairs*.

Professionally more important and productive was my developing friendship in the late 1920s with two of the country's great publishers, Alfred A. Knopf and Cass Canfield. Perhaps because we were young men of roughly the same age, we three always got along well with each other, and our friendships proved lifelong. Knopf's firm had been founded in 1915, but by 1925 it was already well known not only for the prominence of its authors and their books, but for the beauty of design and typography of the so-called Borzoi publications. Knopf had taken a degree at Columbia in political science or history and had a profound interest in these fields. He was one of the few publishers who actually read most of the nonfiction books he published. Furthermore, he made a systematic effort to discover promising writers among younger men and to maintain personal contact with them.

I made Alfred's acquaintance at a lunch to which he invited me. He had no specific message nor concrete proposition. We discussed for a couple of hours what I was doing, what I planned or hoped to do, what particular interest I had in history, and other related topics, in return for which he spoke freely of his own views and aspirations as a publisher. In the end he suggested that I might be the man to write a general history of international relations from 1870 to perhaps the peace settlements of 1919–1920. I had already given much thought to Bismarck as a master diplomat and an almost unique example of the successful statesman who knew when to stop; who recognized the interests of others and the need to respect such interests. I told Alfred that I had already made a start on such a study, and he more or less promised to publish the book if I should write it.

The first product of our association was the completion and publication of a rather detailed and lengthy volume entitled *European Alliances and Alignments, 1871–1890*, admittedly a heavy title but withal an accurate one. It was, indeed, a difficult book to write, not only because of the complexity of the subject matter, but also because of the wealth of documentary and other source material. At some length I showed how Bismarck, determined to protect the gains he had made since 1864 and to forestall any effort on the part of France to prepare a war of revenge, gradually built up the system of alliances, agreements, and understandings that culminated in the crisis of 1887. By adroit balancing between Britain and Russia, he not only kept France isolated, but forestalled a constantly threatening conflict between Russia and Austria-Hungary. It was a most intricate structure, which I attempted to illustrate by charts and maps. All in all, I think I had reason to be proud of this work. It also aimed at seeing the European world as a whole, with the interests of many powers so intertwined that an aggressive act by any one of them would jeopardize the entire structure. Because of the difficulty of the subject, I devoted two or three concluding pages of each chapter to a summary appreciation, a practice which I have followed with other books and which, I believe, has well served to fix the major features of the argument. Of equal value were the bibliographies appended to each chapter. These were not mere listings of authors and titles, but critical appraisals of books and articles as they bore on the subject in hand.

European Alliances was published in 1931, beautifully printed and bound. I could never have anticipated the chorus of praise by which it was received in this country and abroad. Many critics emphasized the breadth of its conception, taking account of many economic, military, and ideological factors as well as the achievements of individual leadership. The *Boston Transcript* described it as "a book of extraordinary range, remarkable mastery of facts, and rare skill in using them for reaching useful conclusions." According to Professor Seymour of Yale, it was a "book of the first historical importance." Professor Peardon, writing in the *Political Science Quarterly*, declared: "Its publication must constitute a major event in recent American historical writing." Professor Lybyer of Illinois, reviewing it in the *American Political Science Quarterly*, declared it simply "a masterpiece." In the *Journal of Modern History*, the English historian W. N. Medlicott, described it as "a notable example of the combination of objective judgment and mastery of detail."

Since the key subject of the volume was Bismarck's alliance system, German scholars took a particular interest in it. Professor Herzfeld, writing in the most important of German professional journals, the *Historische Zeitschrift,* termed it "the most conclusive treatment of the subject, measuring up to the highest standards of monographic work." Other German historians declared it to be "nothing short of a classic" of which "the American historical profession may be proud." The *Times Literary Supplement,* while bemoaning the fact that it lacked unpublished archival material, nonetheless rated it highly: "Professor Langer's lucid and able narrative deserves high praise as a very readable and objective study of the nature and growth of the Bismarckian system of alliances."

I may be pardoned for citing even this brief selection from among the uniformly enthusiastic greetings of my book. It was, indeed, without a rival in its field and has remained so for forty years. During the Second World War, the plates were melted down, but after conclusion of the conflict Knopf felt the demand justified resetting the type. The second edition, with chapter bibliographies brought up to date, gave the book a new lease on life, which was aided by publication in paperback.

My association with Cass Canfield began at about the same time as my acquaintance with Alfred Knopf. Canfield, who had only recently acquired a controlling interest in the venerable publishing firm of Harper and Brothers, was eager to strike out on fresh lines. He proposed that I edit a series of perhaps twenty volumes reviewing the history of modern Europe, not in textbook fashion, but in a broad way, designed for that mythical person, the general reader. Each volume was to run to about 100,000 words and to have some fifty contemporary illustrations. I was to plan the series, find the appropriate authors, review and criticize the manuscripts, and, in general, serve as adviser to the publisher. I do not recall whether it was explicitly provided that the publisher should abstain from interference except in serious crises, but, in fact, except for occasional suggestions or to call attention to possible difficulties, Canfield did leave the conduct of the enterprise entirely in my hands.

What attracted me particularly to Canfield's proposition was not the financial return, which was never more than modest, but the possibility of transcending the traditional historical approach and attempting to see Europe as a cultural unit in which certain ideas and forces produced similar or at times contrary impacts. I insisted that so far as was humanly possible, each volume of the new series, while basically political history, should take account of philosophical currents, literature, art, and science. Each volume should give a clear notion of all aspects of human expression within a certain period. Of course, this was a tall order, and occasionally some author, well versed in political and even economic history, would abandon his assignment when faced with problems of a more strictly cultural nature. Almost without exception, though, authors have told me that the writing of their volume was an education in itself, and not exactly an easy one.

According to my plan, the series was to have a running start of a few volumes, and then become more detailed as modern Europe developed its characteristic forms. The general title was to be "The Rise of Modern Europe," beginning with the mid-thirteenth century and ending with 1920 (later extended to 1945). The early volumes were to cover the periods 1250–1453, 1453–1510, 1510–1559, and 1559–1610. As will be seen, the traditional dividing dates were frequently ignored as being too strictly political. I spent much time and thought on planning the twenty volumes, and I can see now, after more than forty years, that there were serious weaknesses in the plan. All the early periods were too long to permit the treatment envisaged for the series. Some of the later volumes, too, were ill conceived, certain ones planned to cover short five-year periods, while others again were too long. This weakness was partly corrected by the readiness of the publishers to accept manuscripts of 125,000 or even 150,000 words. But I saw no way to avoid being myself the worst transgressor of the limits I had set for others. I had reserved for myself the period from 1832–1852, which seemed to me generally neglected and yet of particular interest because of the progressive industrialization of European society and the rapid spread of the ideas of liberalism and nationalism. I think I failed to realize that among other things, I would have to deal comparatively with half a dozen major and several minor revolutions of 1848–1849. At any rate, try as I might, I failed even after several rewritings to condense the manuscript to 150,000 words. I have never dared count the actual number of words in the published volume, but I am only too conscious that it is the longest in the series, and yet I cannot see how justice could have been done to the theme in fewer words.

One very valuable feature of the series is the bibliographical essay at the end of each volume, in which authors do not attempt to itemize the enormous literature for each and every period, but rather to discuss changes in historical interpretation and to cite analytically the most modern and reliable works. I might have known, even when planning, that these essays would be of minor or no interest to the "general reader," but that they would be invaluable guides to advanced students preparing themselves in special areas or subjects.

In the last analysis, the success or failure of the project would depend on the authors. I was far more fortunate than I could have expected in allocating the various volumes, for I found that the basic concept was regarded by many able historians as a real challenge. I was able to enlist some of the senior members of the profession, and my only serious failure in this respect was the decision of Carl Becker not to add yet another commitment to those he already had. I had gone to Ithaca to try to persuade him, and we had long and interesting discussions. He was enthusiastic about the project, and I thought that he would finally agree to do the volume on the later eighteenth century. But he said that he was so slow a worker that it would be an injustice to me to create impossible expectations. I did enlist a number of his former students, however, as well as other younger men of promise.

I wish we had been able to see the entire enterprise completed with the original cast and within a reasonable time. But over the years several authors reneged for one reason or another, others died, and the majority became involved in some way in the Second World War, which meant that scholarly work had to be put on the shelf for most of these men. The first two volumes of the series, by Professors Brinton and Artz, appeared on schedule in 1934, but thereafter almost all authors fell behind. At present eighteen of the twenty volumes have been published, and only those on the Reformation and on the First World War are still lacking. Years ago, the publishers rather reluctantly decided to experiment with paperback editions of one or two volumes, and these were published most attractively in the Torchbooks series. They proved to be a marked success, and since then all volumes have been made available in this form, much to the satisfaction of college teachers and students who can acquire these basic books at moderate prices.

During the interwar years, I did a good deal of public speaking, book reviewing, and general writing on current questions of international import. The 1920s were plagued by all the explosive issues that emerged from the "peace settlements," while during the next decade the ominous figure of Hitler loomed larger and more menacing on the horizon. Dealing with these matters publicly was not very satisfactory, because the majority of Americans had turned their backs on the League of Nations and showed no inclination to become involved in the World Court or other new-fangled experiments. Among a certain social elite, however, it became fashionable to demonstrate concern with these matters. Expensive luncheons in elegant hotels were organized to give this clientele an opportunity to see and hear speakers, both domestic and foreign, who were meant to dispute with each other and provide a stimulating intellectual show. Whenever some ostensible gain was made in the direction of peace, there was as much rejoicing as at other times there was despondency. On adoption of the Dawes Plan, one would have thought that that most absurd and tiresome of problems—reparations—was at last mastered. And the Locarno Treaties gave rise to unbridled rejoicing.

Whenever I was called upon to speak or comment at such gatherings, I always tried to stress the realities and warn the audience against exaggerated expectations. But I lost the urge to participate and instruct after an experience in Springfield,

Massachusetts, where, at an elaborate and expensive luncheon meeting, I was to respond to the remarks of Sir Ramsay Muir, the British historian, on the meaning and significance of the Locarno Pacts. After Muir's lengthy, eloquent, and enthusiastic address, I attempted to show that the pacts, though important, left many dangerous issues unsolved and that one should not be carried away by uncritical enthusiasm. Thereupon Muir, a man much older and more eminent than I, jumped up and denounced me as one of those vicious people who care nothing for peace but are always talking in terms of war. When at last he had finished, I was quite hot under the collar and eager to reply in kind, but the genial chairman, who shall remain nameless, hastily adjourned the session and left me branded a war-monger. What the audience wanted to hear was what Muir had to say, and it was not surprising when, a few years later, the Kellogg-Briand Pact outlawing war was hailed with the wildest enthusiasm as the beginning of a new era.

These extracurricular activities, if they did little or nothing to convert the American public to a realistic view of international relations and the responsibilities of the United States as the power which in a crisis would hold the balance, at least provided a welcome addition to the family budget. When the financial crash came in 1929, President Lowell of Harvard had just put into execution his long-cherished plans for a substantial upward revision of professors' salaries. He was determined not to backtrack at the shock of general crisis, so that Harvard remained one of the few universities in which there was no reduction of salaries during the entire depression years. In fact, the academic world actually benefited from the constantly falling prices.

And, yet, we always seemed to need more funds, as the new house was a burden and my mother required financial support. We continued, nonetheless, to plan as we worked. Since Cambridge in summer was a poor place for children, we sent the older boy to a supposedly high-grade camp on Lake Winnepesaukee only to find, when my mother and I once visited him, that he was stricken with a severe attack of poison ivy, readily understandable in view of the lush growths of the weed in the near vicinity of the camp. On his return home, he brought a case of impetigo, which he unwittingly transmitted to his grandmother. These episodes were enough to sour me on expensive summer camps, and I was delighted, somewhat later, to find a cottage at Annisquam on Cape Ann, which I could rent for the entire summer for only a little more than I had paid for the boy's stay at camp.

The so-called "Mellon Cottage" was actually a large and roomy summer place, practically on the beach where the Annisquam "River" flows into Ipswich Bay. It had a large upstairs porch overlooking the ocean, where the two boys insisted on sleeping in all weathers. More important for me was a downstairs annex consisting of a bedroom, bathroom, and a sunporch with a western exposure, which made it cool in the morning and hot in the afternoon. The entire village was quiet and off the beaten track, on the back or western side of Cape Ann, so that it was protected against northeastern storms and perfectly delightful in the evening when, from the porch facing west, one could watch the sun set over the sea.

Annisquam, which is about four miles from Gloucester, was forty or forty-five miles from Cambridge. In the 1930s it was still a tedious two-hour automobile trip over narrow, winding roads and through many towns. But its advantages were immense, and the house was so desirable that I rented it for ten successive years. Since we still spend the summer in Annisquam, though in a different house and with excellent highway connections with Cambridge, I think I can say that over some forty years I have done at least three-fifths, if not three-fourths, of all my writing in the quiet mornings by the sea. Of course, trips to Cambridge for books every couple of weeks were unavoidable, but were compensated for by long afternoons on the beach and in the water. Generally speaking, the ocean water was too cold for comfort, but one became used to it and enjoyed all the more the occasional, unexpected warm currents. The youngsters were almost no trouble at all. They had a small sailboat in which they raced on weekends and busied themselves at other times.

I will not rhapsodize further about this heavenly spot, which has meant so much both to my health and enjoyment and to my professional career. From 1930 onward (excepting always the war years in Washington), I made it a practice to accept almost any paying job that was offered me during the academic year, on condition that I remain absolutely free in summer. I could do more creative work in four hours each morning at Annisquam than I could in a week in Cambridge.

The year 1930 marked another important departure in my life. It had to do with music, which was never far from my thoughts and activities. We had bought a Henry Miller grand piano to replace the old upright. Both my wife and I played as often as we could, she reasonably well and I far less so. It became evident to me that I would never get satisfaction from piano playing, not only because I lacked talent, but also because I had never had decent instruction. My wife, who was studying the violoncello, reminded me of the violin which I had bought in Vienna and carried inconveniently around much of Europe. Why not get out this attractive instrument, find a good teacher, and continue with lessons?

On Church Street there was a small but highly reputable music school, the Longy School, established years ago by one of the Boston Symphony players who wanted to ensure sound instruction in theory and performance according to the standards of the Paris Conservatory. I went there for advice and had a long interview with Miss Hull, the director of the school. She suggested that at my age (thirty-five) it was hopeless to become a really proficient player on a stringed instrument, especially since I had another profession that would prevent the necessary practice. Why not take up the viola, which is less difficult and usually in greater demand among amateur quartet players? The idea appeared eminently sensible, and I arranged for lessons at the school under M. Louis Artières, who played at the first viola desk of the Boston Symphony. Artières helped me buy a reasonably good instrument and proved a very helpful, sensible, indeed lovable mentor. He pointed out to me at the beginning that to become a good player was out of the question, but that if I would practice regularly, even an hour a day, I could become sufficiently proficient to play viola in the average amateur quartet. Throughout the five years of our association, he always showed patience and understanding. He gave me interesting music to work on, and if, as occasionally happened, I came to him poorly prepared, he would say, "I understand perfectly that you have a profession and many other commitments. You will do the best you can, and not worry much about what you must leave undone."

Artières, like so many Symphony men, was a graduate of the Paris Conservatory. He had spent the war years in one of the big bands, blowing a wind instrument. A musician to the very tips of his fingers, he demanded that whatever I did should be done right. For the first time in my life, I had the feeling that musically I knew what I was doing. I loved the work and moved heaven and earth to keep up with it. Normally I would get home from the university at 4:30, have a cup or two of tea, and then go up to the study to practice uninterruptedly for at least an hour. Much of it was hard work, because physically I was ill adapted for viola playing. My arm was too short to hold a large viola with any comfort, and my hands were stubby and short where long hands and fingers are usually required. I managed, nonetheless, to progress reasonably well. Before long, I began to play simple quartet music with friends, and presently we were getting into Haydn and even Mozart.

Since my wife played the cello parts, all we needed for a quartet were two violins or a violin and a piano. There was never any difficulty on this score. Indeed, we had the most extraordinary luck in finding really competent first violinists as leaders. There was a succession of them, all graduate students who stayed with us for three or four years. They were all highly qualified and conversant with the literature. Some were actually professionals or the next thing to it. Second violins were also readily available among friends or students. I remember them with gratitude and great satisfaction, for most are now, years later, eminent professors in some of the leading universities.

We made it a practice to reserve Friday evenings for quartet. On those days our partners would generally come to dinner, and we would get to work without delay. Occasionally, we would get an extra viola or cello and play string quintet. At other times, we would play piano quartet or quintet, or flute or clarinet quartet. The literature is, of course, enormous. We always played some Haydn, Mozart, or Beethoven, but we also played lesser-known composers and tried our hands at Brahms and even more modern composers. Our evenings of music were among the most precious in my life, and I was happy, indeed, when, during our five war years in Washington, we were able to organize a good quartet and play almost every Friday evening, even though we were all working six full days a week and time for practice was at a premium. After the war we resumed quartet-playing in Cambridge until it became increasingly hard to get people together regularly, and I myself began to develop arthritis in my fingers which made playing difficult at times. I had bought a much better instrument from M. Lefranc, the first violist of the symphony, and my teacher had bought me a really fine bow in Paris. I hated to put them aside but have continued to get endless satisfaction listening to professional chamber music, which my own quartet experience has been a great aid in understanding.

Before I leave the subject of ensemble playing it may not be amiss to recount an episode during World War II in Washington. In the summer the American Society of Ancient Instruments, consisting of several Philadelphia Symphony players, was billed to give a concert on ancient instruments in the lovely setting of Meridian Park. Rowena, my second wife and I were on hand at 3:40, fully twenty minutes before concert time. But by then the sky had become heavily overclouded and presently a torrential thunderstorm was upon us. Everyone fled, and the concert was postponed until the morrow.

On the next day the very same phenomenon recurred. By concert time seats were so drenched and the terrain so flooded that a concert was out of the question. The would-be players looked forlorn and utterly disconsolate. My wife, who had previously made the acquaintance of the leader, appealed to me to do something. "Imagine," she said, "these poor men sitting in a hotel room on such a hot and sultry day, bored to tears and more than a little irked. Why don't you ask them to our home for a cold drink?" I protested, but naturally to no avail. I was

delighted to find the entire group enthusiastic about the proposal. Before long we were all in cabs and soon made ourselves
comfortable with appropriate libations.

It was hardly likely, however, that professional musicians
would long be content to sit and engage in desultory talk. "Why
don't we play?" one of them asked, suggesting some modern
quartet. But they had only their ancient instruments with them.
I was able to offer my viola and also the violin which I had
bought in Vienna long before, and our daughter, Betty Burr,
who was studying the cello, could provide that. But how to get
a second violin? Our daughter, then about fifteen and full of
energy, flew off in a downpour of rain and returned with her
best friend's instrument.

The quartet of instruments was now complete, but strangely,
each of these excellent musicians disclaimed any ability to play
the viola. The solution, they argued, was that I should take on
the viola part of a Schubert quartet. Knowing that I was being
framed, and that the Schubert quartets were not intended for
beginners, I resisted and protested, but finally gave in, thinking that our guests had only themselves to blame for what
might follow. To my amazement the result was nothing short
of miraculous. Playing with three professionals, I was carried
along and outplayed myself completely, as my daughter was
quick to point out. It was a thrilling experience, and I gratefully accepted the applause that was lavished upon me. It was,
musically speaking, my day of glory, a day I shall never forget.
As for the American Society of Ancient Instruments, they then
treated us to a private concert. Not until the third day were
they at last able to perform for a larger audience in idyllic
surroundings.

In the previous period, I served from time to time at other
institutions for limited periods. During one semester, I com-
muted by automobile twice a week to Wheaton College, in
Norton, Massachusetts, enjoying the thirty-five-mile trip in the
beautiful spring weather. On another occasion, I went to New
Haven once a week to conduct a seminar on European diplomacy at Yale. I recall returning in the early evening on the
Merchant's Limited during the depth of the Depression, when

there would be only a dozen persons in the dining car. But I best remember my semester at Columbia, when I offered a full-time program. Leaving my family in Cambridge and returning home every couple of weeks, I looked for a nice bachelor's apartment in the vicinity of the university. Since I was being well paid by Columbia, I was prepared to go as high as $25 a week for an apartment. To my great disappointment, I found that at that price I could get only a couple of rooms on an inside corridor, with a window on an air shaft. I finally settled for one attractive room, only to discover that it was part of a five-room apartment, with only one bathroom. The other rooms were all occupied by young married couples, of whom both parties went out to work. In the morning there was a desperate struggle to get into the bathroom to shave, and in the evening I was overcome by a medley of culinary fragrances. Finding it all intolerable, I gave up my room in a week, and accepted the invitation of my wife's aunt to live with her on Eleventh Street. This meant a long subway ride to Columbia or even to a concert at Carnegie Hall or to a theater performance. I found life in New York pretty dull and in the evening usually walked from 116th Street to the 72nd or 59th Street subway station. On one occasion I walked all the way down to Eleventh Street. There was, however, one countervailing feature: At lunch or dinner I became well acquainted with some of my colleagues in the History Department, notably Westerman, Schuyler, Baron, and Nevins, who remained my valued friends for life.

The year of the Nazi triumph in Germany, 1933, was also the year of our most extensive tour of Europe. Drawing on the honorarium received for preparing the first consolidated *Foreign Affairs Bibliography* and on miscellaneous receipts, I decided to take the entire family—wife, two children, and mother—on an extended automobile tour, which would make it easy to lunch in the open as we chose, and relieve us of the tiresome business of always having to make hotel reservations in advance. I had one of the smaller Studebaker cars, for which I had had made wrought iron frames. Each of these was fitted to a front fender and could be secured by a movable arm and padlock. Since cars still had runningboards, it was possible to store a good deal of smaller luggage within expansible frames available for the purpose. Trunk space was taken up largely with two spare tires.

Equipped for all eventualities, we drove to New York and boarded the *Manhattan* late in May. The ocean voyage to Le Havre was delightful. The car was unloaded, and we set out for Paris. Unfortunately the oldest boy, Leonard, quickly developed a grippy fever which obliged us to lay over in Rouen for several days, where we became acquainted with the strange methods of European medicine.

In Paris we found delightful lodgings in the small Hotel Voltaire on the Quai Voltaire, too convenient, I fear, to the open-air bookshop along the Seine. Naturally, we saw and admired most of the enchanting sights of Paris, and I had an opportunity to confer at length with French colleagues, notably Pierre Renouvin. After Paris we motored in leisurely fashion to southern France, by way of Chartres, Bourges, Avignon, etc. The weather in France was almost uniformly pleasant, so we stopped from time to time to buy provisions and had our breakfasts and lunches in picnic fashion along the roadsides. In the evening we always looked up some plain but attractive restaurant and had a square meal. When eventually we reached the Riviera, we spent several days at the little fishing village of Le Levandou where we were able to relax and refresh ourselves.

Our route then took us along the entire French and Italian rivieras to Genoa, Pisa, Siena, Florence and Rome, as well as many intervening hill towns. The weather in Italy, while not really cool, was certainly not warm and was usually cloudy or overcast, my mother being greatly disapointed in her vision of "sunny Italy." We toured south from Rome to Naples and Pompeii, after which I could not resist Sorrento and the exceedingly difficult, winding road around the peninsula to Amalfi and Atrani. Ultimately, we went as far as Paestum, where the temples proved to be more beautiful and impressive than I had imagined. Fascism was not especially evident in Italy, which seemed reasonably quiet and contented, though *squadristi* and especially *carabinieri* were everywhere in evidence. Turning north again from Paestum we took an eastern route, through

Ferrara and Padua to Venice which, for us as for most people, was a highlight of the trip, though life in the island city was not quite what it had been even a dozen years before.

Thus far, our journey had gone off without a hitch. On the whole, we found the hotels very clean and mostly equipped with running water in the rooms. The Depression had by no means ended and prices were still low. The equivalent of $2.50–$3.00 in American money would secure a pleasant double room, and a decent dinner could be had for 75 cents–$1.00. We had been about five weeks on the road and had seen more than one could really digest. Since my mother and the boys were getting tired of the constant driving, we made for a new base, carefully planned in advance. We crossed the long Brenner Pass to Innsbruck and thence to the Carinthian lakes. On the beautiful Millstätter See, we succeeded in finding an attractive, ground-floor apartment, only a stone's throw from an excellent market garden and from a hotel which controlled a small but useful beach, a diving tower, and other resort equipment. Here we established my mother and the two boys, who made out very well, except that my mother was terrified by the numerous beggars who stopped at the window and in some cases demanded food or other contributions. During our journeys in Austria, we got the impression that Nazism was more popular than we had supposed. Nazi formations were forbidden, but swastikas and "Heil Hitlers" were on many walls.

For my wife and myself the great objective of our European trip was a tour through the Balkans and back to Austria. Driving south from Villach, we crossed the high Alps over the Loibl Pass to Zagreb and thence to Belgrade. Zagreb was a surprisingly attractive city, with many modern buildings and elegant shops. The countryside in Croatia was charming, but the roads were unpaved and deep in fine white dust. Usually there were two or three roads running parallel, everyone using the one which either for dust or mud seemed least objectionable. There was really little to choose between them. Everywhere flocks of geese were sunning themselves in the warm, soft dust. They refused to be disturbed by automobiles or anything else, and the chief of the flock would come to the car door, hiss and spit at us, and give us a piece of his mind. Eventually the flock rose in leisurely fashion, and we were allowed to pass, only to come upon another flock a hundred yards further on. Chickens, too, were an infernal nuisance, for they always decided to leave one side of the road to run to the other, directly in front of the moving car. It seemed that there were always more geese and chickens on the road we selected than on the parallel ones. Our progress was extremely slow, and we frequently had flat tires from running over horseshoe nails in the dust. From time to time, we would catch up with another car which had raised such a cloud of dust that it made itself completely invisible. Passing was out of the question, and I was troubled to find after an exhausting day, that we had not gotten beyond Brod on the road to Belgrade. At Brod the innkeeper, who spoke German, made light of the world depression and remarked in an offhand way: "Here we can always have a nice fat goose and some green vegetables." Perhaps the goose population of Croatia has in this way been gradually reduced.

We crossed the Save from Zemun to Belgrade by a precarious ferry and began to understand the historic importance of the place from seeing its superb location. The city had been badly mauled in the war and was dirty and neglected. But considerable reconstruction, road building, and general beautification was underway. Since there was little of interest to be seen, we drove southwest to Sarajevo and thence to Mostar and the Adriatic coast. The weather was generally cloudy, cool, and showery, which at times made driving difficult on the slippery roads. The country was mountainous and thinly settled, but forested with some of the most beautiful trees I have ever seen. We repeatedly met pack trains plodding along on the narrow forest road. Thinking that anyone driving more than a Ford must be at least the vice governor, the drivers hastily took their mules into the woods to let us pass. Sarajevo was a larger town and of the utmost interest for me in following the events leading to the assassination of Archduke Francis Ferdinand and his wife in June 1914. The Serbs left no doubt that they regarded the assassins as heroes martyred in the interests of the Serbian nationalist idea.

I suppose that even now few tourists ever visit the rough

center of Yugoslavia. We found it charming and the inhabitants big, upstanding peasants, very hospitable to strangers. They were hard working in an old-fashioned way, harvesting their wheat and corn by sickles and scythes. The road through Mostar, an interesting Moslem town, to the Adriatic was very wild and for the first time I saw quite substantial streams gushing out of the rocky mountains and plunging into canyons below. All the way to Dubrovnik the country was arid and deserted, running along a ridge above the sea. One might have taken it for a moon landscape, except for the occasional sheepfolds which were the only indications of human activity.

I consider Dubrovnik and the neighboring Gulf of Cattaro (Kotor) among the most beautiful and charming places I have ever seen. Dubrovnik (famous as Ragusa until recent times) played an important role in the Middle Ages in Levantine trade and has retained the atmosphere of the small, congested, walled-in, medieval town, beautifully situated on a headland of the Adriatic. I found bathing after many days of dusty rides, most inviting. The water, which must have been $72°$–$73°$ Fahrenheit, was so clear that one could see bottom at twenty feet. The Gulf of Cattaro, not far south along the coast, is sparklingly blue, studded with green, wooded islands, the favorite seats of Orthodox monasteries. No doubt the Adriatic coast is now a much-frequented tourist attraction. In 1933 when, for economic reasons, travel was light everywhere, this charming area was still remarkably undisturbed.

Determined to omit nothing of historic interest, we decided to go to Cettinje, the capital of Montenegro. It could be reached from Kotor only by the military road built by the Austrians up the face of the Lovchen Mountain, which proved to be a tedious and rather frightening drive. I counted twenty-five successive hairpin curves before reaching a small plateau. Another half-dozen twists took us into the capital, a town of little more than 50,00 inhabitants. At a respectable looking café, we were most agreeably surprised to be told that since Montenegro did not brew beer, it imported Munich beer from Germany. I cannot now recall with certainty how many successive bottles of it we consumed.

Montenegro, if it taught me nothing more, made clear why

this wild mountainous country was never effectively occupied by the Turks. From Cettinje a very bad and utterly deserted road led us to the Albanian frontier, where an obliging peasant woke up Andrei, the customs official, by poking the ceiling of his bedroom through an open window. Andrei eventually emerged, shrouded in a cloud of flies. There was something irregular about our visa and consequently considerable delay, but eventually he allowed us to pass and we drove on to Tirana over a wretched road. I might add that the State Department had supplied us with special, diplomatic visas for the Balkan states, which ensured easy passages without much baggage inspection. On the way to Tirana we passed the ruins of Kruja, Scanderbeg's famous fifteenth-century castle, of which very little remains.

There was nothing to be seen in Tirana, which is not an ancient city like Durazzo, its port. We were soon on the road again, driving due east to the town and Lake of Okhrid. I felt as though I were driving through a desert—almost no habitations and no inhabitants, a bad, dusty road, and little vegetation. Because of the road conditions throughout most of the Balkans, we were constantly having flat tires and on several occasions broken springs. Since the local blacksmiths had no spring steel, they forged new leaves of wagon-rim steel, which were better than nothing, but not much better. All the more thrilling, then, was the sight of Lake Okhrid, a brilliant blue mountain lake with the town on the further side and many signs of human activity. We found a comfortable lodging and that evening dined on the finest lake fish I ever hope to eat again.

From Okhrid we cut across northernmost Greece to just north of Saloniki, which we felt obliged to omit for lack of time. Instead we followed the beautiful Vardar Valley north to Skoplye, a busy and interesting place, and thence eastward towards the Bulgarian border. Beyond Kumanovo we met with disaster. On a deserted road we broke an axle and were completely stalled. We had no choice but to lock our baggage in the car and start walking back several miles to Kumanovo. But presently, a Ford jitney overtook us and lo and behold, among the passengers was a Montenegrin who had been in America for eleven years and had served in the United States Army. He had, however, retained the Montenegrin's sense of hospitality and felt impelled to accompany us to Kumanovo and back to Skoplye, where he found a garage that agreed to send out a truck and tow the car in. What a trip that was, over the hot dusty roads! The truck had nothing but a very frayed rope, and it was not long before the rope broke without the driver's even knowing it. I blew my horn, and then ran after him in a cloud of dust. Eventually he realized that he had no tow, stopped, and turned back with me. We started again and the same mishap was repeated several times. But, thank God, the driver became more alert and eventually got us back to Skoplye. He remained in town for three days until we were in shape once again to continue our travels. The garage at first telegraphed Belgrade to send by air a new rear axle for a Studebaker car. The reply was negative. Had it been a Ford there would have been no problem, but a Studebaker was all but unknown in Europe, and there seemed little likelihood that appeals to Budapest, Vienna, or even Munich would have brought better responses. We had almost despaired when one morning the very competent local mechanic greeted us in the greatest glee. He had discovered that the Studebaker axle was a trifle smaller than the Ford and had spent the night in grinding a Ford axle to fit. The entire garage world, as well as our Montenegrin mentor, rejoiced with us as we admired the gleaming product. The repair was made and off we went, assured that the new axle was as good as the old.

Arriving finally at the Bulgarian frontier we found ourselves in one of the politically hottest spots in Europe. Macedonia, in Yugoslav possession, was claimed by Bulgaria, which harbored the Macedonian Revolutionary Committee. Large-scale raids by the Macedonian *comitadjis* were frequent, and the Yugoslav army had been obliged to erect forts every kilometer along the border, these forts being connected by deep wolf-traps, which somehow or other the raiders occasionally managed to cross. It was not likely to be easy for us to cross the border. In fact, we learned to our grief that there was only one official crossing point and that was much further north at Nish. So we were detained for hours during which we were questioned several times, and I barely managed to slip some compromising lists of names of prominent Macedonians on either side of the frontier that had been entrusted to me into the envelop of automobile papers which had already been examined. Meanwhile the officials kept telephoning Belgrade and Sofia for instructions, and finally the naive, not to say stupid, American tourists were allowed to pass. First, the gates on the Yugoslav side of no man's land were opened and closed behind us, and in due course the gates on the Bulgarian side were reluctantly opened to admit us.

By this time our Balkan tour had already become more exciting than we could have wished, but one more ordeal awaited us. Sofia turned out to be a dull town, with a small modern center of government buildings and business offices, and hundreds of hovels and muddy roads. At one point, in leaving, we skidded into the deep roadside ditch and had to be pulled out by a team of oxen. On our way to the Danube, we crossed the famous Shipka Pass to Gabrovo, and thence through a prosperous part of Bulgaria. On our arrival at Rustchuk on the Danube, we were confronted with the problem of ferrying the car across to Rumania. The river in its lower reaches is very broad and imposing, flowing at two or three knots, with considerable steamship traffic up and down. There was no regular ferry, but fishermen were prepared to do our job for a generous price, namely, the equivalent of fifteen American dollars, which then seemed exorbitant but in retrospect appears quite modest, considering the difficulty of the operation. Having no alternative, we agreed and watched with horror as our precious car was being wheedled onto the gunwales of a small scow, where it was tied down by none too sturdy ropes.

Off we went, floating down the majestic Danube and heading for the Rumanian port of Giurgiu several miles downstream. Each time a steamer passed, it left a wake which rocked our "ferry" to the point where it seemed certain that the car would be dumped into the river, with all the legal complications devolving from such a catastrophe. The passage was ultimately completed, but our frayed nerves were further tried as the Studebaker had to be maneuvered across the decks of two ships that lay at the dock at Giurgiu. From there an excellent road took us the short distance to Bucharest, a far more modern, prosperous town with all desired conveniences. It was a good place to catch one's breath and recuperate.

Rumania was already reaping the financial returns of its substantial oil wells at Ploesti, which we visited briefly on our way. We were not wholly surprised, then, to find an excellent macadam highway running over the beautiful, forested Carpathian mountains to the Hungarian frontier. I will not take more space to itemize the details of our travels. We passed through the German (Saxon) part of Transylvania, which German settlers had occupied since the Middle Ages. Noting the purity of the language spoken by the people, I was told by a bookshop owner that the Church and the schools made every effort to preserve the traditional language although surrounded by Hungarians and Rumanians.

Budapest, our next objective, is another of the beautifully located cities of the world. Unfortunately, the cool and rainy weather made sight-seeing all but impossible. Time was running out, so that after a few days in the Hungarian capital we drove on, past Lake Balaton to Austria and the Millstätter See, where mother, genuinely frightened by the many vagrants that constantly appeared at her grated window, was relieved by our reappearance.

In the weeks that followed, we motored to Vienna, thence to Prague, and over the mountains to Dresden. There was little evidence of the political overturn that had occurred only a few months before, but in Berlin I had a chance to talk to a number of fellow historians. They were, naturally, distressed by Hitler's sudden advent to power and the drastic enabling acts extorted from the parliament, which made the Führer a veritable dictator. The outrages against Jews and Communists boded ill for the future. I found that some of my colleagues had joined the party in the hope of exercising a restraining influence. They took me to the North Berlin headquarters of the S.A., where burly and aggressive fellows were lolling around prior to some new exploit. I was even permitted to visit the first concentration camp, Oranienburg, which had only recently been opened and which I may have been the first foreigner to inspect. What the concentration camps were later to become and the unspeakable atrocities committed in them, the whole world knows. But in August 1933 Oranienburg at least seemed like a fairly innocuous detention camp, where most of the 960 detainees were standing or sitting around, doing nothing in particular. Some of them, like former President Ebert's son, were pointed out to me, though I was not permitted to converse with them. There seemed to be but few persons of importance. The majority looked like workers, probably Communists who had tried to engage in street fighting. Nothing much seemed to be happening to them. In fact, the camp, a former brewery, gave the impression of easy-going detention. Of course, I realize that appearances can be deceptive and probably were. As a historian I would have been interested in meeting Hitler, and a request to that effect was sent to his office. The reply was that the Führer would be pleased to receive me, but only after the great Nürnberg party rally in September. Since I had to be back in Cambridge for the new school year, I was denied this experience.

I had better luck with an appeal to the former Emperor William, who lived in exile at Doorn in the Netherlands. His adjutant fixed a date and an exact time when my wife and I were to appear at the castle gate. We left the family comfortably situated at Scheveningen, the seaside resort near The Hague. We then motored through clouds of bicycles and over innumerable bridges to arrive at our destination just in time. An adjutant ushered us into a guest house and asked us to speak English, as the Emperor no longer had much opportunity to retain his fluency in that language. We were then told the exact time when we would be received briefly by the Empress before proceeding to lunch. Since it was clear that the Emperor maintained a full court ceremonial, we were happy that we were fully instructed, even to the point of laying down our knives and forks the moment the Emperor laid down his.

I must say that William II had a good deal of personal charm. His dominant feature, it seemed to me, were his gray-blue eyes, which could easily twinkle humorously. Although he must have known that I had written critically of him, he received us most cordially and we sat down about twelve to a very good lunch. The conversation was general, but from references to the current situation in Germany, it was clear that the imperial court rather expected that Hitler's victory might be the prelude to a Hohenzollern restoration. This idea would seem preposterous, but on the eve of Hitler's advent to power, the possibility of a restoration, with one of the grandsons of William II as emperor or king, was seriously discussed at the very highest levels of the German government. How vain such notions proved to be.

According to instructions, we adjourned after lunch to a smoking room where the Emperor indulged in a cigar. He was in excellent spirits and recalled his occasional visits to the old Emperor Francis Joseph. These visits, he said, filled him with real dread, for he was convinced that his host ransacked the whole world for the worst possible cigars, the memory of which still made him shudder. After a half hour of amiable talk on the window seat, the Emperor retired to rest. He and his consort bade us good-bye, we were escorted to the guest house, and permitted to take our leave. I would not say that this visit to Doorn was of much consequence—a meeting with Hitler would have been more rewarding. But it was interesting to see at least one side of the Emperor's personality and to get some notion of what life at an imperial court was like.

The last couple of weeks of our European tour were spent in England. We had a calm crossing from the Hook of Holland to Harwich and after a short stay in London toured the countryside of southern England before taking ship at Southampton. There were already more private automobiles in England than on the continent. Though they were mostly small, they presented a problem on the narrow roads, most of which were edged with curbing. The weather was beautiful, however, and I recall with great satisfaction our visit to Stonehenge and our drive through the New Forest, studded as it was with superb patches of holly. We were all well as we boarded the *Washington* for our return home.

This chapter may appropriately end with a reversion to my

professional activities. In 1935 Knopf published a sequel to the *Alliances and Alignments,* a two-volume study entitled *The Diplomacy of Imperialism, 1890–1902.* This was so formidable an enterprise that only a generous grant of a year's leave of absence, financed by the Bureau of International Studies at Harvard and Radcliffe, under the direction of my colleague, Professor Sidney B. Fay, enabled me to complete it in reasonable time. I think that of all the books I have written, *The Diplomacy of Imperialism* is still my favorite. It deals with a fascinating period during which Bismarck's continental system disintegrated, the European powers began to divide into antagonistic groupings, and, above all, the European countries, with their enormous technological superiority, subdued or established control over the undeveloped parts especially of Africa and Asia. It was the high tide of imperialism and brought with it wars and threats of wars, while the old European issues such as the Balkan and Near Eastern conflicts periodically flared up. The book gave me a longed-for chance to deal with world problems in their concatenations and interactions. In one chapter I even had the temerity to examine the nature of imperialism, its motives and objectives, the forces, economic, religious, strategic, nationalistic that found expression not only in the spectacular events of the period, but in the tides of public opinion. I worked hard on this book, rewriting the material on the struggle for control of the Nile watershed no fewer than three times as I sensed that it became more and more crucial. And so the book, while not neglecting European alignments, dealt with all the ramifications of the Egyptian problem, the South African War, the emergence of Japan, the war in the Far East, and the efforts to partition the moribund Chinese Empire. The expansion of European diplomacy to the world arena led to a new interest in sea power, which allowed me to discuss the origins of this crucial feature of modern international relations.

In the forty-odd years since the appearance of *The Diplomacy of Imperialism,* no one, to my knowledge, has attempted to improve upon it or to tackle this complex of problems anew. Like *European Alliances,* the book was reset and published in a second, one-volume edition after the Second World War. Despite its rather high price, it has continued to fill a real need. I believe that now, forty years after the original publication, it is selling as well or better on both sides of the Atlantic as it did at the outset. Under modern conditions historians cannot reasonably expect their works to be long lived, so this particular book has always given me great satisfaction. I have never for a moment forgotten my debt to Alfred Knopf for his continuing interest and encouragement.

It is no exaggeration to say that my book put diplomatic history on a basis even broader and more universal than its predecessors had. Reviewers, while frequently questioning some opinion or interpretation of mine, were so enthusiastic as almost to give me a swelled head. Walter Millis called it "a panorama of the imperial years—at once vast in its scope, magnificent in detail and exact in its intricate balance." Professor Seymour declared in the *Saturday Review of Literature*: "The critical scholarship of the author is matched by his capacity for lucid exposition, and his control of detail by a power of synthesis which is reminiscent of the best of the French historians." My friend, Professor Raymond Sontag of Princeton, noted some weaknesses in the book, but considered it "one of the truly great historical works of our generation." The *English Historical Review*, in an appreciation by Professor Harold V. Temperley, declared it "an admirable example of research in published and printed materials," while Professor Robert Seton-Watson termed it "a most stimulating and indispensable book, which towers above any rivals." Finally, Professor Baumont, the eminent French historian, writing in the *Revue Historique*, pronounced it a book of very great interest "absolutely indispensable for all who study or want to learn about this period."

I ought perhaps to say that the English historians, most of whom were inclined to judge the efforts of "colonials" rather severely, felt that I had been unduly critical of British policy in a number of instances. In 1952, when the new editions of the *Alliances* and *The Diplomacy of Imperialism* appeared, the anonymous critic of the *Times Literary Supplement* introduced his lengthy review by saying that the two books "will dominate

academic life for a long time to come, and will shape the out-
look of countless students of European history." Because of this
he bemoaned their reappearance, for he quarreled with almost
every one of my major opinions. He was, of course, entitled to
his own views, which I found stimulating as well as provocative.
In those days editors of learned journals still believed that
important books should be reviewed at length by the most
competent authority in the subject. To my regret, I note that
nowadays the reviews have become so short as to be all but
worthless, and some editors prefer to give important works to
younger men who, even if their knowledge is limited, are expected to contribute new and provocative ideas.

CHAPTER VIII

Diplomatic Historian

THE THIRTIES were for me a highly gratifying decade. *The Diplomacy of Imperialism* had appeared in 1935 and been warmly commended by reviewers on both sides of the Atlantic. The next year I was promoted to full professor and, at age forty, was named the first Archibald Cary Coolidge Professor of History, an appointment which gave me the greatest possible pleasure. The History Department had by this time grown considerably but remained a group of most congenial colleagues. So far as I can remember, there was never, in all these years, any fundamental difference of opinion or effort at factional conflict. I played a full part in the department meetings and did a good deal of speaking both in the university and outside. I tended to disagree with President Lowell on many of his key programs, but never to the point of wanting to make an issue of them. The president favored admitting students by preference at age sixteen, which from my own experience I thought unfortunate and less rewarding than admission at eighteen. Similarly, the undergraduate house plan struck me as altogether too lavish for boys of college age, and my objections to the tutorial system also remained unchanged. But Mr. Lowell retired in 1933, to be succeeded by James B. Conant, a scientist whom I did not even know. In justice to Mr. Lowell I will say that I think the house plan at least has worked out much better than I anticipated. In recent years especially, the houses have become centers of cultural activities, often of considerable interest.

On the other hand, I should note that I was obliged to with-draw my boys from the nearby public school when they showed signs of falling under the control of school gangs. I spoke at length to the principal about this problem, and he assured me that, distressed as he was by the situation, his authority ended when the boys left the school building. He was quite aware that this particular gang, which passed our house on its way to school, was collecting tribute from various boys every morning under threat of severe beatings. Though a firm believer in the advantages of public school education, I felt obliged, like a number of my colleagues, to find another solution for the school problem. After some experimentation with other private schools, I enrolled my older son in the Browne and Nichols School, which over the years I found very satisfactory. It was an old-fashioned school much like the Boston Latin School, with an essentially classical training and with teachers able to maintain discipline.

I regret to say that relations with my mother, however, were not satisfactory. She was now living alone in her attractive Lexington house and garden, but flatly refused to hire anyone to do chores or heavy work for her. My brother Rudolph was professor of mathematics at Wisconsin and rarely came East more than once a year, when his visits led more to recrimina-tions than to the happiness of reunion. And Walter put in only an occasional appearance. His relations with his mother were less clouded than Rudolph's, but he was generally uncommuni-cative and gave less occasion for argument. After the stock market crash of 1929, many of his pupils were withdrawn from the New Mexico school for financial reasons, and in 1930 he had had to abandon his project. On his return to the East, he purchased an estate located on the banks of the Charles, in Newton, and seemed well on the way to recovery. But on a severely cold night (December 9, 1931) the school burned down, largely because all the fire hydrants were frozen. Walter was forced into bankruptcy and decided to return to advanced study. He joined the Psychological Clinic at Harvard, received his Ph.D. degree in 1935, and then went to New York to join the Rockefeller Progressive Education Association. A year later he decided to go to Vienna for psychoanalysis by Anna Freud, which was rudely interrupted by the Nazi invasion of Austria in 1938 and the forced flight of Freud and his associates to England, an episode in which Walter played an important role. A handsome portrait photograph, inscribed by Freud, testifies to the crucial aid he gave to the master and other Jewish analysts. In the absence of my brothers it was I who had to listen to my mother's complaints and do the considerable work on the place. At the time, I wondered why my mother could not derive joy rather than sorrow from the success of her three sons. But I see now that having concentrated her affection on us, she simply could not reconcile herself to our leaving her, especially for other women, who had made no contribution to our success and, indeed, were reaping the benefits of her sacrifices and efforts. Ultimately, when advancing age and infirmity obliged her to give up her house and live with us, her resentment tended to diminish, and in her old age I believe she found peace and such happiness as is still permitted the aged and dependent. Her grandchildren were certainly a great source of interest and joy to her, and they in turn were devoted to her.

Yet another enterprise on which I embarked, in 1937, calls for mention: I was to undertake a thorough revision of a well-known handbook, Ploetz's *Epitome of History,* drawing for assistance on a dozen or fifteen scholars, specialists in various fields. In each of the successive editions of what was renamed *An Encyclopedia of World History,* I have related the long and chequered history of this valuable reference work, so I will only note a few salient facts here.

Originally compiled by a German scholar, it provided all the data for the history of Germany and Central Europe, and to a lesser extent of other European countries. Its great success led to the publication of an English edition, which provided much more detailed treatment of English history and of countries related to Britain, and an American edition did the same for the United States. By 1930, this patchwork book was owned in part by various publishers here and abroad. It was then that Houghton Mifflin bought up all existing rights and invited me to edit a fundamental revision. With the help of others, I did this in a few years, carrying the story back to prehistory, revising and correcting the older sections, and expanding the scope to include the entire world. As *An Encyclopedia of World History*, it appeared in 1940 and has had a number of revised editions, each of which has brought the chronology down to a recent date. In the present, fifth edition, the main facts of historical development cover the entire world through the year 1970. It contains all essential maps in black and white and over a hundred genealogical charts, many of which are original and unique. The analytical table of contents makes it easy to locate the desired subject matter, and the extensive index to identify specific names and events. I know of no historical handbook that has anything like its coverage or, for that matter, its reliability. No wonder it has sold widely and been warmly praised by many of its users.

The political and especially the economic stringency in Europe led to the migration of many scholars to this country. Their numbers became formidable in 1934 when the Nazi regime undertook a thoroughgoing purge of the universities, dismissing all professors who had even remote Jewish ancestry. I find my correspondence file for this period loaded with appeals from my own students for help in finding employment, and similar requests from colleagues in other universities whose positions were abolished in the interests of economy. To this now came the pitiful letters from abroad soliciting aid in finding a position. Though the situation was pathetic, there was little one could do. In the long term, to be sure, the United States benefited greatly from the addition of some of the world's leading scholars. After 1945 there could be no question as to where the intellectual center of the world lay.

The appointment of Hitler as German Chancellor and the complete triumph of the Nazis in the spring of 1933 soon brought an end to the so-called period of fulfillment during which a number of objectionable provisions of the peace treaties were liquidated by negotiation. It has often been said that if more statesmen had read Hitler's ponderous *Mein Kampf* they would have foreseen and perhaps forestalled some of his moves. This may be so, but recall that the book was written after Hitler's first bid for power, the almost childish Beer Hall Putsch of 1923, and that *Mein Kampf* is an extraordinary medley of amateur politics and amazing insights into international problems and possibilities. It is doubtful whether many people in the 1920s would have taken it seriously. The book is important primarily as a revelatory document. Many of its programs and designs were in fact realized, but others again were not. The basic policies advocated in *Mein Kampf*, such as expansion to the east, liquidations of the Jews, etc. were by no means original with Hitler. As I showed in an article published in the *Yale Review* in 1938, on the eve of the Czech crisis, entitled "When German Dreams Come True," these notions were held by many Germans, notably by some of Germany's intellectual leaders. Many later writers have done this better and certainly in greater detail than I could. The point is that in Hitler there appeared a man with the reckless courage to realize them.

It is now generally recognized that the critical point was Hitler's announcement in March 1936 that the Rhineland was to be rearmed. This was indeed a serious matter, but it was unlikely that Hitler's new Germany would long have tolerated so important and valuable a frontier area remaining unarmed and militarily undefended, when the traditional enemy, France, was building the unprecedented, defensive Maginot Line across the border. I had my doubts whether the United States would ever accept the complete disarmament of Texas in the face of even a weak power such as Mexico.

The failure of Britain and France to act was evidence that many British and some French statesmen were inclined toward appeasement: They knew that the peace settlements of 1919 were the reflection not of a sense of justice, but of a passion for revenge. They were willing to see these settlements undone, if it could be effected in a moderate and decent way. It was in Hitler's power to move from one success to another so long as he neither antagonized the other powers nor drove them to form a common front for resistance. Thus, no power seriously considered making a major issue of the reunion of German Austria with its co-nationals in Germany. Indeed, I am convinced from my own observations in Austria in 1933 that in the countryside, if not in Vienna, there was considerable pro-Nazi sentiment and that the effort to represent Hitler's action as an affront to public opinion in Austria was largely misplaced.

It was the brutal seizure of the entire Czechoslovak state, a violation of solemn promises, that left no room for doubt that Hitler would march from one conquest to another and would soon dominate the whole continent. I could fully understand German efforts to undo the most objectionable features of the 1919 peace treaties, and even their desire to unite the German minorities in other states with the Reich. But from my travels in 1933, I would say that the so-called Sudeten Germans had enjoyed a large measure of cultural autonomy under the Czech regime and had no strong antipathy to membership in the historic Bohemian-Moravian state. It was impossible to see the Nazi campaign on their behalf as anything but the prelude to the disruption and absorption of all Czechoslovakia preparatory to the subversion of Poland, the Balkan States, and even the Ukraine.

From then on, my aversion to everything the Nazis stood for in domestic policy was extended to the conviction that they represented a menace not only to Europe, but to the whole world. I recall sitting with my brother Walter in his automobile listening to Hitler's impassioned speeches. I confess I was never so frightened for the future of the world. The Führer's speeches, two hours of constant crescendo, struck me as the ravings of a madman who was dangerous not only because he had a great and powerful nation behind him, but because the strongest armed forces in the world were at his beck and call. I might mention that some thirty-six years later my brother was to attain considerable acclaim by the publication of a secret report prepared during the war, entitled *The Mind of Adolf Hitler*, a percipient evaluation of the Führer's personality which was promptly translated into ten or twelve foreign languages.

The year 1938 was crucial not only for Germany's neighbors and for the peace of the world, but for me personally. I had always liked lecturing and was reputed to be good at it. I hardly knew, then, what hit me in February 1938, when, in the middle of a discussion on the condition of the Italian peasantry, I was suddenly overcome by a wave of emotion so severe that for a few moments I was unable to speak and became so dizzy that I had to hold on to the podium for support. It would, I am sure, have been altogether natural if I had pleaded sudden illness and dismissed the class. But I had always prided myself on my self-control. Not knowing what was up, I eventually recovered enough balance to complete my lecture. It was naturally greatly distressing to find that the same thing, akin to stage fright, happened in each lecture, usually within the first ten or fifteen minutes, but not always with the same virulence. Again, I might reasonably have resorted to the use of a sedative, as many public speakers do, but I was determined to find out the cause of my mysterious affliction and master it if I could.

Lecturing now became a chronic ordeal, and I found myself becoming panicky even before entering the classroom. During the spring vacation my wife and I went to Bermuda in the hope that a short rest might help. This, again, brought disappointment. My brother Walter, who was himself completely baffled, recommended me to Dr. Hanns Sachs, one of the refugee Viennese analysts and editor of *Imago*, the journal which attempted to relate psychoanalysis to literature and the arts. I had a number of long discussions with Dr. Sachs, whom I found one of the most original and interesting personalities I had ever met. Nevertheless, I must confess that nothing he could suggest helped in any way to relieve my affliction.

During the summer, when I had no lecturing to do, I pondered my problem. An obvious possibility was that the acute tension in world affairs was telling on me and that I was reacting in advance to the impending cataclysm. But this explanation seemed to me inadequate. I had never been emotionally affected by the First World War, nor by the systematic study of international relations in the interwar years. I had approached, or seemed to myself to have approached these problems and dangers in the cool, analytical spirit of the surgeon about to embark on a difficult operation. It was so even during the month-long Czech crisis of September 1938. There must, I felt, be some other motivating factor. I sometimes felt that I was facing a hostile group, ready to attack me at any moment. This feeling was quite pronounced and seemed significant because it did not affect me if I was addressing another, more advanced class, or some *ad hoc* group of students or outsiders. But I could never find anything in my past or present experience sufficiently serious or outstanding to occasion such a reaction.

Eventually, I began what I suppose were regular analytic sessions with one of my brother's close Viennese friends, Dr. Jenny Waelder, whom I came to admire greatly, and for whose patient, understanding efforts I developed a boundless respect. I found my sessions with her highly instructive, and I have always felt that, if nothing more, analysis was a most effective method for learning about oneself. My affliction proved absolutely recalcitrant, however. I had to live with it for some twenty years, during which every occasion for public speech was a certain ordeal, to be avoided whenever possible. I rather doubt whether my distress was ordinarily noticeable to my listeners, but its effect on me was devastating. I am firmly convinced that this affliction reduced my capability by at least a third and that for the rest of my life my effectiveness was substantially impaired.

The first months of the Second World War found me far removed from even the essential news of the conflict. I was to have a sabbatical year during the autumn of 1939 and, being plagued by my lecturing difficulties, I set off by myself for a trip to Mexico and Central America. I thought that perhaps in Mexico City I might do a little archival work on the French intervention of the 1860s, and I went equipped with letters to influential persons in the Mexican foreign service. But I was sent from pillar to post and found so little of value that I gave up all idea of work. I felt lonely and despondent and found some consolation solely in an alto recorder, which I had brought with me and on which I assiduously practiced Telemann sonatas.

Here and there, however, were moments of interest. Traveling by ship from New York, I stopped for a week's stay in Yucatan to visit the Mayan ruins. I found Merida a rather intriguing place, with many elegant houses dating from the midnineteenth century when sisal (henequen) was in great demand and brought high prices. Local families grew so rich that they could import the finest French furniture and fittings.

I made a point of visiting one of the sisal plantations which, since the Mexican Revolution of 1911, had been confiscated and divided among the peasants. That Mexico was still in process of social revolution was at once brought home to me. There were Lenin Halls, and the Communist hammer and sickle were displayed everywhere. The priests had been expelled, and the churches closed. But the millenium had not yet arrived. Sisal no longer held its envious place on the world market, and it proved difficult to cultivate on a small scale. The peasants were obliged to form cooperatives if only to maintain the lookout towers to warn of fire. While in Merida I went to the cinema, where a racy American film was being shown. Near me sat an Indian woman with her baby in her arms. I could not help wondering what was going on in her mind as she watched the antics of the Hollywood smart set. It seemed too bad that this was virtually the only view of American life that the cinema was transmitting, even to the undeveloped parts of the world, in the 1930s.

From Merida an admirably organized tourist company took our small group first to the ruins at Uxmal and then in four and a half hours over eighty rough miles to Chichen-Itza, one of the finest Mayan ruins, deep in the jungle. Small, individual cottages had been erected for visitors, and the guides, who were available during the cool hours of the morning and late afternoon, were admirably trained and extremely helpful. My guide did his best to persuade me to ascend one of the temples, but the steps were too steep and narrow, and I contented myself with admiring the ruins, which are so perfect in conception and proportion that they can be fairly compared to the best Greek temples. Later in my tour, I visited several other sites, including Quirigua, in Guatemala, which consists largely of six calendrical stelae, buried in a huge banana plantation. While lost in wonder at the achievements of the Mayan people, I found it impossible to recapture anything of their mentality. Their gods were all such terrible and terrifying figures that one must conclude that the Mayans spent their lives trying to conciliate these monstrous demons.

After a week in Yucatan I embarked on the next ship for

Vera Cruz and had real difficulties in reaching Mexico City because of a railroad strike. While in the capital I made the acquaintance of a congenial couple with whom I visited most of the buildings within a considerable radius that were decorated by the murals of Rivera, Orozco, Siqueiros, and other Mexican masters.

I was surprised in the various commercial galleries by the modesty of the prices of prints and even paintings. I burned with desire to purchase at least one of several items that appealed to me strongly. Unfortunately, since the funds available to me were strictly limited, I suffered one real disappointment. I was much attracted by a painting by Siqueiros of an Indian woman completely shrouded in her cloak, the face hidden. As a study in drapery it was superb and the color, a silvery gray, was indescribably beautiful. I decided that I could not live without it, even after learning that it was priced at $100. But I foolishly reserved my decision in order to give the matter full deliberation. The next morning I was back at the gallery, prepared to take the plunge, only to find that on the preceding afternoon a young American had bought and paid for it, promising to pick it up the next day. While I was bemoaning my fate, the villain appeared, driving an expensive sports car. He proved to be a very decent chap, wealthy no doubt and something of a playboy, but very well versed in modern art history. Though delighted that I shared his love for the painting, he never even remotely suggested any readiness to sacrifice it in my favor. The best I could do—and it was far from a sour compromise—was to buy (for $60) an ink drawing by Rivera of a miner hard at work, a highly dynamic work much admired by all the young members of the family.

I found these Mexican artists very impressive, not only for their design and coloring, but for their subject matter. Unlike the art one would expect to see in Europe, these paintings were almost without exception, propaganda for the social revolution that was transforming Mexico. The early Rivera murals in the National Agricultural College at Chapingo were least so and appealed to me more than the later ones, such as those in the Ministry of Education and in the Cortez Palace at Cuernavaca.

Orozco's murals were, on the whole, even more brutally direct than Rivera's. "You feel the great dark masses in motion," I noted in my travel diary, "and you feel the terrifying uncertainty as to the outcome. . . . One can learn more in two hours of the revolutionary mentality from these murals (in the National Preparatory School) than one can ever derive from books and lectures."

Another vivid reminder of social revolution was my two visits to Leon Trotsky, whose last refuge in exile was in Mexico City. There was reason to believe that Trotsky, concerned not only for his own safety but for that of his records, was interested in selling them to some major library. Dr. Keyes Metcalfe, the director of the Harvard College Library, had asked me to contact Trotsky and try to arrange the sale. I had no difficulty in making an appointment, though I was somewhat shocked to find that Trotsky lived some ten miles outside the city in the suburb of Coyoacan. Eventually, I found a reluctant taxi driver who agreed to search for the place, which turned out to be at the farthest end of the Avenida Viena, a thoroughfare that fell far short of its impressive name. It was, in fact, an almost uninhabited, unpaved street, full of ruts and much obstructed by free-roaming pigs, goats, and chickens. Trotsky lived in a large compound heavily guarded by his followers. They led me through various barely furnished rooms to the great man's study, which was crudely furnished with a raw wooden table and a few comparable chairs. There, on October 2, 1939, I had a two-and-a-half hour talk with Trotsky, followed on November 7 by a second conference. Having spent some years in New York, Trotsky spoke English reasonably well, though he preferred to speak German. He was pleasant and cordial throughout and permitted me to examine his papers, the sale of which was finally consummated.

Trotsky looked to me somewhat younger than his sixty years. He was about 5′ 8″ in height, straight, and rather broad. His head did not seem unusual, except that the face was broad and the features large. Both mouth and nose were large and prominent. The eyes—a gray-blue—were not particularly striking, possibly because they were concealed by heavy, thick glasses, and he had a mass of steel-gray hair, which waved freely in Einsteinian fashion.

Trotsky spoke at some length of the difficulties of writing the history of revolutions, because of the disappearance or willful destruction of crucial records. He observed that revolutions appeared different when in the making from what they looked like after they have succeeded. Having been a great admirer of Robespierre, he was now inclined to admire Danton as the more practical politician. This remark may have reflected his feelings about his own attitude and role and that of his ruthless opponent, Stalin. As for the current situation, so soon after the Hitler-Stalin Pact and the Nazi assault on Poland, Trotsky declared his conviction (quite possibly correct) that Stalin was the most scared man in Europe, with his army greatly weakened by the great purge and disaffection in Russia on the rise. He was, therefore, obliged to make a deal with Hitler if only to save his own skin. This is certainly not the whole story, but I repeat it for what it is worth. It was surely true, that in August 1939 Stalin was ready to do anything to avoid involvement in the war.

After visiting Oaxaca, I flew to Guatemala, a country which I enjoyed for its wonderful climate and scenery, and more particularly for the fine textile work of the Mayan Indians, who are a great majority in the population and still retain many traits of the pre-Spanish period. The worship at the church in Chichicastenango is really worth seeing, with its curious amalgam of pagan and Christian ritual.

My tour took me as far as Quezaltenango, at an altitude of 8,000 feet, where it was far too cold for an extended stay. But fascinating above all was a trip down the River Dulce, which runs through the coffee region down to the Atlantic. I had a letter of introduction to Mr. J. P. Armstrong, an Englishman who was president of the International Railway of Central America, an enterprise far less imposing than its title. We became good friends during my short stay, perhaps because together we listened daily to the BBC report on the war, which could be heard on the Armstrong radio. He urged me not to miss the River Dulce and helped arrange for me to fly over the mountains in a Ford trimotor plane to the coffee region, where there was a small guest house at Panzos. The area was inhabited almost exclusively by Germans, all of whom were evidently Nazis. They were definitely not delighted to see strangers and I am sure I was regarded as a spy. But they put me up for the night, and early next morning I boarded a small river steamer, which, with a rather strong current to help, made the trip down the Poluchic River to Lake Izabal, a large inland basin. From the lake to the Atlantic coast is a matter of some five fabulous miles. The river runs through a narrow canyon, a veritable tropical paradise, known as the Rio Dulce. On both sides was thick jungle, with lianas dropping from the canyon walls and a chorus of tropical birds enlivening the trip.

Mr. Armstrong had arranged with the United Fruit Company to have me met at the little port of Livingston and brought back to Puerto Barrios, the terminus of the railway. Imagine my surprise, then, to find a large, ocean-going towboat waiting for me. For once I had the feeling of being really important.

On the whole I found the Central American countries, except Guatemala and Costa Rica, uninteresting, not to say dull. Yet I recall with pleasure one incident that took place in San Salvador, which was otherwise a dismal place. In Puerto Barrios, I met a prosperous-looking tobacco merchant who revealed an intimate knowledge of modern painting and was delighted to find that in a feeble way I shared his interest. He gave me the address of a local painter in San Salvador who, he assured me, was as talented as he was unknown.

On reaching San Salvador, I found the artist living not far from the center of town in an almost unfurnished garret. He was obviously flattered to have anyone take an interest in his work and showed me a number of his pictures, which stood thick along the walls. I soon found myself agreeing with my Puerto Barrios acquaintance about the quality of his work. There were at least three items that I would have been glad to buy had my financial situation been less precarious. Eventually, I came away with only a charcoal drawing of an Indian woman with a scarf on her head. For this, I am ashamed to say, I paid all of $15, consoled only that the artist clearly considered the sum a veritable landslide. The drawing is really quite fascinating and over the past decades has worn exceedingly well.

I arrived home just before Christmas to find my mother quite seriously ill, the weather atrociously cold, and everything pointing to a major blizzard. The contrast with tropical Central America was painful, and I had not found abroad the hoped-for relief from my troubles. Now I can appreciate the benefits of the trip, but at the time, I felt hopeless and despondent, especially after resuming my teaching under the same handicap.

In the autumn of 1940, when the fate of the world hung in the balance, I was invited to deliver eight Lowell lectures in January of the new year. These lectures, on an agreed subject, are delivered in the Boston Public Library and are open to the public without charge. After only brief deliberation, I accepted the invitation despite all the disheartening experiences I was having in public speaking for three reasons: First, I could not bring myself to give in to my affliction; secondly, I had noticed that my difficulties were less when addressing a strange audience; thirdly, the honorarium was not to be lightly despised by a family of limited means in which four members were taking expensive music lessons.

I chose as the subject of my lectures "The Conflagration of Ideas in Pre-War Europe," meaning by "war" the First World War. My basic objective was to demonstrate that the ideas so agitating Europe in 1940—the threat of nazism, fascism, and communism, the intellectual restlessness and confusion, the rise of the revolutionary spirit, especially in the Western countries, the cult of a new, conservative, or integral nationalism, the doctrine of *Volkstum* and the need for expansion, especially among the Germans, the conviction of race superiority and the growth of anti-Semitism, the glorification of violence, and finally, the formation of elite shock troops that were to overthrow the existing social and political order and introduce the new, higher, nobler, more natural, and humane culture of which Nietzsche dreamed—antedated the First World War. Even if not widespread or formidable before 1914, they were greatly stimulated by the experiences of the war and came to fruition in the succeeding generation.

Basic to my argument was the proposition that with the rise of modern industrialism and science, many of the old tenets of European society had given way. There was a revolt against traditional religion, against materialism, against the democratic-parliamentary system, against what was felt to be the irresistible mechanization of man and society. Europe and the world were faced by a fundamental, deep-seated revolt, confronted by new doctrines and new programs of great variety, but all directed at the destruction of the old order and the establishment of a new, integrated society, without class or class struggle.

It is obviously impossible to sketch even in light detail the "conflagration of ideas" of the late-nineteenth and early-twentieth centuries. The subject inspired one of my few excursions into what is called the history of ideas—an excursion that I thought on the whole successful. The late afternoon audiences were substantial, attentive, and appreciative. As I expected, I suffered less from "stage fright" than in my Harvard classes, which in small measure at least, restored my self-confidence— that I worked like a beaver on the preparation of these lectures is attested by the masses of reading notes attached to each one. I wrote them out far more fully than was my wont and intended to publish them as soon as possible. But I still wanted to devote much study to them, and circumstances soon drew me into government service, which for years ended all systematic scholarly work.

CHAPTER IX

The War Effort

THE DOWNFALL of France in June 1940 was a hard emotional blow for many Americans who had traveled in France and for many others who remembered, from the First World War, the traditional comradeship in arms. Even more severe, however, was the realization that Britain might next succumb to the ferocious air attack of the Nazis. President Roosevelt, convinced that such a catastrophe would be a direct and immediate threat to American security, persuaded his fellow citizens, in intimate radio talks, that all possible aid, short of military intervention, should be accorded the embattled British.

Among other things the President, in the spring of 1941, sent on a mission of inquiry Colonel (later General) William J. Donovan, a hero of the First World War, a defeated Republican candidate for the governorship of New York, and at the time a successful corporation lawyer. Both an astute politician and a master of men, Donovan had a profound interest in and an exceptional knowledge of world affairs. After visits and professional discussions in many countries, the colonel reported favorably on Britain's chance of survival, provided it could count on unlimited aid from the United States. In addition, Donovan urged upon the President the crucial need for organizing a coordinated foreign intelligence service, without which the government could not hope to keep abreast of the world situation or formulate sound policies in time to make them effective. He proposed the establishment of a new agency, responsible directly to the White House, which could draw on the universities for experts with long foreign experience and specialized knowledge of the history, languages, and general conditions of various countries. The President was quickly convinced of this need. In the summer of 1941, that is, before Pearl Harbor, he set up the Office of the Coordinator of Information and appointed Donovan the first coordinator. He was directed to bring together and analyze the vast and diverse volume of foreign intelligence constantly flowing into Washington agencies from all parts of the world.

Donovan's was a truly charismatic personality. He had an exceptional gift for arousing the interest and enthusiasm of others and of enlisting their loyalty and devotion. Prominent among his early assoicates were Colonel Edward Buxton, Donovan's deputy, a quiet, kindly, and understanding business man, and General John Magruder, who had had long experience in military intelligence work and was completely won over by Donovan's plans. For the rest there was soon formed a veritable galaxy of prominent lawyers and bankers, manufacturers, foreign service officers, and merchants.

His first move was to name President James Phinney Baxter, III, an expert in American diplomatic history who was president of Williams College, as chairman of a select board of analysts, who in turn were to direct a larger staff of experts in various foreign fields. This program was submitted to a small luncheon group at the Tavern Club in Boston in July 1941. The response was decidedly favorable. To me the notion appealed as innovative and full of promise. Baxter, an old friend and former colleague, invited me to serve as chairman of the board and director of research. He and I promptly set to work to invite or persuade outstanding scholars in the social sciences to join the board and begin enlisting a staff.

One problem that probably had not occurred to either Donovan or to us was that of federal salaries, carefully classified by the Civil Service Commission. In 1941 the official schedule provided for a salary of $8,500 for the highest grade. This was meager, to say the least. It was exactly the equivalent of my Harvard salary, which I had supplemented to the tune

of $1,200 by repeating one of my courses at Radcliffe. Neither
I nor most other scholars could afford government service at
so severe a sacrifice, especially since it involved moving a
family to Washington. Only after long but futile arguments
with the civil service did Donovan take up this crucial question
with the President, who finally ruled that Donovan's agency
should not be subject to civil service regulations. Even so, I and
my colleagues were to receive only what we had been earning
at the universities, and during the war the highest civil service
grade was usually excluded from federal pay raises voted by
Congress. For us government service was no gold mine.

Anyone at all acquainted with official life in Washington
knows that the establishment of a new agency demands endless
effort and unremitting determination. The existing agencies
are quite naturally convinced that they are fulfilling their function and that the intervention of inexperienced interlopers will
not only diminish their own position, but will also lead to
duplication and confusion. All recognized the fundamental
principle that knowledge is power, which they had no inclination to share with an upstart.

This being so, as founders of the Research and Analysis
branch, we spent much time running hither and thither, ex-
plaining our objectives and our hopes, petitioning for toleration
and cooperation, and waving our presidential order. All this
was of little avail. In fact, we were badly hampered by our own
ignorance about the details of our mission. No one would or
could enlighten us as to what we should do and how to go
about it.

We decided before long that our wisest course would be to
collect and evaluate such information as came to us from the
State Department cables, the newspapers, radio intercepts, and
the military. We began to issue an attractive pamphlet, "The
War This Week," which consisted of a succinct review, ably
edited by the late Donald C. McKay. Although the most critical
intelligence, such as the Roosevelt-Churchill correspondence,
was, of course, withheld from us and from just about everyone
else, "The War This Week" proved a useful digest, and we soon
built up a considerable clientèle among high officials of the

government, who alone were eligible to receive it. But the very success of this initial effort provoked opposition. The matter was referred to the Joint Chiefs of Staff with the argument that important information was being bandied about town. The chiefs thereupon ordered its discontinuance, and Donovan for once lost his temper. Talking to me, he asserted that scholars no doubt were smart, but they were not discreet: "They are like chorus girls, who have beautiful legs and like to show them." I know that he felt the liquidation of "The War This Week" to be a serious setback to his basic plans, but he could console himself that it was abolished only because it was too good, too striking an example of the rightness of his concept.

As other branches of the Office of the Coordinator began to develop and impinge upon existing agencies, there was more and more surreptitious agitation in high places for its abolition. I must not say too much on this subject, because my knowledge of the detailed maneuvering is so fragmentary. But it is clear that after Pearl Harbor the situation changed drastically. No one will ever forget the shock of the Japanese surprise attack. It was a Sunday afternoon, and my wife and I were visiting the Corcoran Art Gallery. On leaving at dark we were met by newsboys hawking the latest reports. I hurried home, and then drove to the office, where Colonel Donovan and the chief staff members were assembled. With the utmost gravity he gave us a full report of the catastrophe and the American losses in men and materiel. None of us needed to be told that thenceforth all efforts on our part would have to be redoubled.

Under the direction of General Marshall, plans were soon being made for a counterblow to the Axis position by the invasion of North Africa. Much of the crucial undercover work was carried out under Donovan's direction. As a result of the useful studies made by the Research and Analysis (R and A) branch of the logistics of a landing and invasion and the invaluable role played by "consuls" such as Robert Murphy and William Eddy, the agency was renamed in June 1942 the Office of Strategic Services (OSS) and placed directly under the guidance and protection of the Joint Chiefs of Staff. Colonel Donovan was promoted to the rank of brigadier general, and

I took over as chief of the R and A branch when reasons of health obliged Baxter to withdraw.

Although I served as chief of R and A from September 1942 until the dissolution of the OSS in 1946, I find it difficult to recount its work and accomplishments. My chief claim to leadership was the extent of my published work in international relations, but I found myself for the first time in a strictly administrative position, which became ever more burdensome as the organization grew. By the end of the war, the staff comprised some hundreds of trained professionals, including men of such outstanding ability as Ralph Bunche. There was also a large number of able secretarial and clerical personnel.

I went to England in September 1942, in the company of the late Conyers Read, our learned and energetic chief of the British Empire section, and S. Wilmarth Lewis, the director of the already huge collection of published and unpublished materials that was being assembled on the most diverse problems of the war. In these days of fantastic speed and comfort in air travel, it is hard to recapture the conditions of 1942. Our transportation was a great lumbering seaplane operated by the American Export Airlines. It was equipped to sleep sixteen individuals on the long, tiresome trip to Newfoundland and thence to Ireland, whence a less monstrous machine would take us, with all windows sealed, to the Bristol airfield. Instead of sixteen passengers we numbered twenty-six, mostly Army officers. Under the circumstances we drew lots for the upper berths, while the losers (I among them) stretched out and sometimes slept head to foot on the lower bunks. The weather was fine, however, and the huge plane had a smooth passage once it got off the water.

At this time the OSS already had a substantial office in London, directed by William Phillips, a Foreign Service officer of ambassadorial rank and the younger brother of Dr. John C. Phillips, the ornithologist and employer of my youthful days. Colonel Donovan arrived for a few days of consultation with the divisional chiefs of the OSS and with their British counterparts. Like him, I visited British installations, discussed with American and British officials all aspects of the intelligence analysis problem, and made countless friends. Among these I cannot refrain from mentioning especially Colonel Alfred Gruenther and General Walter ("Beetle") Smith, with both of whom I was to work intimately in later years. These and other American officers had heard me lecture at the Army War College and treated me as a friend. Smith had just been appointed General Eisenhower's chief of staff, and Gruenther was one of his right-hand men.

In rereading the little diary I kept during my three weeks in England, I find an interesting reference to "Beetle Smith." "A pretty young man, very alert and very positive . . . I am sure that we shall get along very well with him. His opinion of the R and A is flattering in the extreme, but he reminded me that the prejudice of the military against civilians is a hard thing to overcome." These remarks, from so high a military officer, help to explain Smith's attitude as director of Central Intelligence in 1950, when he insisted that the Office of National Estimates was the crux of all intelligence work and did so much to establish cooperation among the various agencies. Of all this, and also of Gruenther's role in founding the National War College, more will be said later.

London, although partly demolished and in strict blackout after dark, made an excellent impression on the visitor. It was an unique example of voluntary austerity. Restaurant prices were appallingly high, yet the meals were frugal and unexciting. But people took it all in good spirit and even ignored air-raid warnings on the plea that most of them were futile.

While in London, I was able to fit in a couple of nonprofessional visits. I called on Harold Laski and found him more amiable than at Harvard. More interesting was my visit to Anna Freud, who was living with her mother and a brother in one of the suburbs. She was and no doubt still is a most charming and delightful lady. She inquired in detail about my brother Walter and about the Vienna analysts who had gone to the United States, notably Hanns Sachs, Grete Bibring, and Jenny Waelder, all of whom, through my brother, I had come to know well.

I think the reader may be amused by an account of a concert I attended at the Albert Hall for the benefit of United Aid to China. Sir Adrian Boult conducted the BBC Symphony Orchestra with Myra Hess as soloist. We were taken to our seats by beautiful Chinese girls in gorgeous native costume and then listened to an almost entirely German program: Mozart's "Haffner" Symphony, Beethoven's Fourth Piano Concerto, and Schumann's Concerto in A minor, for pianoforte. The final number, to be sure, was Variations on an Original Theme, by Elgar. This we omitted, as being perhaps anticlimactic. We were satisfied with a superb concert of enemy music, performed by an English orchestra for purposes of China relief. This was a long call from the fanaticism of World War I.

By and large I found as much confusion among the British agencies as among the American, due no doubt to the pressure under which all were working. An exception was the British Joint Intelligence Committee, which met weekly to coordinate information acquired by the various agencies and was presided over, not by the traditionally influential Admiralty, but by the Foreign Office. The British have always had a greater understanding of and respect for international relations than Americans, who tend to regard the State Department as at best a necessary evil. There was no question that the Americans had much to learn of secret intelligence operations from the more experienced and adept British.

Most of my work took me to Oxford, which was almost devoid of students and dons and had been given over to government work. The nearest agency to the R and A was the Interservice Topographical Division, a much smaller organization, and I think never as effective as its American counterpart. Another agency at Oxford was the press-reading group at All Souls, which culled what intelligence it could from foreign newspapers and broadcasts. I was astounded to find in its ranks some of my very good friends, whom I regarded as the most qualified students of international affairs: men such as Charles K. Webster, Alfred Zimmern, H. A. R. Gibb, David Mitrany, etc. I have never understood why the British failed to assign these men to crucial posts in the war effort. Clearly Donovan had a higher opinion of scholarship and made far greater and better use of the country's academics than did our British allies.

I returned home at the end of September, after several delays due to weather. I might interject here that though the Secret Intelligence branch of the OSS never became a major source of intelligence for our studies, we were infinitely obliged to it for the effective work of its representatives in Stockholm and Lisbon in obtaining for us German, Russian, and other newspapers, journals, and books without which many of our operations would have been impossible. Donovan's hunch that most of the needed information could be obtained from printed materials (often from quite aged books) was proved altogether correct. The strength of R and A lay in the research training and experience of its personnel.

As the war progressed, the Joint Chiefs of Staff assigned more and, indeed, even more difficult operational assignments to the OSS. These fascinated Donovan and gave full scope to his imagination. More and more of his attention was focused on these tasks, many of which required him to be abroad. Compared to plans for sabotage of enemy installations, aid and supplies to resistance groups, the penetration of enemy positions, etc., the work of the R and A lacked drama and excitement. Hence, the books that have been written on the OSS have little to say of it and devote themselves to the narrative of adventure and heroism. But Donovan never lost his interest in R and A and its work. On the contrary, he rated it highly and interfered little, though he never failed to have visiting notables shown around, if only to see men and women busy at desks or typewriters.

The work of the R and A was so varied and so conditioned by the requirements of the war that it is extremely difficult to give a coherent account of it. At first we were ignored, if not opposed, by other agencies, and most of our reports were unsolicited. Our Projects Committee decided which problems were important or apt to become so, and directed and criticized the product. The staff complained that first-rate studies never reached the people who should know of them. It is quite possible that instead of devoting myself to the organization and standards of the work, I should have made more of an effort to get around town and solicit customers. But this was simply not my nature, and I recalled, from my World War I experience, that if one shell in ten struck anything worth striking, the batting average of the artillery could be considered good. Like Donovan, I believed that if we could effectively fill a need which certainly existed, customers would eventually beat a pathway to our doors.

And so it was. In the planning of the invasion of North Africa, all sorts of abstruse information was required and the contributions of our African section, headed by Sherman Kent, who for many years was to play a key role in foreign intelligence work and actually wrote a book on the subject, were gratefully received. The landing in Sicily and the Italian campaign were to tax our Italian section, and here, if I am not mistaken, we first began to make careful target studies for Air Force bombardment.

By 1943 our staff had outgrown its Library of Congress quarters. The headquarters of the OSS, including the R and A, had been moved to the other end of town to a group of buildings evacuated by the Public Health Service at 23rd Street and E. A few blocks from there was an abandoned skating rink into which I agreed to move our staff, despite protests and jeers. Actually it was a great convenience to have the staff nearer at hand, and after much remodeling, the new quarters were fairly well adapted as well as airy and light. I forget how long the R and A was housed there, but it was not for long. Presently the entire branch, administration as well as staff, was moved into an apartment house at the corner of 23rd Street and E, not too far from the rest of the OSS. Naturally, such quarters, no more air conditioned than our previous lodgings, presented many inconveniences. But there was ample space, and we gradually adapted to it. I might add that the research units of the State Department and then of the new Central Intelligence Agency continued to be located in this apartment house until, years afterward, it was demolished to provide space for the extension of the State Department itself.

I hesitate to detail the many-sided work of the R and A

over several years, partly because I carried away no records whatever when I resigned in 1946, partly because in advanced age my memory has become dim and often untrustworthy, and finally because it is more or less invidious to speak of one activity while omitting others. It stands to reason that R and A reports were classified and therefore limited in circulation. But after some thirty years, all restrictions were removed, and they are now open to public inspection in the National Archives.

As the war progressed the burden of my work grew constantly as special units were sent to perform needed tasks abroad. By the end of the war there were R and A units in London, Caserta, Cairo, and Kunming. Fortunately, I was well supported in what needed to be done. The chief administrative officer, Louis Ream, was experienced and efficient. He took the entire budgeting process off my hands which, as anyone conversant with government knows, can be very time consuming indeed. My successive secretaries, Mrs. Mildred Brockdorff and Miss Frances Douglas were all that one could ask for and warded off many queries and complaints that could only have worried me. As it was, we were working six full days a week, on hot days and cold. If I remember correctly, it was only when the temperature rose above 90° that we were permitted to dismiss the staff and close shop. On many occasions, when urgent work had to be done, staff members would return to work in the evening, and, I should add, staff members of other agencies would come to assist in matters within their competence. I recall that my Harvard colleague, Alexander Gerschenkron, the eminent economic historian, who was then with the Federal Reserve Bank, could always be relied upon. Since he had complete command of Russian, he gave invaluable support on several projects. I cannot refrain from commending the devotion, loyalty, and spirit of cooperation among staff members, at least among those of the war agencies. These "Indians" are definitely the forgotten men in all histories of high policy and grand strategy.

Speaking of Russian affairs I need hardly emphasize the importance of every last shred of intelligence that could be

secured on that secretive country. Almost anyone would admit
that the outcome of the war hinged largely on the success or
failure of the Russian forces, which in turn depended largely
on the availability not only of tanks, airplanes, and trucks, but
also of munitions. How were we to form an independent judgment on Russian capabilities and needs? Very few of our
economists, even among the ablest, had any knowledge of the
organization and workings of either the Soviet or the Nazi
economy. The economics of the New Deal, which had brought
many of them to Washington, were too fascinating and immediately important to study the functioning of the dictatorships.

Our economics section, headed by my distinguished colleague and life-long friend Edward S. Mason, was extraordi-
narily able, imaginative, and dynamic, staffed by a number of
brilliant young scholars, who were for many later years to play
important roles in Washington. They had no difficulty in
recognizing the problems and mapping out approaches to
their solution. There was only one serious obstacle—ignorance
of the Russian language and hence inability to read many of
the crucial materials.

According to Geroid T. Robinson, professor of Russian history at Columbia and author of a well-known study, *Rural
Russia under the Old Regime* (based on two years of archival
work in Russia in the 1930s), ignorance of the language vitiated
the value of the reports on Russian affairs produced by the
economics section. The latter replied that such work could not
be abandoned to the Russian section because it knew no
economics. Actually, I think Robinson and some of his staff
knew more of Russian economics than the economics section
knew of the Russian language; but fortunately, it never became
necessary to rule apodictically on this important issue. Both
Mason and Robinson were outstanding men, whose prime interest was in getting the work well done. It was soon arranged
that on Russian problems appropriate members of each section
should work together. This was the natural and successful solution. The R and A studies on Russian needs and productive
capabilities were among the most effective of our products.
Towards the end of the conflict, various sections working

together produced an extended analysis of Soviet capabilities and intentions that may justly be called the first national intelligence estimate. In the budding "cold war," it was highly regarded by General Embick and the Joint Chiefs of Staff and may well be described as the very acme of intelligence analysis.

Before leaving the economics section, more than mere mention must be made of its contributions on the German side, where the economists had a better command of the language and where, too, close collaboration with the German section was gradually established. Using captured Nazi materiel, the economists discovered the key to the serial numbers of captured truck tires, engines, and other Nazi industrial products. Presently they could tell with astonishing accuracy which factory was producing what amount of what product, where the bottlenecks were (as with ball bearings), and which plants it was urgently necessary to destroy by bombardment. Similarly, by the careful analysis of the local Nazi press (collected in Stockholm), it became possible to determine, through the officer obituaries, where different Nazi units were and sometimes what their losses were in recent engagements. I submit that these items were military intelligence of the highest order, attained by altogether new and ingenious methods. No other nation during the war was, or so far as I know, has since been able to bring such concentrated intellectual power to bear on wartime problems as did Donovan's R and A.

During the concluding year of the war, the German section had the crucial role of studying for the occupation and military governments of territories conquered from the enemy. This section was peculiarly fitted for this assignment because it had on its staff a number of German refugees with considerable firsthand knowledge about conditions and procedures. I think here of the late Hajo Holborn, professor of history at Yale, the late Franz Neumann, of the New School for Social Research, and Herbert Marcuse, whose later revolutionary role was then indiscernible. These senior scholars were supported by younger men, almost all of whom were eventually to fill chairs at our major universities. To mention Franklin L. Ford, Carl E. Schorske, Robert L. Wolff, H. Stuart Hughes, and Paul

Sweet is only to cite those whom I knew best. Holborn was later to write an excellent book on occupation policies and military government, and all that need be said here is that by dint of hard and sustained work the R and A was able to make a major contribution in a difficult and troublesome field.

I do not remember that members of our staff had any important part in the studies for the organization of the United Nations. These were firmly controlled by Leo Pasvolsky of the State Department, who drew on his own staff for support. I was one of a small group of Donovan's staff that accompanied him to the San Francisco Conference in the spring of 1945, but my function was primarily to be available if R and A help was required. Actually Robinson and I spent most of our two weeks working out memoranda on our relations to the Soviets. General Embick laid these before a select group of high army officers and we had an exciting afternoon of discussion with them.

Wartime in Washington meant mostly hard work in often inadequate quarters and frequently in unbearable humidity and heat. In the early part of the war my wife and I were divorced after having drifted apart for some time. In 1943 I remarried, my bride being Rowena Morse Nelson, the divorced wife of a professor at Duke University. She brought me four additional children of varying ages. We were fortunate to rent a comfortable, middle-aged house on Newark Street, just above 34th, where we remained until our return to Cambridge in 1946. The children liked their schools and easily made friends and once or twice a year we were able to get away for ten days to Capon Springs, a mid-nineteenth century resort most of which had burned down years ago. The surroundings were beautiful and the accommodations comfortable but simple. The spring water was as good as I have ever tasted, and since the inn had a farm attached to it, we had enough meat to eat, which was not always true in Washington.

Capon Springs had a small golf course attached to it, and my wife and I could not resist trying our hand. The results were challenging and the mountain air stimulating. Like many others, we became enamored of the game. After the war, when we went to Florida annually to check on property owned by my wife's family, we began to take golf lessons and to get increasing satisfaction from the game. Back in Washington during the war there was no chance to play except on Sundays at the public course in Rock Creek Park. The course was excellent, but attracted almost a thousand players on Sundays. My wife and I still think back occasionally on that precious day of rest, when we tumbled out of bed at 6:00 a.m., drove through the Park just as the ducks were lifting their heads from under their wings. On arrival at the course we racked up our clubs, had a very decent breakfast in the lunchroom and around 8 a.m. were able to start out, always with another couple. The waiting, especially at the short holes, was something incredible, but everyone seemed patient and courteous. We were all in the same boat. We wanted to play golf so we put up with war conditions. If lucky, we were home by three in the afternoon.

I am one of those pathetic individuals who has always loved sports but has never had much aptitude for any of them. I felt obliged to give up tennis when I noticed the ball hitting me in the tummy before I could see it coming. My golf has been better than my tennis, but I was forty-eight when I took it up and at that age not much can be expected. At times I have played in the lower 90s or upper 90s but I consider anything around 100 quite satisfactory. In any event neither my wife nor I have ever flagged in our devotion to the game, which provides exercise in beautiful surroundings, as well as other satisfactions. On our return to Cambridge we joined the Oakley Country Club, an old but well-kept course overlooking Boston, but now surrounded by residential areas. There we have played in spring and autumn, while in our long summers at Annisquam we have had membership in the Essex Country Club, where tennis is much more popular than golf, leaving a splendid 18-hole course to less than a hundred golf-playing members. Any golfer will willingly say that this is about as close to paradise as one is apt to come in this vale of tears.

CHAPTER X
A Dual Existence

MY CAREER as a Washington bureaucrat was interrupted before long by the intrusion of novel, but nonetheless genuine, historical problems. In autumn 1943, I recived an invitation to call on Secretary Cordell Hull at his apartment. I was baffled but, of course, accepted. I found him alone and at leisure, and we had a pleasant cup of tea together. He spoke to me at length about American policy towards Vichy France, which had from the start been distasteful to the American public.

Despite the public clamor, Hull was convinced that our policy had been wise, that we had derived many substantial advantages by maintaining contact with Vichy, and that, if the American public had any notion of the complexities involved, it would see the situation in a different and more favorable light. He asked whether, as a professional historian with all the records placed at my disposal, I would undertake a retrospective analysis of the past few years of our relations with France. While much intrigued by the suggestion, I reminded the secretary that I already had a full-time job and at best could work on the proposed study only in the evenings, which would delay completion considerably. Moreover, I could not, as a professional historian, undertake to write an apologia. I would have to be free to demand any and all records, to consult all those who were directly involved, and above all to express my own conclusions.

Hull's reply was that he had not been thinking of an apologia nor had he supposed that I would undertake one. He simply thought that greater knowledge of the facts would influence American opinion. If, he remarked, the government's policy had been wrong, it was important to know how and why. I might interject here that the secretary was unwittingly touching on a problem that was to be of overriding importance in the future. It seems to me that if the government had taken the country more into its confidence on South Vietnam and had relied less on secrecy and subterfuge, one of the worst crises of recent American history might have been alleviated if not obviated.

Having agreed to the secretary's proposition, I began thenceforth to live a double existence. Each day the State Department arranged to have what records I desired deposited in a locked room where I could work in the evening undisturbed. My day shaped up in this way: My wife was good enough to make the tedious trip to town by bus each day to join me at lunch and so provide a break in the day's business. I tried to get home for dinner by six, after which my wife and I went off to a driving range and practiced golf for half an hour before I hurried back to my nocturnal assignment. At times she would return with me to the State Department and, while I studied the official dispatches, would scan the printed newspaper and magazine material. We aimed to get back home by 10:30.

I need hardly say that the job, while arduous, was intensely interesting. It is not often that a historian has a chance to work with such recent materials. Furthermore, Admiral Leahy, now back in Washington, supported the project wholeheartedly and discussed many matters with me at length. Ray Atherton, in the department, gave me all possible aid, as did Robert D. Murphy, who was deeply involved with the preparation for the invasion of North Africa.

By dint of hard and systematic work, I was able to present Secretary Hull and Admiral Leahy with a first draft of my study towards the end of 1944. This draft was read by a number of the top officials of the department, all of whom were delighted with it. One might conclude that their pleasure reflected relief at my generally favorable conclusions. But I think it derived chiefly from my demonstrated conviction that our Vichy policy had given us an invaluable listening post on the continent, an opportunity both to maintain contact with a traditional ally and to use our influence to restrain the forces making for collaboration with the Nazis, and a certain hold on the French navy and colonial empire.

This completes the first phase of my trials and tribulations with our Vichy policy. The question at once arose whether this enlightening account of our problem should not be published. The decision was decidedly in favor, but I could not hope to act on it for some time, because after the liberation of France in 1944, Pétain, Laval, and other Vichy leaders were put on trial for treason. The published records of the trials were extremely voluminous, and it was no simple matter to analyze them and also keep up with the numerous volumes of recollections and experiences that began to multiply. The eventual publication was, therefore, delayed.

The six months just before and just after the end of the Japanese War were for me a period of such confusion that I search in vain for any guiding theme. The R and A was at the height of its power and influence and so busy that it constantly demanded more of my time. My own university was the first to honor it by conferring upon me at commencement, 1945, the honorary degree of LL.D., with a most appropriate citation making me the representative of the numerous members of the Harvard faculty who had gone to Washington and contributed to the outcome of the conflict.

Hard upon this happy event came an invitation from General William J. Donovan to join him and a few of his staff in a hasty mission to China, where preparations were being made for secret operations against the Japanese occupying forces. I think the general thought of this as a useful break in a stiff routine, for the R and A contingents in various places were all, so far as I knew, operating smoothly and effectively. That was largely the work of William Applebaum, a member of our staff and an unusually capable efficiency expert. Applebaum had just returned from an extended visit to all R and A outposts, where he had effected many valuable improvements in organization and operation. The outpost chiefs invariably congratulated themselves on having survived the "Apple-Bombing."

I found all in order at the R and A posts and for the rest immensely enjoyed seeing some of the gorgeous scenery at the mouth of the Shatt-el-Arab, the great oil refineries at Abadan, the tea plantations on Ceylon and the brief glimpse of India and China.

Just as we were leaving China, news came of the Japanese surrender. I think I should say that the R and A and I believe the OSS as a whole, had no important part in the war in the Pacific. At the beginning, after the loss of the Philippines, every effort was made to assemble all possible information about the islands, and General MacArthur had vast quantities of intelligence collected from former American businessmen, educators, etc. for his planners. But the general had, from the outset, determined to have his own intelligence staffs and had insisted that everything in the Pacific theater should be under his control. On several occasions he or his subordinates made efforts to enroll R and A personnel, but always on the condition that they sever all connections with the OSS and allow themselves to be integrated with his own intelligence unit. To this Donovan would never agree, so we heard little of the war against Japan, except from the Chinese angle.

The situation started to change after the surrender of Germany when all efforts became concentrated on the Pacific. The R and A was gradually brought into the picture through the intervention of General S. W. Embick, who had been recalled from retirement by General Marshall to serve as chairman of a political strategy group, with the mission to study such political problems as might confront the armed forces as they advanced into new territories. Embick, a highly educated and keenly intellectual man, had almost immediately recognized that the R and A could do invaluable background work toward the solution of his problems. So far as the Pacific was concerned, his question was whether it was essential to bring the Soviet armies into the war against Japan at any cost, or whether, if cut off entirely from the home islands, the huge Japanese forces in China could long resist surrender.

The reply of R and A was anything but Delphic: It was quite unnecessary to offer the Soviets any concessions to induce them to intervene, for it was unthinkable that a great power with a high stake in East Asia would allow itself to be excluded from the peace settlement. Intervene the Soviets certainly would, but only at the last possible moment, so as to minimize their losses. And as for the second part of the question, we were convinced that if the Japanese Islands could be completely blockaded and all connections with the Chinese mainland severed, the armies in China, deprived of essential munitions and supplies, could not possibly hold out.

It is common knowledge, of course, that none of these arguments persuaded the military authorities. One can easily understand their fear of massive losses if an amphibious invasion of Japan should become necessary. Hence the unexpected dropping of the first atomic bombs on Hiroshima and Nagasaki. No one will deny that they accomplished their purpose and probably saved countless American lives. But in R and A the general opinion prevailed that Japan could have been effectively blockaded by sea and land and would, for that reason, have been forced to surrender before long in any case. The thought of the new atomic age filled us with horror, and we wondered whether in the circumstances the game was worth the candle. Possibly, the atomic age was coming anyway, from one direction or another, but it would have been at least some consolation if the first step had been taken by others.

Almost one of the first moves made by President Truman after the surrender of Japan was to order the dissolution of the OSS. General Donovan was allowed to resign without much expression of gratitude, and a committee was set up to decide on the division of the carcass. I was not one of those who were brought into the deliberations of the judges, nor had I expected to be, for I never had the slightest interest in the jockeyings for influence and power. Without having specific knowledge of all the maneuverings of the autumn, I was given to understand that the President acted on the advice of the Bureau of the Budget, but I suspect other powerful influences were also brought to bear.

Some months later the President quite unexpectedly conferred on me the highest civilian award, the Medal for Merit, "for extraordinary fidelity and exceptionally meritorious conduct." The citation, over the President's own signature, noted that as chief of the Research and Analysis branch of the Office of Strategic Services Langer "was charged with the collection, intensive analysis and dissemination of social, political, economic, and topographic intelligence concerning many regions of the world. At the request of the Joint Chiefs of Staff, the State Department, the War Department, the Navy Department and various other agencies, he directed and led in pioneering the production of vast quantities of studies, surveys, handbooks, and guides which were of inestimable value in the prosecution of the war. Few operations of such scope have ever been carried out in time of war by the research brilliance and prodigious effort of one man. He distinguished himself by the manner in which he discharged his responsibilities and his accomplishments reflect great credit upon himself and upon the United States Government."

No one could ask for more lavish praise than this. Yet it seems likely that when, in the autumn of 1945, the President precipitously ordered the liquidation of the OSS, he had but little knowledge of the organization and possibly even less of the R and A. The one redeeming feature was that among the ruins of Donovan's great agency, one wall was left standing intact—the R and A. The Bureau of the Budget recommended its assignment in toto to the State Department, the agency that in peacetime needed its services most and yet had no comparable establishment of its own. Colonel Alfred McCormack, an official with long experience in military intelligence, was appointed as special assistant to the Secretary of State to coordinate all intelligence operations within the department. I, who had never even met Colonel McCormack, was to continue to serve under him as chief of R and A. So far as my branch was concerned, everything went on much as before, except that the top personnel left in ever-increasing numbers to return to their universities.

McCormack's assignment was no sinecure. Few officials of the State Department welcomed the incursion of intelligence specialists, since they were firmly convinced that, reading the diplomatic traffic, they knew all they needed to know about foreign affairs. McCormack soon became involved in an epic organizational conflict. While he insisted that all the intelligence work of the department should be consolidated, the secretary finally yielded to the permanent officials and decided that the R and A staff should be broken up, and its regional sections assigned to the various regional desks. McCormack, who felt deeply on the subject, resigned at once, and I was appointed to succeed him. My sympathies were all with his views, but I agreed to serve for six months from February 1946 and make a real effort to get the program to work. I was well acquainted with many of the chief officials of the department, and I think succeeded reasonably well in establishing coordinated action through an Intelligence Committee. But I did not flatter myself that a real solution had been found and was anything but sorry when my term as Special Assistant to the Secretary of State for Research and Intelligence ended and my good friend, Colonel William Eddy, agreed to take over and wrestle with the problem.

It had always been my intention, once the war was over, to return to my university, resume my teaching, and devote all available time to my projected volume on the early nineteenth century for the Rise of Modern Europe series. Indeed, I had no desire to continue with studies in diplomatic history. The Vichy study was a sort of "extra-tour," dictated by circumstances.

But fate determined otherwise. Well before I left Washington to rejoin my family at Annisquam in August 1946, I had allowed myself to be lured into another historical enterprise, and one of major dimensions. The Council on Foreign Relations had obtained from the Rockefeller Foundation a substantial four-year grant to finance the writing of a scholarly history of American policy during the entire war. I was the obvious man, it argued, to do the job, which would be of national interest and importance. I protested, but not too much, because the assignment was challenging and because, frankly, I was relieved not to have to lecture for some years. Having found that, as in the case of the Vichy study, the official papers would be available to me, and having been promised access by Admiral Leahy to such Chiefs of Staff documents as had a bearing on policy, I proceeded to enlist the full-time collaboration of Dr. S. Everett Gleason, whom I had known and liked for years and with whom I had been associated in the R and A.

I then discussed the matter at lunch with President Conant of Harvard, only to find him lukewarm at best. He doubted whether the Harvard Corporation would agree to grant me another four-years leave and seemed to think that, with my great knowledge, I could conduct my undergraduate work with my left hand, leaving the guidance of graduate students and the writing of the history to my right hand. I pointed out that in the social sciences even the preparation of lectures in an under-graduate course required constant reading and study and that the new project would involve a tremendous amount of re-search and even travel. But he remained essentially uncon-vinced and finally suggested that I discuss the matter with Provost Paul Buck, who was largely handling matters of this kind during the president's absence in Washington.

Buck was a professional historian and a specialist in Ameri-can history. My conference with him was a relatively simple matter, for he saw at once the great value of making available to the public a competent and coherent account of the war. He was worried about my graduate students, but completely satis-fied when I blithely said that I would offer a full-year seminar, each year, at no expense to the university. I entered upon this commitment without realizing all its implications. With the return of young men from the war, the universities were quickly swamped by students at all grades. I found that instead of the usual eight or nine students, I had for several years as many as eighteen qualified and serious students, which meant an alto-gether unexpected burden of discussion meetings and grading of reports.

Without losing much time, Gleason and I managed to rent office space in Harvard Square just behind the Widener Library. For a few months at least, I had the added services of my excel-lent secretary Frances Douglas. We collected all kinds of pub-lished materials and occasionally felt obliged to interrupt our

work by prolonged visits to the Washington archives and consultations with officials. These visits alternated with stays in
New York City to examine the voluminous Morgenthau Papers,
and to Hyde Park to exploit those Roosevelt Papers that had
been ordered and catalogued. It was not long before we realized that we had been entirely too optimistic in thinking we
could complete the work in four years, especially since we were
determined to produce more than a diplomatic chronicle and
to attempt to set American policy in the political, economic,
and military framework of four years of war.

Meanwhile, my favorite editor, Alfred A. Knopf, was busy
producing the Vichy study, which we decided to call *Our Vichy
Gamble*, reflecting the chance we took in preferring the hated
Vichy regime to the glamor of De Gaulle's Free French movement. My reading of the proceedings of the Pétain and Laval
trials only reinforced my earlier conclusions. It would have been
pleasanter for me to have been able to join the chorus praising
De Gaulle, but I was forced to conclude that Pétain, for all his
political predilections and obvious senility, did what he could
under trying and dangerous circumstances, to protect the
French people from the worst aspects of Nazi domination.
Even Laval, while he committed the stupendous blunder of
publicly wishing for a Nazi victory, seems to have thought he
was working for the best of his country. Fully convinced of the
coming German victory, he thought a friendly though defeated
France might fare better than the recalcitrant victims of Hitler's
fury.

Our Vichy Gamble was published in April 1947 and at once
created a sensation, for it was the first study of a wartime problem based on the official records. Just about every commentator
reviewed it at some length. I was all ready for a general and
severe panning, so was rather gratified by the general tone of
the commentaries. Few writers tried to label it an official apol-
ogy. On the contrary, many noted that my views could be re-
futed on the basis of the material I so generously supplied.
Most of the critics thought it a well-written, exciting book, interesting whether one accepted its conclusions or not. Even
Eric Sevareid, who saw nothing persuasive in the argument,

held it to be "a completely fascinating account," and *Time*, which published my picture with the famous caption "Expediency First," conceded that the book was "the most thorough and respectable defense the United States policy had had." There were, of course, those like Lewis Gannett and Leon Edel who found little if anything to say in its favor. But my historical colleagues rated it highly. Carlton J. H. Hayes of Columbia, recently American ambassador to Spain, wrote: "It is authentic *history*, fully documented, objectively presented, lucidly phrased. It is as illuminating as it is interesting and sane." Lindsay Rogers praised it and Leo Gershoy declared that I had made "a monumental historical contribution," while Arthur Schlesinger, Jr. thought "Langer fully establishes the essential correctness of our Vichy policy." Even at a later date, so competent a critic as Eugene V. Rostow (writing in *World Politics*, I, 1949) could not overcome his ambivalence. He thought I had seen everything through the eyes of a small collaborationist clique at Vichy and had failed to appreciate the degree of support for De Gaulle. His conclusion was strange to say the least: "All the standard reasons advanced in defense of our Vichy policy turned out to be wrong. Yet," he argued, "the policy was right, not for the reasons given by Langer, but because at the time of our weakness it seemed the least dangerous of alternatives."

Since I was never arrogant enough to think I had found the answer to even the less thorny problems, I took what adverse criticism there was in my stride. But I became genuinely disturbed when, within a couple of months of publication, several French banks and a few individuals began to challenge statements in the book and threaten me with libel actions. To this end they sent a special agent to New York who discussed with prominent corporation lawyers the ways and means to set things right.

It so happened that the French agent turned to two of the leading law offices of New York, namely Sullivan and Cromwell and Coudert Brothers, and, to my great good luck, were then referred to Allen Dulles and Henry Hyde, respectively, who were partners in the firms and had been my associates and

friends in the OSS. These gentlemen, after reading the voluminous records of the two French banks during the war and producing the judgments of three high French courts (especially
that of the National Commission of Purification) to the effect
that their conduct had been "above reproach," set themselves
to explain that I was a professional historian in good standing,
had been a high official of the government, had based my account on official documents supposedly trustworthy, and that I
had no interest nor intention to denigrate the reputation of any
Frenchman.

Letters passed frequently between New York and Paris, and
I went to New York for personal conferences with the French
agent. I explained that the sources of my information were wartime reports of several important American agencies, reports
which must have been planted by enemies of the banks or of
the Vichy regime. I agreed to make the necessary changes in
any future editions and in the forthcoming French edition. I
promised further to publish in the *New York Times* and in two
Montreal newspapers an explanatory statement.

The agent expressed himself as well satisfied with my response to his charges and the matter was closed on the above
basis. But the affair dragged on from June to December 1947,
when the *New York Times* finally printed the statement, with
my regrets that misleading reports had led me to malign a
number of patriotic and incorruptible Frenchmen. But I may
as well mention here the quite unpleasant aftermath. In May
1948, while my wife and I were enjoying a short stay in Paris
after a strenuous lecture tour in England, I received a cable
from my colleague Gleason saying that plans were still afoot to
start a libel suit, and that my New York lawyer thought it best
that I should be warned. Knowing that the French police regularly scanned all incoming messages, I took this almost as noti-
fication that the police would soon be on my trail. I must say
that I did not relish a further stay, even in beautiful Paris, or
a trial in courts with which I was quite unfamiliar. My wife
and I spent a couple of uncomfortable, not to say apprehensive
days until we were safely aboard the steamer at Cherbourg and
heard the engines turning over. Perhaps the whole episode was

based on a misunderstanding. In any event, nothing more was heard of this alleged threat.

As though my unexpected tour of duty in the State Department in 1946, our desperate efforts to get on with the projected history of American foreign policy, and the tribulations of *Our Vichy Gamble* were not enough, two other projects cut in on my available working hours. Late in May 1945 Roger Scaife, the director of the Harvard University Press, had proposed that I edit an entirely new historical atlas, consisting of perhaps 300 maps and costing about $100,000. The existing historical atlases, though derived for the most part from the excellent German folio atlases of the 1870s and 1880s, were outmoded and inadequate. With the world moving at a dizzy tempo, it was urgently necessary to bring the old material up to date and to add the many maps required to cover modern developments. I have always loved maps and I took to the idea enthusiastically. I outlined three folio volumes—ancient, medieval, modern— which could then be reduced and divided into special sections —American, European, East Asian, Latin American, even African—to be sold chiefly to meet the needs of college courses. I was convinced that expense could be minimized by reducing the data on many maps and printing them in black and white, which in many instances would be the most effective medium. I consulted at length with Arthur H. Robinson, one of the chief geographers of the R and A and a man of unusual imagination and technical ingenuity. We were all agreed and all enthusiastic. The Syndics of the Press approved the project and on July 9 the Harvard Corporation voted to appropriate $100,000 to it. I began to give much thought to the enterprise, as did Robinson, and we actually began to plot out some of the maps. I wanted to go back and at least attempt a map showing the drift of the continents. I read the relevant German literature on the subject, which was very persuasive. But when I consulted one of my expert friends, he promptly replied: "Bill, don't touch that. It's all a lot of hokum." Ironically, he himself, some thirty years later, discovered some of the conclusive paleontological evidence for the drifting apart of the continents, and the theory is now generally accepted.

The rest of the atlas story can be quickly told. The study of costs indicated that merely drafting the maps would cost about $85,000, and that the corporation's stipulation that the whole enterprise be completed in three years was entirely visionary. It was probably fortunate for me that the project had to be abandoned, but now, after the passage of another generation, the need has become even greater, and nothing has been done to meet it. The job is actually far too much for a single scholar. A commission of five or six paid historians, geographers, and designers should direct the undertaking and organize teams of consultants. This could, of course, be done only if some great foundation were to appropriate not a couple of hundred thousand, but several million dollars to the project. I am sorry that pressure of other work made it impossible for me to press for some action. I am astonished, however, that this major need in the field of humanistic studies has continued to be overlooked.

Another, much pleasanter, aspect of my government service was as a member of the Board of Consultants of the National War College. During the 1930s I had gone to Washington regularly in the spring to lecture at what was then the Army War College. Through a course of lectures by outside authorities, the select members of the war college had been given an opportunity to hear objectively about some major problems of foreign affairs and to have an hour or more of hard-headed discussion. The National War College, established in 1945, was more ambitious. It was to consist not only of a small selection of the most promising officers of all the services, but also of delegates from the State Department, from the Central Intelligence Agency, the FBI, the Treasury, and other agencies actively involved in foreign affairs. During the war I had met Major General Alfred Gruenther, who told me how much he had profited from my Army War College lectures. He was now, under Admiral Hill, the deputy commandant of the new National War College, and requested my help in planning the curriculum for the new institution. My chief proposal was that the student officers be required to prepare at least one fairly lengthy report. After all, I argued, how can officers hope to judge the soundness of reports submitted to them, unless they had had at least some experience in grubbing through the sources, noting the differences of opinion and the standards of research, etc.

This proposal appealed to Gruenther and it was practiced for a year or two. But the pressure of a very intensive program, the difficulties of getting various source materials quickly enough, and the general unfamiliarity with systematic research led to its modification and temporary abandonment. But the National War College, on whose advisory board I served from 1946 to 1951, proved a great success. The students were carefully selected to this highest of military schools, and other agencies soon came to appreciate the value of having at least a few of their men get a basic understanding of modern warfare and military problems. For a few years the chief difficulty was that outstanding students were recalled by their services for some important mission. But eventually, the Chiefs of Staff and other high authorities realized that this was merely robbing Peter to pay Paul, and that it was a matter of importance to have even the ablest men complete their year at the College. The training was also stimulating for those few scholars who were appointed periodically to the faculty and who, in exchange for their contribution in the field of international relations, were given valuable insight into the military aspect of national policy.

I have not, over the past twenty years, maintained close contact with the college, though for a few years I gave occasional lectures. I was the more gratified, therefore, to receive the text of Vice Admiral M. G. Bayne's commandant's address of welcome to the incoming, twenty-ninth class of 1974–1975. In an admirably organized review of the objectives and procedures of the ten-month course, the commandant noted that the appointment as student to the college by either military or civilian agencies, was itself a clear recognition of achievement and promise, just as graduation from the course was practically an assurance of advancement to high rank. I was naturally pleased to learn that over the years the conception of the college as the highest school for government officials, remained unaltered, and even more gratified to read that whereas a few years ago almost no written work had been demanded of students, now four short papers were required and all students were urged to undertake a "major research paper" on a topic relating to the national security. Toward the end of the course, each class is now taken on a three-week tour of four or five critical areas, given an opportunity to see conditions for themselves, discuss current problems with American representatives, and to meet leading foreign officials. The commandant's remark that this tour was in no sense to be regarded as a junket was surely gratuitous. The National War College is not only an important demonstration of interservice education at a high level, but also an institution of which the country can be very proud.

CHAPTER XI

The Tribulations
of a Historian

WHILE I was still engaged with the French in the controversy over *Our Vichy Gamble,* an even more violent though less dangerous storm of words was brewing in our own country. By way of preface I should say that while, in the 1930s, the question of responsibility for World War I was becoming quiescent, a new form of "revisionism" was flourishing in the United States. The erstwhile isolationists found new arguments in the revelations of congressional investigations and other materials, which, they alleged, demonstrated the stupidity and futility of United States intervention in 1917. Woodrow Wilson had been taken in camp by British propagandists and had been lured into active participation in the war by American munitions makers, bankers, and businessmen with a high stake in an Allied victory.

On June 9, 1947 Walter Trohan, of the *Chicago Tribune,* the chief organ of the neoisolationists, happened to read in the annual report of the Rockefeller Foundation of the substantial grant made to the Council on Foreign Relations to arrange for the writing of a history of American policy before and during the recent war "calculated to offset any debunking of war aims and policies." In the exact words of the Rockefeller Report: "The Committee on studies of the Council on Foreign Relations is concerned that the debunking journalistic campaign following World War I should not be repeated and believes that the American public deserves a clear and competent statement of our basic aims and activities during the Second World War." Trohan saw in this passage a concerted plan to choke off journalistic comment or criticism. The passage was admittedly badly worded, but it only meant that controversy and recrimination might be put on a sounder footing, if more of the facts could first be presented by competent historians.

Trohan's opening gun was presently followed by a heavy artillery barrage opened by no less a person than Charles A. Beard, whose article "Who's to Write the History of the War?" appeared in the *Saturday Evening Post* on October 4, 1947. Beard, a senior member of the historical profession, had long taught at Columbia, was active in many reform organizations, and had authored numerous books on American politics and American life. I do not remember ever having made his personal acquaintance, but I had read a number of his publications and was well aware that he had a large and devoted following among those who were critical of the political, military, and social institutions and policies of the administration. A later generation of youth clubbed all these institutions together under the term "the Establishment," so perhaps one might call Beard an early pioneer of anti-Establishmentarianism. He had been dead opposed to President Roosevelt's policies and especially to our intervention in the war. The same was true of the *Saturday Evening Post,* so author and publisher were entirely congenial.

Beard's article was directed chiefly against government agencies and officials who made their records available to some well-disposed individual, who was then expected to write something akin to an apologia. It was clear to him that the Rockefeller Foundation and the Council on Foreign Relations were intent on getting the official account before the public in order to head off hostile criticism, and Langer was their man. He had already had privileged access to State Department and other records in writing his *Vichy Gamble.* "Presumably," he would again enjoy special favors denied to others. In Beard's opinion "subsidized histories of this kind, prepared to serve a purpose fixed in advance, are more likely to perpetuate errors than to eliminate them. . . . Official archives must be open to all citizens on equal terms, with special privileges for none; inquiries must be wide and deep as well as uncensored, and the competition of ideas in the forum of public opinion must be free from political interests or restraints."

Beard's plea was at once supported by the *Washington Post,* the *New York Sun* (in which George E. Sokolsky described the Council on Foreign Relations as "a stuffed-shirt affair of high-brow internationalists who meet occasionally to discuss the affairs of the world"), and, of course, by other isolationist papers. The ensuing debate was too lengthy and acrimonious to be repeated here. I wrote a letter to the editor of the *Saturday Evening Post* pointing out that Gleason and I had not been given a monopoly of state department records and that there was not and could not be any question of censorship of our conclusions. I suggested that if Beard's search for the truth had carried him even so far as the State Department Bulletin, he could have read, in the May 25, 1947 number, that "it is the policy of the Department that its records be made available to persons not officials of the U.S. Government as liberally as circumstances permit" and lays down the procedures to be followed by applicants. I might interject here that one of Beard's stoutest supporters and one of the most active isolationist writers, Charles Tansill, had in fact been allowed to see State Department records and, what is even more astounding, that Beard himself had never once in his long career, asked to see even a single document. Incidentally, he had accepted a subsidy of $25,000 from the Social Science Research Council to write an earlier book on the national interest, but, he argued—though on what basis remained obscure—that his subsidy was an entirely different matter from ours. So, no doubt, was the $500,000 subsidy given James T. Shotwell for his multivolume *Economic and Social History of the War.* It evidently mattered greatly who got the subsidy from whom and for what.

These points seem to have made little impression on the editor of the *Saturday Evening Post,* who had throughout the war been a bitter opponent of the Roosevelt policies. He replied to me that he would gladly publish my letter if reduced to about 150 words, and to this Beard might then respond as he wished. This offer I rejected out of hand: If the *Post* could afford to give Beard half a printed page for his original attack, it could certainly allow me space for an adequate reply. Pleading that his journal was really anxious to publish my reply, the *Post* editor offered to give me perhaps an additional fifty words. It was clear that this great organ with its huge circulation was not going to publish anything contrary to its own editorial views. I turned elsewhere, and had no difficulty in getting the *Washington Post* (Nov. 9, 1947) to publish my letter in reply to Beard in extenso. To this, Beard published in the same paper, a feeble and evasive reply a week later.

This rather disagreeable episode might be closed by referring to Beard's address to the American Political Science Association as reported in the *Washington Evening Star* on December 30, 1947, when he went out of his way to say that he had no objection to Professor Langer but thought that the materials should be made available to all. This was the last that was heard of the redoubtable Beard, but the *Chicago Daily Tribune* in a a long article on January 16, 1948 entitled "A Hired Liar" launched a violent attack on *Foreign Affairs*, the journal of the Council on Foreign Relations, in which an article by me appeared in company with others such as Mr. Stimson, Mr. McClary, Sumner Welles, and Anthony Eden. Here was sufficient evidence of an interventionist, Anglophile clique. The anonymous writer ended by expressing confidence that Langer would give them their money's worth.

While Beard's charges bordered on the ridiculous, based as they were on "presumptions" and on practically condemning a book before it was written, to say nothing of the errors and misleading statements, I would not want to suggest that there was not then and still is a serious problem of access to government documents. In my opinion *Our Vichy Gamble* did serve to enlighten public opinion about the objectives of our French policy and so headed off much speculation and futile argument. Despite the unfortunate phrasing in the Rockefeller Annual Report, the objective of the Council on Foreign Relations (which existed for the free exchange of all sorts of ideas) was simply to provide the basic facts on which judgment could be passed. Gleason and I were asked to do the job, because we were known to be well qualified, independent, and objective historians. No one in or out of the State Department would have thought for a moment that we would lend ourselves to a whitewash or even that it would be possible to influence our opinion—and no one ever did.

But this still leaves the question of whether public records should be made available to all on equal terms, and after what interval they should be opened to scrutiny. I am sure that if Beard had applied he would have been given the same privileges as we had. It was simply a question of professional competence and of purpose. Obviously, no government wants to have hack writers rummaging in its records in the hope of making a scoop.

Recently, most major governments have reduced the traditional fifty-years closure of archive material to thirty or even twenty years, and they have been far more ready than before to publish important documents. Unfortunately, the publications usually lag far behind the present, and the thirty-year rule is still excessive. In the United States the controversies evoked by the Vietnam War and the Watergate affair have resulted in massive leakages of government records, often leaving the administration in a position far more compromising than if the materials had been made available much earlier.

To find the remedy is not easy, because governments must of necessity keep certain information secret for security reasons, if for no other. Unfortunately, it is far easier to have a document stamped "secret" or "top secret" initially than it is to have the classification reduced or abolished later. If the mountains of government archives were to be systematically declassified, a team of hundreds of highly qualified personnel would be required over a period of many years.

Something can be learned from the procedure adopted for Gleason and me while writing the volumes that so aroused the ire of Beard and others. It was decided at the outset that the manuscript should be reviewed only for security considerations.

For the rest, the innumerable unpublished documents that we adduced were to be declared automatically declassified and open to any qualified historian. Since we were writing about events roughly ten years after their occurrence and since not a single objection was raised to this procedure, even by foreign governments whose papers had found their way into our files, I submit that a sound solution would be to generalize this rule. It would not be unreasonable to expect applicants to submit two or three letters supporting their competence and purpose and their willingness to submit their manuscript for a security check. The interests of the United States extend over an entire, fast-moving world. Even if matters of importance in a democracy could be kept secret for twenty or twenty-five years—and we know that they cannot—it is wise not to keep the country in the dark. Policy makers and other officials will probably be more circumspect if they can no longer reckon on the protection of prolonged secrecy, and the public is apt to have greater confidence in its government if it is better informed about the course of events.

While Gleason and I were working at top speed against an impossible deadline, the international situation degenerated to the point where our efforts might well prove meaningless. The first Arab-Israeli war ended in the establishment of an Israeli state, yet was fraught with all kinds of dangers for the future. The Soviet occupation of Czechoslovakia raised the question of how communism was to be contained. The Berlin airlift, one of the really heroic episodes of modern history, suggested the virtue of persistence. On the other hand, the Soviet atomic bomb put an end to Western monopoly of the horror of horrors. In these times of unknown dangers a short visit to Europe under pleasant circumstances promised a welcome break. My good friend and fellow historian, Dame Lillian Penson, had been named vice-chancellor of the University of London and joined with the Royal Institute of International Affairs (Chatham House) in inviting me to come to England to deliver a few lectures. I accepted with enthusiasm, and my wife and I sailed on the *Queen Mary* early in April 1948. The Marshall Plan was then being debated in Congress. I therefore chose as the subject of my three lectures "The American Attitude towards Europe," the very reverse of the subject frequently treated in other books. For my Chatham House lecture I decided on "The Mechanism of American Foreign Policy," attempting to trace the complicated committee systems through which Congress eventually arrived at a decision. The sixteen European powers which had drafted the European Recovery Plan were following the debates in Congress on the necessary funds. I assured my audiences that after all that had gone before it was unthinkable that the United States would turn its back on Europe. I was more than a little gratified when events bore out my assurances.

We arrived at Southampton after a pleasant crossing and were met by my former Harvard colleague and dear friend, Professor Gerald Graham. After consulting with Dame Lillian and the historical staff at the University of London on April 13, it was decided that my three lectures should be scheduled for April 26–30, leaving us ample time for sightseeing and visits. But when I visited Chatham House the next day, I was besought to undertake a tour covering some of the organization's provincial branches. At first I objected that I never had and never would repeat the same lecture in rapid succession, but I allowed myself to be persuaded that the audiences would be so different as to permit me a good deal of flexibility. And so it proved to be, from Aberdeen to London.

In Durham, I was astounded and gratified to find Lord Eustace Percy, who had been so influential in the days of the League of Nations, among my audience and to be entertained at dinner by him and Lady Percy. Our final step in the provinces was at Sheffield, whence we returned to London. I delivered my three lectures there on April 26, 27, and 30, always to a fairly large and interested audience. My lecture to the Chatham group was on April 29 and was well attended and much discussed. During our days in London we were generously entertained at lunch and dinner, despite the still rigid austerity regime. Dame Lillian assembled a group of historians for a formal dinner, while Professor Charles K. Webster, an old friend, had us dine with him informally. We lunched at Claridge's with Lord and Lady Vansittart, who begged us to come early before all the meat dishes had disappeared from the menu. One afternoon we had tea with Lord and Lady Halifax at their very modest apartment in Kensington, and I recall with pleasure our host's insistence, on our leaving, to go to the street with us to make sure we got on the right bus. We also went to Oxford for a short visit with friends of my wife from her college days. I was kindly received by A.J.P. Taylor, who induced me to give a talk at Magdalen in the evening.

In May we went to Paris for something over two weeks, where I had conferences with many of my French colleagues— Renouvin, Girard, Donant, etc.—as well as with military men such as General Weygand (who seemed old and taciturn), General Bergeret, and Admiral Fernet. The high point of our stay, however, was a lunch given by the Count and Countess de Chambrun at their beautiful home near the Invalides. The Countess is the daughter of Pierre Laval and her utter faith and devotion to her father and unshakable conviction of his patriotism were really quite moving. The company, then, was strictly Vichyite, including M. Isorni, the chief counsel of Marshal Pétain at his trial and now, twenty-five years later, one of the leading French jurists. One could hardly imagine a greater contrast than that between the austerity of the British, including the upper, wealthy classes, and the altogether splendid and lavish entertainment of the Chambrun's with elegant servants and the choicest menu, a world also utterly different from that of the average Frenchman.

I was told by the Count de Chambrun that Madame la Maréchale, the wife of the imprisoned Marshal Pétain, would like to make my acquaintance; so one afternoon my wife and I appeared at her apartment for tea. It was a strange experience: The Maréchale sat as though enthroned with all the leading lights of the Pétainist group around her listening to her plaints against the heartless French government, which refused to alleviate the lonely lot of "the hero of Verdun."

On my return to Cambridge I found my collaborator working long hours on our study of American foreign policy. I pitched in, and never was able to work further on my London lectures, although *The Mechanism of American Foreign Policy* was presently published in England and soon also in Germany.

By this time the first volume of our book, later published under the title *The Challenge to Isolation,* was all but complete. It took American foreign policy and world developments from about 1937 to the conclusion of the Destroyer Deal in September 1940. But when our four-year grant expired in 1949, we were still struggling with the draft of the second volume, which appeared eventually as *The Undeclared War* and ended with the Pearl Harbor attack. We regretted that we had not been able to do much more than half our assignment. The Council on Foreign Relations was eager to have us continue and would no doubt have found the necessary funds, but neither Gleason nor I had the courage and strength. The writing of contemporary history is like the work of Sisyphus. The constant flow of new materials makes it almost impossible to arrive at any conclusion.

CHAPTER XII

Bureaucracy–
Second Phase

ON THE termination of our four-year grant, Dr. Gleason and his family returned again to Washington, where he assumed the position of deputy chief of staff of the National Security Council. His departure was a severe blow to me, because we had both come to depend on discussion of pending problems and because, in general, our collaboration had been so congenial and effective. Critics of the book frequently pointed out that it was impossible to say who had written what or how we had been able to carry through a line of argument so smoothly. Gleason was determined to stay with the project to the end, and in Washington he worked on the second volume in his free time while I continued to strain every nerve to get on with the job. A first draft of Volume II had been completed, but considerable revision and even writing were still necessary.

I seemed fated, however, to be always distracted by other work of such interest and importance that I did not feel free to decline it. In November 1950 General Walter Bedell Smith, who had recently become director of Central Intelligence, persuaded me to accept and then dragooned the Harvard authorities to grant me one more year of leave in which to organize the Office of National Estimates in the recently established Central Intelligence Agency. This statement calls for at least a few words of background information.

For several years after the precipitate dissolution of the OSS in the autumn of 1945, presidential commissions continued to study how the important work previously carried on by that organization could best be reconstituted—in other words, how to make good an egregious error. In 1947 Congress finally passed the crucial National Security Act which among other things established a Central Intelligence Agency and a director of Central Intelligence with the power to supervise and co-ordinate the work of all intelligence agencies. It was, on the whole, a good act, yet for some time its implementation was fragmentary and inconclusive. Only during the Korean War did President Truman take the decisive step of appointing General Smith as director of Central Intelligence. Smith had the reputation of being extremely tough and enjoyed the respect of all the services. As Eisenhower's chief of staff, he had received the German surrender in May 1945, and had then served for two years as United States ambassador to the Soviet Union.

In London in 1942, Smith had spoken enthusiastically about the work being done by R and A. He now made no secret that he regarded that work, namely the analysis and evaluation of all available intelligence and the production of a coordinated, interagency National Estimate, as the crucial part of all foreign intelligence. He saw to it that the research work in the State Department was once more set up as a separate unit and let it be known that he would require all military and other intelligence agencies to participate actively in the drafting of national estimates. There was to be within the Central Intelligence Agency an Office of National Estimates under a small board of National Estimates consisting of outstanding, experienced civilians and military men. This board would allocate the work to be done and would be supported by a highly competent staff, most of whom would be specialized in some particular region or discipline. This staff would analyze the problem and assign the preparation of a rough draft to the appropriate Washington agency. The draft would then be critically analyzed and revised, after which officials of the various agencies would review the revision, tabulate the comments and objections of their agency, and eventually meet in prolonged discussions usually presided over by a member of the Board of Estimates.

It will be seen that this process required time. It was not, in fact, ever envisaged that estimates would be short-term evaluations. They were meant to be long-range studies of the objectives and capabilities of certain powers or of the factors controlling a specific problem. It was not unusual for such estimates to be months in preparation, sometimes with footnotes registering dissent by one agency or another when complete agreement proved impossible. General Smith invariably read these estimates carefully and at times gave them rough treatment. When once approved by the overall Intelligence Board of which Smith was chairman, they became the official statement of the government, subject, of course, to modification at any time if new and important intelligence became available.

Due to my past experience, Smith asked me to return to Washington, become an assistant director of the Central Intelligence Agency and organize the Office of National Estimates. This was in November 1950, just as I had resumed my teaching and, I might add, just as the Chinese forces intervened in large numbers in the Korean War. The Harvard authorities were naturally reluctant to have me leave again, but were unable to resist when Smith enlisted President Truman to support his appeal. I was granted until February 1, 1952 either to be back in Cambridge or to sacrifice my professorship.

I hastily packed a bag, leaving my wife to follow with the family. After long discussions between the general and myself, the organization was decided on as outlined above, and I was instructed to take any personnel from any part of the agency. I eventually assembled a staff of fifty or sixty, which Smith was sure would prove inadequate. I pled with him that I did not want so large an office that much of the time would be lost in administration. He finally yielded, on my promise to add to the staff if necessary, but it was never increased. The members, all exceptionally gifted and competent people, insisted that they preferred long and hard hours to becoming enmeshed in endless red tape. The members of the Board of Estimates and the staff therefore worked in the closest and most intimate relation, to the benefit of all. Some staff members were eventually appointed to the board, and over the long pull, a number rose to high positions in the government, attaining even the rank of ambassador.

It took some doing to induce the various agencies to send for discussions men who were not only competent in the subject matter, but were authorized to speak for their agency and their chief. But the drive and the overriding authority of General Smith made for rapid progress. My only disagreement with him was over footnotes. I contended that an estimate littered with them would be of no value to policy makers. It would merely notify them that there were large differences of opinion, while the great objective should be to arrive at the utmost limits of agreement. Smith finally agreed to leave the matter to my judgment but warned me not to be too tolerant. In the final discussion of an estimate, which in some cases had involved hours and hours of often heated debate, Smith ruled with a firm hand, and footnotes did not become a major problem. I must say it was a great pleasure to work with a man who had so clear a mind and such determination to attain his objective. He was convinced that national estimates were of the utmost importance as the basis for sound decision making, and I think that no other nation then had and perhaps does not now have, so systematic and effective an organization of intelligence evaluation.

I was sorry and not sorry when my term of service came to an end in January 1952. By this time the Office of National Estimates was a going concern of real stature in the government. Sherman Kent, my colleague of OSS days and a devoted friend, was to take over my position and promised to continue to operate with a small, select team. This he did in the twenty-odd years before his retirement, during much of which I continued my contacts with the agency through periodic consultations. I was much gratified, too, when my invaluable former secretary, Miss Frances Douglas, joined the Office of National Estimates and eventually became its chief administrative officer. Smith's health did not allow him to serve long beyond my own term, but he was succeeded as director of Central Intelligence by Allen Dulles, and he eventually by Richard Helms, both men with important OSS experience and the imagination to make intelligence work contribute as it should to the crucial problems of foreign policy.

In violation of chronological continuity, it will be well for me to close out the story of my thirty-year association with the problems and organization of foreign intelligence by referring to the President's Foreign Intelligence Advisory Board, revived by President Kennedy in 1961 soon after the Bay of Pigs debacle. The new board, chaired at first by James Killian and later by Clark Clifford, had only eight members, all experienced in the military, diplomatic, and scientific operations of the government. I was the only strictly intelligence official among them. The function of the board, which had offices next to the White House and a small but highly competent staff, was to oversee all or any of the intelligence activities of all agencies. Empowered to demand any papers, to question any officials, and to make any recommendations to the President, the board generally met for two days every six weeks or two months and worked intensively on general or specific issues, often of widely differing character. It ordinarily ended its sessions by drafting recommendations to the President, which in President Kennedy's time were usually discussed personally with him before the board disbanded.

President Kennedy had a real appreciation of the importance of carefully evaluated intelligence, and took a lively interest in the board's work. His interest was not, however, shared by President Johnson, who rarely consulted with the board, despite the gravity of many of the problems arising from the Vietnam War. Nonetheless, the board worked uninterruptedly, and its authority over the intelligence community was as fully exercised as before. Indeed, members made increasing efforts to transcend the strictly Washington problems by checking on operations in the field. When traveling abroad, they met with intelligence agents. At one time or another, I myself reviewed the situation in Paris, Rome, Madrid, Athens, Ankara, and Teheran.

Looking back over nine years of service with the board, I can only say that it was performing a most useful and necessary supervisory function. With advancing age, however, I found the meetings very strenuous and, what was more important, the problems were becoming more and more technical, so I was well satisfied to have President Nixon accept my resignation at the time of his inauguration.

The reader will have no difficulty imagining what sort of existence we led during the fourteen months preceding my return to Cambridge in January 1952: at a government office all day, engaged for the most part in long and arduous discussion or controversy; in the evening work at home, often until 11:00 p.m. immersed in proofreading and in writing the last chapters of *The Undeclared War*. Gleason did what he could in revision and polishing, while our good wives also plunged into work. My wife, for example, was almost entirely responsible for the excellent, analytical indices which, with books running to 776 and 941 large-size pages respectively, were nothing short of heroic achievements. And, be it noted in contradiction to the charges and innuendos of our opponents, none of us received even a penny for the effort. All royalties earned by the books went automatically to the Council on Foreign Relations for support of further research.

The Challenge of Isolation was published in 1952, while *The Undeclared War* appeared in September 1953. To discuss the reviews of the second volume would be otiose, for they obviously had little to add to the reviews of the first. The great majority were favorable, not to say enthusiastic. While they did not all subscribe to every conclusion of the authors, they commended in the highest terms the comprehensiveness of the account, making it "a world history of a critical time." They had nothing but praise for the solidity of the scholarship, for the cool and dispassionate style, for the readiness to criticize as well as approve American policy. Leading experts stamped it a monumental contribution to scholarship. Arthur M. Schlesinger, Jr. (in the *New York Post*, September 3, 1953) called it a "stunning exercise in professional history at its best"; Samuel F. Bemis (in the *New York Times*, September 6) thought it "a work of which American scholarship and men of good will everywhere may justly feel immensely proud"; while Lindsay Rogers (in the *Saturday Review*, September 26) declared that it "will long remain a monument of American historical scholarship."

But just as the first volume had its Beard, so my erstwhile "friend," Harry Elmer Barnes led the pathetically feeble assault on the second. Barnes, now on the staff of the *Chicago Tribune*, published several pamphlets. The first was a classic exposition of the thesis that President Roosevelt and his henchmen knew of the coming attack on Pearl Harbor and permitted it to take place as an excuse for leading the country into war. This preposterous notion, according to most reviewers of our book, was not supported by even a scintilla of evidence. A second pamphlet reviewed all the maneuverings and deceptions by which the minions of Wall Street gradually led the feckless Americans into the war to save the wily British.

But the third pamphlet, published, probably in 1954, without indentifying place or publisher, but evidently like the others by the America Renaissance Book Club in Chicago priced at fifty cents for fifty pages, was entitled *The Court Historians versus Revisionism* and was largely a personal attack on me for having sold my skills for vile pelf. Despite what he considered the wrong-headedness of the authors, Barnes had to admit that the book was probably "the most elaborate example of the work of court historians in the whole history of historical writing and the smoothest and most adroit job ever turned in by a court historian, from Sallust to Robert Sherwood. . . . The excellence of this exercise in court historiography is exactly what an informed person would expect of a man possessing the great intellectual ability, amazing industry, vast learning, and high literary talent of William Leonard Langer." What a tragedy that such gifts should be employed for such sordid purposes! I could not possibly, in brief scope, review Barnes's entire invective, laced as it was by errors and by amazing information acquired at second or third hand. Surely one of the most ludicrous of Barnes's notions was that after my return to Harvard in 1927, I had come to move among "the best people" in Cambridge and Boston, whose Anglomania knew no bounds. The Harvard atmosphere was no longer congenial to a stalwart revisionist, especially one of German descent, so I decided to shift my ground by "parachuting to safety" by becoming a confirmed interventionist. It must have been at least a consolation to the author that the Langer-Gleason books would supply enough material to stimulate revisionist writing and publication, and "provide a great armory of ammunition for Revisionists, who can take these facts and give them their logical and realistic historical application."

Barnes could not resist ending his abuse on a sad note. Great were his lamentations: "As I recall the William Leonard Langer of 1923 to 1940, I still would like to believe that, although he has now attained riches and eminence as a result of his voluntary servitude, nonetheless, he has moments of acute nostalgia for the old Clark [University] days when, even if he earned only $4,000 a year [I never had more than $3,700], he eagerly searched for historical truth, independent, and unafraid, and breathed the fresh air of scholarly freedom, as befitted a brilliant and rising young craftsman."

Fortunately, I never suffered the nostalgia nor pangs of conscience which Barnes so vividly evoked. Both Gleason and I felt that we had done a creditable, honest job and were happy to be awarded one of Columbia University's *Bancroft Prizes* for American history. Barnes and his fellow isolationists continued their assaults on Roosevelt and his policy, but I am sure I am right to say that for American and foreign scholars the basic account of the critical years before Pearl Harbor is still that of *The Challenge to Isolation* and *The Undeclared War*.

After several years of strenuous work with next to no chance for recreation, life in Cambridge seemed to hold unusual attractions on our return in 1952. Through my brother Walter's alertness and concern, we had been able to buy a fine old house on Berkeley Street, within seven or eight minutes walk of my Widener study. We took possession in September 1946 and immediately embarked on renovations and modernizations, for the house, built in 1855, required a number of changes and improvements, notably in its lighting and in our need for many more bookshelves. Futhermore, like most old Cambridge houses, it had no garage. On applying to build one, I was told that if I had been wounded or captured by the enemy and held prisoner, there would be no difficulty, but my government service in Washington counted for nothing. It was all irritating, but eventually we were able to build a garage and even to secure additional telephone service.

Our family on our return in 1946 was large and included my aged mother and her nurse. My two sons, Leonard and Bertrand, had both quit school and enlisted in the armed forces. Now they were back and ready to resume their studies. Leonard married in 1947 and Bertrand in 1950. Both started families and both have had successful careers, the older son in banking, the younger one first in computer work, then in real estate. My one stepdaughter, Betty Burr, was a student at Radcliffe, but before graduating married a young engineer, Pier Antonio Abetti, the only child of an eminent Italian astronomer. My wife's oldest boy, Duncan Nelson, graduated from Wesleyan and went on to a Ph.D. at Harvard and a position as professor of English at the University of Massachusetts in Boston. Of the two younger boys, Evan studied at Harvard, and George has become a professional musician. In 1947 my mother died at the age of seventy-nine. She had been living with us for some years and had gradually lost her mind. To us she was a pathetic figure, who at best could grasp some remark about the weather and at times even failed to recognize her sons.

Having many friends in Cambridge, we led a rather lively social life, including frequent theater performances and countless concerts. We were regular subscribers to the Boston Symphony and to various other musical enterprises. I kept up my regular weekly quartet playing and even arranged to squeeze in an occasional hour of practice. Unlike many other people of our age, I never developed the intense dislike for modern music of some of my friends. In fact, I always thought one of the most stimulating and gratifying rewards of concert going was the growing appreciation of music hitherto meaningless. I confess that as a young man I rather disliked Brahms, thinking him uninspired and academic. Now, I have long since become an enthusiastic Brahmsian. I have even grown to enjoy a good deal of twentieth-century music, though not as yet Schönberg nor all of Stravinsky or Bartok. Even today, for all our concert going, I frequently play on the stereo, before retiring, some elusive musical composition, finding that by more frequent hearing it becomes more meaningful and enjoyable.

The one sad feature of Boston musical life is the lack of an opera house. The regular grand opera performances of my youth had died out, and the opera house was used only for the spring visit of the Metropolitan Opera Company and occasional performances by visiting ballet groups. It had, in fact, become a white elephant, and no one was surprised when it was torn down to make valuable building space available on Huntington Avenue. As fate would have it, opera and ballet both revived within a few years. But neither Caldwell's Opera Company of Boston, which has attained national renown, nor the Boston Ballet Company have any better quarters than rundown movie palaces. In fact, one performance was staged in the indoor gymnasium of a local college. The existing facilities are wholly inadequate for the purpose and are uncomfortable and unpleasant for the audiences. The destruction of the Opera House can now be regarded as a major tragedy.

Any professional man, certainly any academic person in his fifties, is bound to be involved in many projects and organizations. There were, for example, the annual meetings of the American Historical Association after Christmas, which over the past quarter century increased their attendance from 400–500 to several thousand. This made personal contacts more difficult and tended to reduce the gatherings to what was called "the slave market," where young men were looked over for prospective jobs. The huge numbers also required a great expansion of the program, so that most of the sessions were planned by chairmen who then recruited speakers and commentators. The subject matter became less and less important. Many of the papers are now on perfunctory subjects and are given primarily to allow the authors to show themselves for appraisal. It is truly astounding how the real contributions to historical scholarship continue to sink in number and quality.

Far more stimulating were the semiannual meetings of the American Philosophical Society in Philadelphia and the monthly meetings of the American Academy of Arts and Sciences in Boston. I had been elected to both these venerable learned societies and took an active interest in them, serving not only on various committees, but also on their councils. The American Philosophical Society had a strictly limited membership of 400, drawn from all conceivable scholarly disciplines. This meant that only about twenty new members, plus a few foreign honorary members, could be elected in any one year. A great attraction of both organizations was the opportunity they provided to hear about problems and activities in a large variety of fields and to form acquaintances and even friendships with scholars eminent in their disciplines. The Century Association in New York, of which I also became a member, tended to emphasize architecture, the fine arts and literature, but also provided opportunities, at luncheon or dinner, for free discussion and exchange of ideas.

But the highlight of the early fifties was an extended tour of the American West. I had long since promised my stepsons that when I had completed work on *The Undeclared War* I would relax by taking the family on a trip to the West Coast and especially to the Rocky Mountains. The five of us set out early in June 1953 in a Cadillac which was both comfortable for passengers and adequate for our baggage. I decided to cross the continent by car, though I knew that some 1,500 miles of the journey would be pretty tedious. It seemed to me highly desirable that the youngsters should have some idea of the vastness of the country and of the great expanse of the Middle West, but there is no point in chronicling our itinerary in detail since thousands of tourists have been over the same ground or part of it. Starting from Denver we drove through the gorgeous Colorado Rockies, visiting national parks and scenic areas. After a short stay in the Navajo country we went on to the Grand Canyon, where we committed our first but never regretted miscalculation. We were all agreed to go down the canyon all the way to the river, not on foot, of course, but on mule back. So eager were we to make the arrangements that we bought tickets for the next morning without first taking a look at the canyon. An imposing sight! But also scary when one realized that the mule trail was a narrow ribbon running along the precipices. I have never done well in high places, but did not want to turn back. So I consoled myself that presumably the mules themselves would do what they could to avoid suicide. Next morning a troupe of about a dozen set off with a guide. I was disagreeably surprised to realize that in the steep descent one's weight would be thrown into the knees. In twenty minutes I was ready to give up, but where was I to go and what to do? So I bore the agony as well as I could until we reached the plateau and had a rest. We had been urged by the authorities that a marvellous view could be had from the plateau and that the lower part of trail would be insufferably hot. But no: We had to do it all and did, in fact, ultimately reach the river, where we lunched along the bank before starting back. We were dead tired and all but prostrated by the heat, yet had still to face several hours of a return trip. The guide would occasionally give us each a thimbleful of water to keep us from expiring. The trail going up looked even more frightening than the way down, but the mules performed admirably and returned us safely—obviously, since I sit here indulging in reminiscence.

Having survived the canyon trip, we went to Las Vegas. Our route took us to the Mojave Desert, and I foolishly allowed the family to persuade me to drive the length of Death Valley —in late June! The road from Baker to the southern entrance of the valley and through the valley adds another seventy-five miles. I think we all realized how stupid we were, but we drove on grimly, wondering all the time what we should do if the car broke down. Fortunately, we reached the warden's lodge at Furnace Creek, only to be roundly lectured on the danger of being in the desolate valley in a temperature of 110° without even having given advance notice. The inherent dangers were demonstrated when, on the road from Furnace Creek to Panamint Springs, one of our "nonblowable" tires blew out, and we had to wait some time for it to cool before we could touch it. The water at Panamint Springs was heavenly, and I think we each consumed about a gallon before the innkeeper tired of bringing more.

The rest of our two-month tour covered the Pacific coast states and took us into Canada, where we followed the great mountain barrier at far as Jasper. Turning them homeward we visited Yellowstone and the Badlands before crossing the Middle West and stopping for a look at Niagara Falls. We were back in Annisquam early in August, weary but much refreshed and ready to plunge into the accumulated work.

CHAPTER XIII

Regional Studies

EVEN AS AN undergraduate, I had been dissatisfied with the compartmentalization of knowledge which permitted the study of a country's literature without reference to its history. So disturbed was I by my own ignorance that when planning the Rise of Modern Europe series, I was determined that in each period an effort should be made to integrate the traditional political-military history with other cultural aspects, although obviously no author could be expected to treat all facets in equal detail or with equal authority. It was a stiff assignment, but the results were certainly worthwhile: Many students have expressed their satisfaction in at least glimpsing the entire culture of an age.

A regional study program does not necessarily deal with a vast area or a complete culture. As applied in the R and A branch of the OSS it was restricted to individual countries or groups of countries, with emphasis on the integration within the chosen area of all aspects of life. In each section historians might rub elbows with economists, anthropologists, writers, politicians, and scientists. Furthermore, men of various competences and from various sections of the organization might collaborate closely in the treatment of specific problems, with reference always to contemporary conditions and with the requirements of a great war.

I recall with pleasure that in 1943 or 1944 Mr. John W. Gardner and Mr. James A. Perkins, both members of the

Carnegie Foundation, called on me by appointment. For some years that foundation, acting through the Social Science Research Council and the American Association of Learned Societies, had been encouraging "area studies," which meant primarily the promotion of university instruction in important though neglected foreign languages. The armed services had opened schools for the teaching of Russian and Japanese, and eventually the Committee on World Area Research and Area Research Training Fellowships was to provide fellowships for students in these fields. But these commendable and generally successful efforts were only slightly related to the R and A, which was not intentionally an educational institution, but an out-and-out research organization devoted almost exclusively to the problems of the war. My visitors were impressed by the R and A approach to the analysis of complicated situations and, in the course of lengthy discussions, asked whether some similar system might not be introduced in our universities. I gave them what encouragement I could, and it was in fact the Carnegie Foundation that, in 1945, financed the establishment of the Russian Institute at Columbia and shortly after the Russian Research Center at Harvard.

In these new centers the language, the history, the economics, and the general culture of the Soviet Union were intensively studied in an integrated way. It was impossible for me to take an active part in these experiments, but my Harvard colleague and R and A colleague, Donald C. McKay, was instrumental at Harvard, as was Geroid T. Robinson, also of the R and A, at Columbia, in setting up the Russian institutes. Both centers proved markedly successful and continued to enjoy the financial support of the Carnegie, Ford, and other foundations. Within a generation this country, hitherto so woefully ignorant of Russia, of Soviet institutions, objectives, and policies, developed an impressive number of scholars and officials conversant with these affairs, who produced a substantial literature on numerous aspects of Russian history and literature, on the revolutionary movement, and on the existing regime.

In 1954 I was asked by the Harvard administration to attempt the establishment of a related Center of Middle Eastern

Studies, for which several American oil companies, in need of trained personnel, were prepared to supply financial support. Having for years offered a course on the history of the Ottoman Empire, I was naturally much attracted by the idea, though it was a more formidable challenge than had been the Russian Research Center. The Middle East is territorially huge and widely dispersed with particular linguistic and religious problems. Moreover, it was a field poorly cultivated by scholars. There were some outstanding authorities in biblical and Christological studies, but professional Orientalists were mostly interested in the history, literature, and culture of the Arab caliphate and paid little or no attention to the Turkish or modern period. I made no claims to being an Orientalist, but I understood my assignment to be chiefly to set up the center, to establish the necessary relations with various departments of the university, and to find a competent director. I was fortunate at the outset in enlisting the support of the late Mr. Derwood Lockard, an anthropologist who had had long intelligence experience in the Middle East and was keenly aware of current problems. He proved a popular and invaluable associate director of the center until his retirement in 1972. As for the director, we had our eye from the beginning on Sir Hamilton A. R. Gibb, professor at Oxford and one of the few outstanding authorities on the Arabic, Turkish, and Persian cultures alike. It seemed improbable that he could be moved, but after some negotiation he agreed to come, not at first as director of the center (that decision he reserved for the future), but as Jewett Professor of Arabic and University Professor, which gave him freedom to associate himself with any department of the university.

Sir Hamilton, who arrived in 1955, told me later that much as he regretted leaving Oxford, he saw at Harvard the opportunity for a great extension and expansion of Middle Eastern studies, with the chance of securing much needed financial support and attracting able students. I emphasized to him that my directorship was intended, at least by me, as purely provisional, and that I would gladly turn it over to him when he felt ready to take it. I think he was mildly astonished by this offer, but accepted it at midterm 1956. He remained director until he suffered a severe stroke in 1964 which eventually obliged him to retire. He must, I am sure, be regarded as the real artisan of the Middle East program. A man of great charm and a scholar of worldwide reputation, he inspired confidence and enthusiasm both in students and in important outside agencies. It was through his efforts that the Rockefeller Foundation made the center a capital grant for endowment, and other foundations and businesses continued to provide funds for operating expenses.

The university had made it clear from the outset that, however desirable an expansion of Middle Eastern studies, especially in the modern period, it could not provide the funding of so formidable an undertaking. Early in the center's history, however, the Agha Khan provided the endowment for a professorship in Iranian studies. His grandson, the present Agha Khan, was then an undergraduate at Harvard and was so inspired by Professor Richard N. Frye as well as by the program of the Center that he persuaded his grandfather to offer support. Professor Frye became the first incumbent of the Agha Khan Professorship. But it was left for the center itself to finance greatly expanded instruction in the modern Middle Eastern languages, to support advanced fellows, and in general to defray the considerable expenses involved in the operation. Under Sir Hamilton's direction a great deal was accomplished. He himself took a direct part in the elementary and intermediate instruction in Arabic and in the supervision of the organization of courses and the publication of studies.

In 1955 I was also named director of the Russian Research Center in succession to Professor Clyde Kluckhohn, the eminent anthropologist. At the same time, I assumed the general directorship of regional studies and became a trustee of the Harvard-Yenching Institute, a private endowment devoted to Chinese and Far Eastern studies. This meant that I was now deeply involved in the organization and functioning of regional studies and their relationship to the work of the traditional departments. The problem became more involved with the establishment of the Center for East Asian Studies, largely financed by the Harvard-Yenching Institute.

A related development, though not directly connected with

the organization of regional studies at Harvard, was the extraordinary revival of Armenian studies in this country, to which I also unintentionally became closely committed. In *The Diplomacy of Imperialism* I had devoted considerable space to discussing the emergent Armenian national movement of the midnineteenth century and the efforts of Armenian revolutionaries in the 1880s and 1890s to provoke Turkish reprisals so as to arouse the interest and intervention of the great powers. Since the Armenians were a small nation divided territorially between Turkey, Russia, and Persia, this proved a difficult task and bore fruit chiefly in the terrible Armenian massacres by the Turks in the midnineties. These and later massacres led to large-scale emigration of Armenians to America, where many of them prospered, not only in business and law, but in science, literature, and music. Substantial colonies of Armenians had grown up in Watertown, Massachusetts, in New York City, in Detroit, and in Fresno, California. By the midtwentieth century the second generation had grown up knowing little of the language or history of their homeland. They were reticent about their nationality, for they had been taught by their elders that theirs had been an unheroic role, victimized by the terrible Turks without cause or provocation.

In 1953 or 1954 I had a long talk with Mr. Manoog Young, a graduate student at Clark University. He had been impressed with what I had had to say about the Armenians in my book and realized that they had played an heroic, if hopeless role. They were, in fact, one of the oldest historic peoples, with a glorious record in art and literature, who had played a notable part during the crusades. Yet this was being forgotten and would soon be lost. Could I suggest, he asked, how to salvage the traditions of Armenian culture and revive the systematic study of the people and its history.

We both saw the difficulties in rearousing interest among people who did not even realize that the problem existed. I suggested that if the necessary $400,000 could be raised to establish a professorship of Armenian at Harvard, that would be the greatest stimulus to revival of Armenian studies. The idea, which I regarded as quite visionary, appealed at once to Young, who reminded me that there were many wealthy Armenians in the country. He thought that with a specific program in hand he might be able to interest them.

Young proved himself intelligent, energetic, and dedicated. He organized a meeting of Boston Armenians and invited both me and Professor Richard Frye, who was also interested, not only to attend, but to expound our views on the importance of the problem, on the danger that Armenian studies would soon be a thing of the past, and on the ways to save the situation. There were several more meetings, marked by increasing enthusiasm. Steps were taken to have courses in elementary Armenian offered in the state extension program. Presently, the National Association for Armenian Studies and Research was established, and many Armenians were induced to join. It was my impression that they were delighted that something was being done to reestablish their identity. Young visited other Armenian communities and found them quite prepared to associate themselves with the program.

In fact, the needed $400,000 was raised in a few years, a professorship was established at Harvard in conjunction with the Center for Middle Eastern Studies, and Harvard facilities for meetings and conferences put at the disposal of the Association. My wife and I attended a huge banquet in Memorial Hall at which the governor of the state, President Pusey, leaders of the Armenian clergy, and other Armenian notables either spoke or performed. A professor of English from the University of Ohio, who enjoyed a reputation as an Armenian poet, declaimed one of the great Armenian epics in the national tongue and spoke so eloquently that many of the older people were moved to tears.

So far as I know, this was the first time that a professorship at Harvard had been endowed not by an individual or his family, but by an ethnic community. It was a major achievement, but not enough to satisfy Mr. Young, who promptly set out to raise funds for the development of Armenian studies at the University of California at Los Angeles, at Columbia, and at other places. I will not attempt to recount in detail the further development of this unique enterprise. As I write, the association has celebrated its twentieth birthday. It has acquired its own building in Cambridge, launched a publishing house, and founded a substantial library. Already it has organized and conducted two national conferences on Armenian history, and has conducted several tours to Turkish and Soviet Armenia, establishing contacts and exchanging publications with the Armenian Academy in Yerevan. All this achievement in a mere twenty years is probably unique. It is a great tribute to the imagination and will power of Mr. Young and his associates to have rescued Armenian culture from oblivion, despite the religious and political issues that have long divided the Armenian community.

After this rather lengthy discursus, I should return to the main problem of regional studies, but I will beg the reader to bear with me while I launch on yet another topic demanded by the general chronology of my career. In June 1955 I paid a hurried visit to Europe for two reasons. I had an invitation from the University of Hamburg to accept an honorary Doctor of Philosophy degree, and I had been asked by the Council on Foreign Relations to join a small delegation representing the council at a select conference on international affairs under the auspices of the Nobel Institute at Oslo, which annually awards the Nobel peace prize. I accepted both invitations with pleasure and was met at the Hamburg airport by an old friend, Professor Egmont Zechlin, who was undoubtedly the instigator of the honorary degree. I had seen much of him in Cambridge when, as a young scholar, he had come to the United States on a Rockefeller fellowship. Since then he had become a leading German expert on Bismarckian diplomacy.

I had decided to prepare and deliver my address at Hamburg in German and indeed ventured to choose as a subject the role of Woodrow Wilson at the Paris Peace Conference of 1919. This was a subject that would make the hackles of most Germans rise, for it was a commonly accepted proposition that the harsh Versailles Treaty was a betrayal of Wilson's early promises, that he only betrayed the Germans to persuade the British and French to accept his visionary scheme for a League of Nations. At best, this thesis was only partially true, for Wilson had been convinced, ever since his "peace without victory" speech, that a decisive defeat of either side would result in a ruthless, dictated peace that would leave a great and dynamic power such as Germany resentful and vengeful. After the defeat of Germany, he had done what he could to forestall a dictated peace and had pleaded for a negotiated settlement acceptable to all parties. Even after he had been obliged to abandon this position, he fervently hoped that the projected League of Nations would serve to rectify and revise the most objectionable articles of the treaty. His hopes, as we know, were blasted when the United States Senate rejected the treaty, League Covenant and all. I also presented these views a few months later in two lectures at Bryn Mawr College, which were then published in a small book entitled *Woodrow Wilson and the World of Today* (edited by Arthur P. Dudden, 1957). But I suspect that neither my Hamburg address nor my Bryn Mawr lectures reached a very large public or did much to alter the traditional view of Wilson's policy toward Germany.

It was, of course, impossible for me to judge the purity of my German style or the impact of my argument on my hearers. But the award ceremony was truly impressive, the members of the entire faculty appearing in their picturesque, seventeenth-century gowns, velvet cap and ruff included. I was so taken with this costume that I asked permission to wear it on American academic occasions. The issue was novel, for the costume was worn not by the graduates, but only by the faculty, and only after much debate did the university senate approve the so-called Lex Langer. As a result, I cut an impressive figure at many successive commencements, notably when escorting Harvard honorary degree candidates, and especially in 1956 when Yale conferred on me the honorary degree of Doctor of Humane Letters and the award of the Doctor of Laws to Chancellor Adenauer, whose staff was duly impressed by seeing the Hamburg costume in the Yale setting.

My journey was then to take me to Oslo. It so happened that I found at Hamburg the bosom friend of my graduate school days, Professor Lawrence D. Steefel, on leave from the University of Minnesota. Steefel had written his doctoral dissertation (later published) on the Schleswig-Holstein Question in the 1860s and was still much interested in the problem and its setting. He urged me to join his wife and himself in motoring from Hamburg to Copenhagen, whence I could take a plane to Oslo. I did not require a great deal of urging, and I recall with great pleasure our drive through Holstein and Schleswig to Flensburg, and thence by ferry to the islands and Copenhagen. There was much of historic interest to both of us, and I am afraid that Mrs. Steefel had to put up with an uninterrupted flow of shop talk.

In Oslo the weather was decidedly cool even in mid-June, so that one was glad to be indoors. The conference, which lasted about a week, was dominated by a retired Norwegian banker, evidently of great influence, who seemed quite willing to tell the delegates from most of the Western countries what they should think on various points. Since most of the delegates were men of experience and stature, they were not ready to accept his notions without debate. There was much interesting discussion, but nothing of sufficient significance to stick in my memory. I recall particularly, however, a lavish luncheon offered by the mayor of Oslo, and the pleasure of the company of some of my fellow delegates, especially Arthur H. Dean, who had only recently completed the long and arduous negotiations for the treaty ending the Korean War. Having grown up, like my wife, in Ithaca, New York, he recalled her quite distinctly and asked to be remembered, which he was. Among others I liked particularly the late Professor Mario Toscano, professor of history at the University of Rome and historical adviser to the Italian Foreign Office. Toscano was a great authority on international law and the author of several important books on European diplomacy. He had recently lost his wife and had brought his fifteen-year old daughter to console him. He and I became fast friends, and he was a generous host to us later in Rome.

CHAPTER XIV

The Middle East Embroglio

MY MAIN OBJECTIVE in 1955 was to make a survey trip of the Middle East, which seemed indispensable to any intelligent planning of Middle Eastern studies. By chance the International Congress of the Historical Sciences was to hold its quinquennial meeting in Rome in September. For the first time, Soviet delegates were to attend and, in fact, participate in a session on the origins of the First World War. This was an occasion hardly to be missed.

The congress met daily for a week at Mussolini's great convention hall outside of Rome, which certainly had many advantages, but involved a considerable drive through the heavy and all-too-hectic Roman traffic. When it became known that the Soviet delegates and those of the satellite countries were going to launch an attack on the policies of the Allied and American governments during the First World War, Professor Toscano urged me to reply. I think I effectively pointed out that the Communist charges were based largely on the documents published by the very governments they were attacking, and then asked why the Soviet government had kept its records under lock and key? After the session one of the Soviet delegates asked to speak to me privately and explained that Soviet historians had no say whatever in these matters, which touched questions of high policy controlled by the Politburo.

I must not become involved in further details of our tran-
sient stay in Italy. We drove south past the ruins of Monte
Cassino and on to Naples and Pompeii. My wife had spent a
year in Italy but had never been to Sorrento or Amalfi. My
former colleague and our dear friend, the late Professor Gaetano
Salvemini, was also living at Sorrento in the devoted care of
admiring friends. Salvemini had taken so active a stand against
fascism even in the 1920s that he had been harried from his
professorship in Florence and obliged to flee first to Paris, then
to the United States. Since at that time he was in dire financial
straits, I induced the Harvard Corporation to pay $300 for
three lectures on modern Italian history in the pre-Fascist
period, in connection with the course for which I was responsible. I think this modest sum was his first income in this country,
but he was soon engaged to give lectures in other places and
was eventually appointed the first Lauro de Bosis Professor of
Italian history at Harvard, a post which he filled until he returned to Italy to be feted and celebrated as a great and
courageous champion of liberal democracy.

Salvemini was a big man, of Calabrian peasant stock, a
dynamic speaker and a first-rate scholar and controversialist.
Now, an old man in failing health, he was lovingly cared for in
the Sorrento villa of his friends. When told that we were at the
door, he was overjoyed. We spent a memorable couple of hours
with him. I always think of him as one of the truly heroic figures
of our time.

In Amalfi we found Isaiah Berlin (not yet knighted) and
a friend sunning themselves to recoup from the Rome conference. Berlin is, I believe, officially a professor of philosophy
at Oxford, but his works that I have read deal chiefly with
Russian intellectual history and are about as stimulating and
brilliantly written as anything I have come across in that field.
My wife has for many years done me the great favor of reading
aloud to me before going to sleep. We have gradually covered
an impressive literature, both fiction and nonfiction, mostly
things that we otherwise would never have gotten around to.
Among our readings were, a few years ago, the entire three
volumes of the English translation of the *Memoirs of Alexander*

Herzen, a great and fascinating human document which comes to mind because Isaiah Berlin has written with such insight not only of Herzen but of the entire intellectual ferment in Russian society in the time of Nicholas I.

But to come at last to our Eastern experiences. We took ship from Naples to Athens and spent about a week visiting Corinth, Mycenae, Nauplia, Epidaurus, Olympia, Lepanto, and Delphi. The ancient ruins, which are so fragmentary, interested me less, especially since the wonderful finds of Schliemann and his successors have been removed to the Athens Museum. Delphi is, to be sure, an exception, as is the Parthenon, but with my interest in the Byzantine and Ottoman periods of Greek history I was deeply impressed with the marvelous fortifications of Nauplia, with the Gulf of Lepanto, and with the small Byzantine churches that still stand in Athens. While in Greece we took a short voyage to Delos and Mykonos, which again impressed me less than they do most people.

Rhodes was quite another matter. Having studied the Turkish siege of Rhodes at some length, I was fascinated by the great fortifications, splendidly restored by the Fascist regime. These late-fifteenth-century walls and structures represent the most consummate military works of the Middle Ages and were held by the Knights Templars for some time against overwhelming Ottoman forces. While on Rhodes, we drove along the coast to Lindos, with its wonderful citadel and view over the blue Mediterranean. My wife even insisted on our crossing the mountains to the valley of the butterflies. I was sure that this was all tourist propaganda and was simply delighted to be proved wrong. We ascended a narrow vale overgrown with gum trees. At the slightest stir or the crack of a stick, thousands if not millions of bright red butterflies would fill the air.

After a week in Istanbul, we had to leave in order to reach Baghdad in time to take the plane to Bahrein. Instead of flying to Ankara, however, we went by train because of my interest in the history of the Berlin-Baghdad Railway project and the rugged scenery. On the train we met a lady musician who was on the way to Ankara to make recordings of Turkish court music, which was rapidly sinking into oblivion. At her invitation we visited the studio when she and a young man were recording music for the kanun and tambour. The names are misleading for a Westerner, for the tambour proved to be a type of zither of great complexity, while the kanun was something like a lute. The music was very strange, yet rather moving.

There was not much to be seen in Ankara beyond the old castle, which commanded the approaches to the city, and the Hittite museum, which had only recently been opened. Our idea was, if possible, to travel by road over the plateau and through the Cilician Gates, to Adana and Antioch. To our surprise, the embassy knew little about the road even as far as Konya and recommended plane travel as the obvious solution. But we were persistent, especially after talking to Mr. Robert Kerwin, an embassy official who spoke Turkish fluently and offered to go with us, since he had not been in southeastern Anatolia for years. We snapped at the opportunity, hired a taxi, and set out for Konya. The road was surprisingly good, and in Konya, where we were comfortably lodged in a new and recently opened inn, we were much interested in both the very old—the tomb of a great Moslem saint—and the very new— an important carpet factory where rugs and carpets in the most divine colors were being produced. This factory had already supplied all the floor coverings for the Hilton Hotel in Istanbul and had established contact with at least one well-known New York department store.

From Konya eastward, through the heart of Turkish peasant country, the road, although at times quite bad, was remarkably good over long distances. Our driver, an amiable and capable young man, had repeated tire trouble, as tires were almost impossible to obtain in Turkey, and the tubes were already patched beyond all reason. We had at least one flat tire a day, on one occasion in late afternoon just as we were descending the wild Cilician Gates, through which the invaders of Asia Minor from the East had usually come. Although the railroad and telegraph lines followed the road, the pass was still desolate and forbidding. My wife and I were returning from a walk during a tire change, when we noticed a black panther watching us from a ledge above.

In Antioch, our chauffeur's tires all gave out at once just as we were entering the square. We no longer had time for much sightseeing, so we hired another car and went on to Aleppo, thence southward through the valley to Homs and Baalbek, about the most gigantic Roman ruins I have ever seen. Our road then took us over the mountains, at breakneck speed, and finally down to Beirut, another city with a fabulous location by the sea.

Colonel William Eddy, who had been born of missionary parent at Sidon and knew the Arab world as few other Americans did, had given us recommendations to notables along the coast. We visited not only Biblos and Sidon, but also two of the great refugee camps of Palestinians, who were living in unbelievably squalid tent towns and had been so lodged since the Arab-Israeli War of 1948. One shuddered at the thought of the children who were born and brought up in these conditions. Time has proved that they provided an admirable recruiting ground for Palestinian terrorist groups, which, having nothing to lose, will readily risk their lives and gladly take their revenge on Israelis or indiscriminately on others.

Through the courtesy of the Ford Foundation office in Beirut, we had the use of a car and driver to visit the Krak des Chevaliers, the great medieval fortress commanding the passes into what is now Lebanon and the Holy Land. The trip was long and tiresome over very rough roads, especially on the last leg ascending the hill on which the fortress stood. As one stands on the parapet and views the landscape, one can understand why no hostile force could move south without encountering powerful opposition. The Krak is in an excellent state of preservation, impressive in every respect, and a splendid example of medieval engineering and fortification exceeded, if at all, only by the fortifications of Rhodes.

We traveled from Beirut over the mountains to Jericho and Damascus. I was amazed, on approaching Jericho, to see the huge volume of water pouring out of the spring. This accounts fully for the successive construction of many cities on this venerable site. Outside of Jericho we visited another refugee camp and also a huge farm established by a refugee Palestinian landowner to train and employ refugee boys for a useful career. The farm was devoted chiefly to poultry and vegetables and was largely patronized by the Arabian-American Oil Company (Aramco) as a source of fresh food.

After a short stay we flew over Kuwait, which seemed like a collection of huts baking in the sun. The plane finally landed at Bahrein, whence a short ferry trip took us to the mainland and to Dhahran. We were the guests of Aramco, very comfortably housed in the guesthouse for about a week, during which we talked to all the high officials of the company, who explained the discovery and operation of the rich oil wells, and were shown the schools, hospitals, and other facilities of the settlement. We were also taken by a short train ride to the El Hasa Oasis by Dr. Vidal, who had studied and written a monograph on this imposing desert garden, with its town of Hofuf. As at Jericho, great gushes of water poured out of the sand, forming a pond of some size, where the Arabs were not only bathing themselves, but also scrubbing their camels and donkeys. We were told that the donkeys, a white variety much prized in the Arab world, could be identified only by their henna markings. Some had red ears, others red feet or a red tail, indeed, much ingenuity was used in deciding the markings. Coffee was served us in the emir's palace, although he was absent, and we spent a fascinating hour in the souk. The town itself was a fine example of the fortified desert settlement, and its gates were closed at night.

On another day we were driven some seventy miles to Ras Tanura, the great oil refinery, from which the petroleum was shipped abroad. A dip in the Persian Gulf, however, proved anything but refreshing, as the water temperature was 78° or 80°.

We found our discussions with the Aramco officials most instructive. They were doing their utmost to operate within the strict requirements of the puritanical Saudi Arabian government, but even then they did not expect to be allowed to stay much longer. That after twenty years they are still there is a tribute to their tact, their ability to adjust and to compromise, and, in general, to make imperialist enterprise unobjectionable to the host country. Life for the American staff was anything but pleasant, but they avoided isolation by founding a theatrical company, by importing motion pictures, by laying out a golf course on the rocky desert soil, with oiled sand for the greens, by maintaining a stable of polo ponies, and so on. As for the natives, the company provided schools for the youngsters, employed all the men who showed ability, and promoted them in the hierarchy as promptly as possible. So much has been written criticizing imperialism and the alleged exploitation of helpless natives, that it was a pleasure to see a great enterprise conducted with so much consideration and farsightedness. To a large extent, I am sure, this policy was inspired by my friend Colonel (later Ambassador) William A. Eddy, an outstanding connoisseur of the Arabs and their culture, who for some time served Aramco in a role analogous to that of a foreign minister. Of course, Aramco has made large profits over many years, but Saudi Arabia has also benefited in countless ways, has become the majority stockholder in the enterprise, and has amassed such wealth as to be able to carry out almost any improvement it may desire.

In Cairo, we were met by a former student of mine and housed in a guest suite at the American University. Our host drove us out to the pyramids as the sky was becoming overcast with black clouds. We feared rain, but were told laughingly that it never rained in Egypt at that season. Hardly had the words been spoken, when the heavens opened and we had a short but heavy downpour. We are, no doubt, among the very few people who have seen the pyramids in the rain.

One of the most fascinating and instructive phases of our Middle East journey was the flight from Cairo to Arab Jerusalem which, because of the tension with Israel, had to circumvent that country by flying to the southern tip of the Sinai Peninsula and then turning north along the eastern shore of the Dead Sea. Since the plane was small and slow and flew at low altitude, we had excellent views of the Suez Canal, Aqaba, and St. Catherine's Monastery. A more arid region can hardly be imagined. Especially along the Dead Sea there was no sign of habitation, only rocky hills and deep canyons.

The Arab-Israeli tension was already great, and was to

break out in war in the next year. It was, therefore, impossible to pass from Arab to Israeli Jerusalem except through the Mandelbaum Gate, a passage that was something of a venture in itself. The "gate" was really two gates, one on each side, with a couple of hundred feet of no-man's land between. Arab boys would take your baggage, rush to the center of the intervening zone and dump it where their Israeli counterparts could rush out and pick them up. When all this was safely accomplished, my wife and I screwed up our courage and made a record dash, which happily was without incident.

In Israeli Jerusalem we were fortunate to obtain, through the King David Hotel, a chauffeur and car which served our every purpose. The driver was a German Jew, who had come to Israel in 1929. He was affable, intelligent, and exceedingly well-trained as a guide. After driving us around Jerusalem, he went on to Tel Aviv and then, for the next several days, took us on a tour of the northern half of Israel, pointing out everything of interest and demonstrating a really solid knowledge of history. It was all fascinating and impressive. Indeed, it was hard to realize how so few determined people could have accomplished so much with what, after all, is unpromising terrain. One cannot avoid admiring the Zionists for their devotion and perseverance, while yet regretting and, in fact, bemoaning the cost to the Palestinian population, which in one way or another was deprived of its land and property and reduced to the wretched status of refugees.

CHAPTER XV

Retirement:
Before and After

A COUPLE OF years after my return to academic work I learned that I would probably be elected president of the American Historical Association for 1957. The office was chiefly honorific, but it did involve the preparation of a formal address to be delivered at the annual meeting of the association. Since the presidential address would be published in the association's *Review* early in January, the text had to be in the editor's hands by September 1.

The president of the association was expected to deal with some broad aspect or some fundamental problem of historiography, something of general interest, requiring no specialized knowledge. Since almost seventy-five such addresses had been made since the founding of the association, it stands to reason that most of the basic problems had already been explored. Had I had anything new to say about diplomatic history, that would have been an obvious choice. But I had nothing important to add to what I had written in the prefaces of published works. After much deliberation, I decided to expose myself to criticism and perhaps even ridicule by speaking of the need for deeper study and more extensive reference by historians to the teachings of modern psychology, notably psychoanalysis. I decided to entitle my address "The Next Assign-

ment," that is, the need for an effort to expand the field of
historical work and deepen our understanding of historical
developments.

I had discussed this subject frequently and at length with
my brother Walter, who was a professional psychoanalyst, and
had often commented that human motives were treated so
superficially and incompetently by historians that they tended
to distort rather than to enlighten the past. Furthermore, I had
done considerable reading on the subject as my interest in it
grew. It seemed to me that a discussion of the problem in
purely general terms would make only a slight impression.
What was needed was reference to specific examples. I thought
I found a good case in the story of Luther's youth. The great
reformer had left a huge mass of writings and correspondence,
which threw abundant light on his relations to his father and
to his choice of a career. As the first part of my address, I therefore went over this example as briefly as possible, only to learn
soon afterward that Erik Erikson, whom I had known for years,
had been working for some time on the very same subject. He
asked me to read the proof of his book *Young Man Luther,*
which I did with much benefit to myself.

Erikson's book, the work of a professional, was naturally of
much greater value and import than my brief remarks. It had
an immediate and lasting impact, and may fairly be called the
pioneer work in what has since been unattractively labeled
psychohistory. Historical and literary biographies published
since 1957 have amply demonstrated that where there is sufficient source material, this new approach can be very enlightening. There are those who insist that the psychological
analysis of a person long dead is an impossibility, because it is
no longer feasible to ask him the vital questions. I would maintain, on the other side, that a voluminous correspondence, such
as that of Luther, Napoleon, or Mazzini has a unique value in
so far as it reveals aspects of the subject's personality without
the remotest thought on his part of its ever being used for
psychical analysis.

My address and Erikson's book stirred great interest among
analysts, many of whom seem to have felt that in their prolonged work with individuals they were not doing much for

society at large. Gradually, however, younger historians, to whom my appeal had been primarily addressed, were attracted by the possibilities and psychohistory is now an active field of historical endeavor.

I wish I could say the same for the second and to me, crucial part of my address. What really interested me was not so much whether psychoanalytic techniques could be applied to the study of historical personages, but whether these techniques could contribute to our understanding of larger movements in history, whether they could help to explain the tides of social development, the often sudden winds of change. I thought the plague epidemic of 1348–1349, the Black Death, might serve as an example. This great visitation, possibly the worst catastrophe ever to have befallen the human race, struck Europe suddenly as a new phenomenon about which nothing was known and which was therefore free to run its course. In a few months it carried off anywhere from a quarter to a third, or even more, of the population. It was unthinkable that such a cataclysm should not have shaken European society to its very foundations and since, for several centuries, new outbreaks of the disease recurred every eight or ten years, it was unbelievable that mankind, living under constant threat of death, should not have been deeply affected in many ways. Economic studies had already shown the impact of such a high mortality on living conditions. My effort was to show that in psychological terms the general distress was reflected in religion, art, literature, and other aspects of human life.

I still think that I made a pretty good case for the disastrous effects of the Black Death and succeeding epidemics, but I gladly recognize that further work along such lines is bound to be extremely difficult. I myself have never found adequate time to pursue the matter further, even with reference to a much more limited subject of study. A basic difficulty arises because much less advance has been made in collective psychology than in psychoanalysis. There have been excellent contributions to small group psychology, and much has been learned about the composition and behavior of crowds. But as yet we know very little of mobs or of changing public attitudes. I think my address, however, has been a great stimulus to historical epidemiology, and through more intense attention to the history of the great man-killing diseases has had an important impact on the larger field of historical demography.

"The Next Assignment" came as a shock to the editor of the *Review* and to many others who probably expected some platitudinous remarks on diplomatic history. The delivery of the address was for me something of an ordeal because after a lifetime of more than ordinary good health, I had now begun to fall on evil days. I had a major operation early in November, with the physician's assurance that I would just be able to preside and speak at the meeting of the association. I delivered my message with knees wobbling and hands firmly grasping the podium. During the winter I had two more bouts with the surgeons, so that the summer at Annisquam was welcomed with more than usual enthusiasm.

I continued to carry a full teaching load and maintained my interest in international affairs, not only through the regional study programs, but as a trustee of the Harvard-Yenching Institute and of the Carnegie Endowment for International Peace. The latter was, I believe, the earliest of the foundations devoted entirely to international relations and the pursuit of peace. While no longer financially capable of competing with the Rockefeller, Ford, and other modern foundations, it enjoyed an enviable international reputation. With a distinguished board of trustees and a highly competent staff, it has been able over the years to do much to keep alive the principles of international law and above all to offer instruction in the conduct of international affairs and diplomacy to the officials of the many newly independent nations. As a member also of the advisory board of *Foreign Affairs*, I have been able to observe how, over the past fifty years, the emphasis in international relations has shifted from the traditional territorial issues and conflicting national claims to the much greater and more universal problems of competition in armaments, population pressure, food and energy shortages, race relations, and many issues arising from the liquidation of imperialism.

In 1959 I was appointed to a fellowship at the Center for

Advanced Studies in the Behavioral Sciences, at Stanford. The center, only recently endowed, was designed to give mature scholars an opportunity to devote their full time to current research, or even to just thinking. Fellows usually lunched together at the center, but they had no duties, and nothing was required of them. Each was assigned a simple but attractive study, without a telephone. Secretarial and library privileges were freely available, and there were agreeable meeting rooms for any who wished to organize a group discussion. My wife and I were fortunate to rent the house of a Stanford professor who was on leave, and were located about as close to the center as possible. We were also next door to the Stanford golf course which, through the courtesy of my friend President Sterling, was put at our disposal.

There is no exaggeration in this picture of the idyllic life dreamed of by scholars. I devoted my time almost exclusively to desperately hard work on my projected volume in The Rise of Modern Europe series and did, in fact, complete a first draft of most of the chapters. As usually happens, the first draft was much too long, and there was still much to be done. We enjoyed seeing something of our friends, however, both at Stanford and at Berkeley. It is always a temptation to recount the pleasures of one's travels, especially if, like my wife and myself, we enjoy motoring and seeing interesting places. I will say no more than that our stay at the center was one of the most pleasant and rewarding of my career. In my opinion the center is serving a most useful purpose in bringing scholars from various disciplines into contact with each other, facilitating the exchange of ideas, and above all, providing what modern scholars need most—the time to work uninterruptedly on their project without the distractions of the classroom and of committee work.

The only serious diversion to my studies at the center involved the writing of a chapter on the United States' role in world affairs as part of the *Report of the President's Commission on National Goals*. President Eisenhower, greatly concerned by the complexity of both domestic and foreign problems and the growing unrest and confusion of the American citizenry, had appointed a Commission on National Goals consisting of eleven eminent private citizens, who were to analyze the chief problems confronting the country and make suggestions as to possible remedies. The commission, financed entirely by private foundations, had no official connections or responsibility. The executive secretary, William P. Bundy, threw himself into the project with his usual intelligent energy. In a short time, he had enlisted the interest of fifteen competent authorities in a large field of study. It was in this connection that he invited me to write the chapter on the role of the United States in world affairs. It was a subject that appealed to me in principle and seemed so important that I could not decline. For some months I therefore rose at an early hour and worked intensely on my contribution. Though the main commission may not have underwritten every word or proposition advanced in my essay, it nevertheless expressed basic approval and incorporated the major lines of my argument in its report. Late in 1960 the report and the supporting analyses were published in both hardback and paperback editions under the title *Goals for Americans*. It was, in my opinion, a splendid synthesis, comprehensible to all, and it sold in deservedly huge numbers.

This extra tour had curious and rather interesting consequences. Not long thereafter, I had a letter from an "Academy of Achievement," in which it was argued that since the *Goals* had suggested that Americans did too little in the way of recognizing achievement, the academy had been organized to correct this situation. At annual meetings, Golden Plates of Achievement were to be awarded to some fifty persons who had made significant achievements in fields of human endeavor: science and technology, the arts, literature, business, education, and so on. I was invited to receive the award for distinguished work in history.

I was at first skeptical of the whole project as an advertising stunt. Yet there was nothing obviously wrong with it and at least some possiblity that it might do good. So my wife and I journeyed to Dallas and spent three very enjoyable and instructive days there. The fifty recipents all proved to be outstanding men, some young, some old, and the ceremonies were conducted without fanfare. Each candidate was given five minutes to explain how he had come to embark on this particular career, and the highest ranking seniors of the Dallas high schools were present to hear these thumbnail sketches. These sketches interested us as I think they undoubtedly inspired some of the youngsters. The young people were given the further opportunity of breakfasting with speakers who interested them and to ask about items that troubled them. In fact, we older people on these occasions formed some friendships which we were to treasure. I remember, especially, our long discussions with the late William Gottlieb, a pioneer of American abstract painting, who had only recently received a high award at an exhibition in Rio de Janeiro. All in all we considered the academy and the meeting most successful. I continued to receive their reports for some time and believe the academy is still active.

My stay at the center was rudely interrupted in June 1960 by a severe fainting spell which had all the appearances of a heart attack. My wife and friends eventually got me to the Stanford Medical Clinic where it was quickly discovered that while my heart was in order, I was bleeding internally. I was transferred to the newly opened Stanford Hospital, given the most excellent care, and in two weeks was discharged to return East by plane. One of my stepsons and a nephew were kind enough to drive the car back to Cambridge, loaded with documents, books, and other paraphernalia.

My illness prevented my attending the commencement exercises at Mills College, where I was to be awarded an honorary degree. It was, however, eventually conferred on a later visit to California. My illness also blasted our plans to attend the International Historical Congress in Stockholm in August, which we were to supplement with a short tour in Finland and Soviet Russia. It seems strange that with my early and continuing interest in Russian history and my connection with the Russian Research Center—the directorate of which I did not resign until 1960—I never actually visited Russia. For years it was impossible to secure a visa, and after the "freeze" illness effectively precluded travel. Later still, during my service on the President's Foreign Intelligence Advisory Board it was thought undesirable for members of the board to visit any Communist country, so that once again I was deprived of an experience I would have valued greatly. Although my wife and I had seen many of the greatest museums in Europe, we both had a keen desire to see the Hermitage collections and were disappointed by our failure to get to Russia, if only for that reason.

In revenge for the frustrations of 1960, we took our car and golf clubs to Europe in the late summer of 1962 primarily to enjoy ourselves, but also to attend to some government business here and there. During a short stay in Frankfurt, we were seized with the idea of seeing Berlin for ourselves. The moment was not particularly auspicious, but it was not much more tense than usual. On arriving in West Berlin I was shocked beyond words by the ruins all about us, the huge piles of rubble, and the open areas, overgrown with weeds, in the very center of the city. Quite as sudden as our decision to go to Berlin, was our inspiration to enter East Berlin—in retrospect a genuine imbecility for there was every likelihood that I might be picked up and questioned at checkpoint Charlie, where one had to leave one's passport until returning. To my immense relief, nothing happened, and now I am glad not only to have seen the famous wall symbolizing the rupture in Western society, with armed guards ready to shoot down any who attempted to escape from the East to the West, but also to have witnessed the gloom and apathy among what seemed to be the sparse population of East Berlin.

While motoring through the castle-studded Dordogne we were able to go through the recently discovered Lascaux Caves, our party being one of the last before the caves were closed to the public because of the air pollution caused by so many humans. The hunting scenes are vibrant and dynamic to the last degree, and remind one rather of Picasso than of the primitive, though impressive, art of the early Middle Eastern civilizations. It is my understanding that a replica of the caves and the paintings is being constructed for the benefit of the public, but I am eternally grateful to have seen the originals in all their pristine glory. At Pau, the birthplace of Henri IV, we discovered that the golf course was the oldest on the continent, built by Wellington's soldiers who, after expelling the French from Spain, wintered at Pau and found a golf course essential to their happiness. The course, no longer one of the finest in Europe, is said to have been in use constantly from that day to this.

It was in Spain that business and pleasure became deeply enmeshed. Arriving in Saragossa in the late afternoon, we found enormous excitement and learned from the newspapers that Soviet ships, loaded with missiles and other munitions, were on their way to Cuba. The United States was reported to have established a blockade and to have threatened to stop the Soviet squadron by force. The world was as close as it has been since 1945 to the outbreak of atomic war.

We hurried on to Madrid, and I contacted the American embassy at once. The American minister and I drove out to the great American air base some miles from Madrid and sat with the commander for some time awaiting successive messages from Washington. I will never forget the sight of the American bombers, lined up for immediate takeoff with their atomic bombs, the crews in full battle array, with faces grim and determined. I wish more Americans could see our forces on active duty, and witness for themselves the efficiency and precision of their preparations. In September 1962 we certainly skirted world catastrophe, but I suspect the Soviets knew what they were doing when they declined the American challenge.

In 1960 President Pusey called on me in my study to remind me that I would be eligible for retirement with the arrival of my sixty-sixth birthday, but that the corporation would be happy to have me continue to sixty-eight or even seventy. I replied that I did not yet feel quite ready to retire and would therefore gladly remain active to sixty-eight, though I doubted whether I would want to go on till seventy. All this was agreeable to him, and I remained on the rolls until June 1964. By that time I felt strongly that I wanted to retire, for I still had many commitments which I could hardly expect to meet unless I had the full use of my time.

On such occasions it is customary to honor a retired scholar with a *Festschrift*, that is, a collection of essays by friends and former students. It had so happened that on my fortieth birthday my good friend Donald C. McKay mobilized some of my former graduate students, and presented me with a volume called *Essays in the History of Modern Europe*, of which he was the editor. Needless to say, I was flattered but also embarrassed, because the volume, though not designated a *Festschrift*, was in fact one and as such was some thirty years premature. Furthermore, I regarded the *Festschrift* as something of an outmoded German custom, appropriate only when professors and students were few in number and were generally working in related fields. I let my future students know that I regarded the practice as undesirable, for two reasons: First, the essays were usually commissioned for the occasion and rarely presented new or important material; secondly, *Festschriften* are usually catalogued in the libraries only under the name of the recipient. This means that such important individual contributions as the volume might contain are generally lost as far as the scholarly world is concerned.

Knowing my feelings on the subjejct, two of my dearest friends, Carl E. Schorske and his wife Elizabeth, had in 1966, unknown to me, hit upon the idea of editing for publication a collection of my previously published (and some unpublished) papers and addresses. These, after some delays, were brought out in 1969 by the Harvard University Press with the title *Explorations in Crisis*. Schorske, presently a professor of history at Princeton, provided the book with a lengthy introduction reviewing and commenting on my work. I must say that I was deeply impressed not only by his generosity, but even more by the honesty of his appraisal. No good purpose could be served by any effort of mine to outline the thesis which he has so eloquently expounded. But I will say that I well recognize myself as a historian, primarily of recent international history, who was constantly groping for some key to bewildering developments and being repeatedly swayed in my interpretations by the hectic developments through which I lived and in which to some degree I participated.

I particularly appreciated Mr. Schorske's observation that I never thought of myself as a specialist but as a historian in the broad, etymological sense of the word: an inquirer. Although I would always throw myself into the task before me, I was never satisfied with historical studies as being pursued by myself and others. They were always too narrow, too superficial. I never managed to interest myself in minor topics, which the French call *pointes d'histoire*, although they are often intriguing and piquant. My articles have mostly been too long, and the same is true, a fortiori, of my various books.

Mr. Schorske is quite right in suggesting that my latest writings were, in spirit, the youngest of all. Whatever problem I tackle always suggests to me other, usually deeper and more difficult, problems that should be explored. Perhaps, this is as it should be: History, properly speaking, is a mature subject. Only through long and arduous work with the sources and the effort, as one German historian has put it, to make sense out of what is essentially senseless, can one arrive at a deeper understanding of the issues involved. Basically a conservative who is unwilling to believe that in the course of thousands and millions of years on this planet, mankind has not learned by bitter experience many of the requirements of social existence, my deepest sympathies have always been with the vast lower classes and their sufferings, the classes of which we know least and of whom we should strive to know more. Here my own origins have given me a deep-seated appreciation of fundamental problems of mankind.

The *Explorations in Crisis* was presented to me in 1969 at a party given by Professor Robert L. Wolff, when I was also given letters of appreciation written by former students and colleagues. These letters were beautifully bound in red leather, and I need hardly say how highly I prize these intimate tributes to my work as a teacher. Because of the tension and unrest in the university, including a bomb scare in the college library on that very day, the presentation party had to be postponed from April to June.

In a sense I have now spent more than a decade in retirement and these have been among the most pleasurable years of

my career. Although arthritic fingers—and the all but insuperable difficulty of bringing four players together regularly—
obliged me to give up viola playing, my wife and I have remained inveterate concert, opera, and ballet patrons and have
enjoyed the rich fare provided by the Boston-Cambridge area.
And, yet, it is but rarely that I fail to play on the stereo at the
close of the evening some piece of music, classical or modern,
that has appealed to me. I have taken a great interest in the excellent Harvard-Radcliffe orchestra and, in fact, served for
several years as president of the Harvard-Pierian Foundation,
whose sole objective is to guide and support that organization.

Retirement has meant that my wife and I were much freer
to travel. In 1965 we drove from Le Havre to Vienna to attend
the International Historical Congress. I was simply delighted
to see the city of my student days, the more so as it had been
so little harmed by bombardment. Since I was then working on
the revolutions of 1848 for my book, I was able to retrace the
entire course of events and to visit many other sights as well.

In the following years we made several annual trips to the
West Coast and to Arizona, where our married daughter was
living at Scottsdale and my old friend Lawrence Steefel had
built a house at Apache Junction. We also developed the habit
of spending a couple of weeks in January in Antigua, in a hotel
furthest removed from St. John's and the tourist centers.
Among longer expeditions we embarked on a tour to East
Africa, where I was especially eager to see the sources of the
Nile, an impressive stream even where it leaves Lake Victoria
and full of interesting animal life in the stretch below Murchi-
son Falls. At that time Uganda was still open to tourists and
there as well as in Tanzania we were astounded by the wild
animal life. We visited the site of earliest man in the great
Olduvai Gorge and drove to and from over the great Serengeti
Plains and Ngorangoro Crater, ending with a night's camping
at the foot of Kilimanjaro. From Nairobi we flew to Ethiopia,
where I hoped to see the sources of the Blue Nile and the great
Nile Canyon. Unfortunately I was taken ill almost at once on
reaching Addis Ababa and remained in bed until I was able to
fly to Rome and then home.

My health had by this time become quite precarious. I had several sojourns in the hospital and a case of major surgery. But I have managed to recover well from these various ailments and have been able until recently to carry on not only my professional work, but my summer gardening activities and a reduced schedule of golfing. Indeed, my wife and I recently undertook a trip to Iceland and the Norwegian coast. Lava-covered Iceland, with its hot springs and snow covered mountains as well as its well bred and congenial population fascinated us to the point of wanting to return for a longer stay. The fjords of Norway are all that they have been long admired for. The weather in early July was superb, with a temperature of 80° Fahrenheit on crossing the Arctic circle. We steamed north to Hammerfest, for which I had a boyhood affection, and to the North Cape. A more enjoyable tour could hardly be imagined.

Professionally, my great preoccupation on retirement was to complete work on my own volume in The Rise of Modern Europe series. It was a formidable undertaking, because my work had been repeatedly interrupted over some twenty-five years, and even in 1968–1969 was diverted by revision of the *Encyclopedia of World History*, which appeared in 1970 in a fifth edition, taking account of all the new nations. Besides, I had given myself far too large an assignment, covering the history of Europe from 1832–1852, including six to ten revolutions of varying dimensions and importance in 1848–1850. The text was completed by 1967, and the book appeared in 1969 under the title *Political and Social Upheaval, 1832–1852*. I deeply regret that the volume is substantially larger than the other volumes of the series, which I consider quite unpardonable in the case of an editor. And yet I think it one of the best books I have written, dealing with a period of extraordinary change and uncertainty. As a volume in a series, it was not so widely reviewed as some of my earlier books, but the comments were definitely favorable, and one of the English reviewers, J. P. T. Bury, declared that my editorial license as to length had resulted in a book "which is probably the most comprehensive treatment in English of these twenty years from

1832 to 1852." He found the work "impressive in its organization, its readability, its mastery of specialized literature and its
erudition." I do believe that I succeeded in knitting together
many strands in the complex history of the continent and in
bringing out many aspects that have long remained obscure.

In studying the period of my volume, I had long been impressed by the rapid growth of the European population and
had done a great deal of reading on the sudden upswing in
1760 following centuries of relative stability. Historians had
shown a surprising lack of interest in what seemed to me a
fundamental alteration in European society, and the economists, who alone showed much concern with demography,
had failed to discover the cause or causes of the spectacular
change. I thought that their effort to deal with the problem
statistically, where statistics were nonexistent or so inadequate
as to be unusable, was unlikely ever to produce a satisfactory
answer.

I had gradually become impressed by the fact that the
sudden rise in population was generally concurrent with the
widespread adoption in Europe of the potato (and maize)
culture. These American vegetables, long known but not much
cultivated, were so highly nutritive that they could fill the requirements of a greatly enlarged population. In 1962, in an
article in the *American Historical Review* entitled "Europe's
Initial Population Explosion," I reviewed earlier efforts to explain the phenomenon and then attempted a review of the
little-known history and importance of the potato culture.

Historical demography has recently attracted many scholars
in both England and France, who have published numerous
detailed studies mostly of a sociological nature, that have revealed many aspects of population growth. Lacking statistical
training, I have not attempted to participate in analyses of
birth and death rates and similar problems, but I have remained concerned with the larger population growth before
the late eighteenth century, the prevalence of infanticide and
exposure of newly born babes, the prohibitions on marriage,
the astounding degree of celibacy, and so on. Meanwhile, I
think that other investigators have increasingly realized that

nothing but a major increase in the food supply would adequately explain the phenomenal upsurge, just as nothing but massive emigration from Europe in the nineteenth century and rapid industrialization could account for the tolerable demographic situation that existed for over a century.

It was a curious coincidence that the great outburst of student unrest began at Berkeley, California just as I retired from teaching. I regarded this as a stroke of luck, for the tension and antagonism that developed between students and teachers would have been heart breaking for me. No doubt, I would have survived as did the majority of my colleagues, but the unrest and violence of the 1960s certainly suggested that in many aspects of American education fundamental changes were indicated. Although the disorders ended almost as suddenly as they had begun, they left their mark and, in fact, basic changes in organization and procedure are already under way in many institutions.

As I look back on the eighty years of my life, I realize that, despite hardships and setbacks, I have been fortunate: My existence has, on the whole, been gratifying. I am neither sufficiently arrogant nor stupid to attribute such success as I have had to exceptional ability, or even to the inspiration and unfailing support of a devoted mother. These were important factors, quite possibly reinforced by the well-known Protestant ethic stressing integrity and hard work. But certain contributions were certainly crucial: It was my good fortune to be born and bred in a city rich in history and outstanding in educational opportunities. Nearby Cambridge had one of the world's greatest universities, wide open to those willing to meet its standards. Furthermore, the years of my childhood were a period of unusual stability and general prosperity. Europe might be shaken by periodic crises, but it is hard now to recall how little they affected the average American. As newsboys, my brothers and I paced the streets until late hours, but not to report the latest developments of the Moroccan crisis or the progress of the German naval program—our job was to furnish the breathless American public with the final scores of the major baseball games. In 1914 I was only one of countless Americans who had only the haziest notion of the Habsburg Empire and the nationalism that culminated in the war against Serbia. In those days it was easier to live—easier on the nerves—than during and after the First World War. In an article entitled "The Well-Spring of our Discontents," published in the British *Journal of Contemporary History*, I attempted to show how most of our present-day woes and tribulations, if they did not originate in the First War, were given a greatly enhanced impetus in Western civilization by that disaster.

I would not say that I ever believed in a former "golden age," or in the ultimate perfectibility of man, or even in the notion of continuing progress. I realize that the story of mankind has been largely one of misery, oppression, and recurrent crises. I do maintain that it was my luck to grow up in one of the brief periods of relative quiet, before men lived with the nightmare of atomic warfare, of frightful overpopulation, of chronic and widespread starvation, and of the threat of exhaustion of natural resources. Individuals, including children, were subjected to far fewer pressures in the early years of the century than they are now.

As for personal factors in my progress from poverty to a certain eminence in scholarship and government, I will not attempt to hide my light under a barrel. I was a happy, energetic child, though with increasing age and further responsibilities I suspect that I have become more sober, though I hope not entirely humorless. I have some basis for these remarks in a beautiful portrait of myself commissioned by my wife in 1954 and painted by the New York artist Umberto Romano. A devotee of Renaissance style and color, the artist painted me among my books, papers, and maps, looking decidedly serious and thoughtful. As a likeness, the portrait was an unqualified success, but I thought at the time that it showed me as too grave, almost grim. But now, I realize that the artist saw me in 1954 much as I have grown to be twenty years thereafter.

Everyone realizes or should realize that one cannot be all things to all men. My many commitments and avocations left me little time for traditional social intercourse. In retrospect I am positively amazed at how much entertainment my second wife managed to insinuate into our busy lives. In any case, I have never felt in the least misanthropic. I have loved my fellow men, have gotten along well with them, and like to think that, by and large, they have admired or at least liked me. I have been ambitious, but have also rejoiced in the achievements of others. Nothing gives me quite the thrill as reading a first-rate historical work. As a teacher of advanced students, I may have been too exacting, if not at times irritable and pedantic. But if I am to trust the later testimony of former students and the quality of their own achievements, I suspect that the high standards and stiff demands of the seminar have born good fruit.

During my career I have worked with people from every walk of life: longshoremen, academics, soldiers, bureaucrats, and businessmen. I have usually found some good in all of them. The various Boston Brahmins with whom I worked impressed me with their high sense of social responsibility and their willingness to work as hard as others. In Washington I managed to hold my own in the incessant struggle for power. I made my way with the "brass" as well as with the "Indians." I found that in the intelligence services, alone of which I can speak with assurance, the patriotism, devotion, and loyalty of the much maligned "Establishment" is hardly recognized and rarely referred to by the average citizen. I am very proud that in these days of controversy and delation, the key task of intelligence evaluation, as worked out in the R and A and then perfected in the early days of the CIA has remained essentially untouched.

Though I have, over the years, built up a reputation for erudition, I must confess that a sense of my ignorance has always exceeded any feeling of knowledge, and this is true of the fields of my specialty as well as of other areas. There simply is too much knowledge in the world today, and the rate of production is so appalling that no one can expect to feel anything but inadequate.

Spending so much time in major research projects has naturally deprived me of the opportunity to read as widely as I would have liked. Science, so important in modern society, is pretty much a closed book to me. I wish, too, that I had had as much time to devote to modern literature, especially poetry, as I had to music. But my interest, at least, has remained catholic, and I have enjoyed my forays into the history of medicine and epidemics. Furthermore, my wife has, over the years, read to me at bedtime, and I am simply astounded at how much modern and classical literature we have covered in this way.

It has been my privilege and good fortune to know intimately many men of outstanding ability and personality: John C. Phillips, Archibald Cary Coolidge, General William J. Donovan, General Walter Bedell Smith, and others too numerous to list. But I would do honor also to my collaborators and assistants: the late S. Everett Gleason, Carl E. Schorske, Robert L. Wolff, Franklin L. Ford, Marshal Shulman, the late Derwood Lockard, and Sherman Kent. All these, as well as many beloved students, have helped to make my life rich, exciting, and rewarding. To all of them, I recognize a real debt of gratitude.

INDEX OF NAMES